Telling Young Lives

Edited by

Craig Jeffrey and Jane Dyson

Telling Young Lives

Portraits of Global Youth

 TEMPLE UNIVERSITY PRESS
Philadelphia

Temple University Press
1601 North Broad Street
Philadelphia, PA 19122
www.temple.edu/tempress

∞ The paper used in this publication meets the requirements of the American National Standard for Information Sciences—Permanence of Paper for Printed Library Materials, ANSI Z39.48-1992

Library of Congress Cataloging-in-Publication Data

Telling young lives: portraits of global youth / edited by Craig Jeffrey and Jane Dyson.

   p. cm
   Includes index.
   ISBN 978-1-59213-930-9 (cloth: alk. paper)
   ISBN 978-1-59213-931-6 (pbk. alk. paper)
   1. Youth—Biography. 2. Globalization—Social aspects. 3. Globalization—Economic aspects. 4. World politics. I. Jeffrey, Craig, 1973– II. Dyson, Jane, 1974
   HQ796T414 2008
   305.235—dc22   2008022365

2 4 6 8 9 7 5 3 1

Contents

Katharyne Mitchell

Foreword

I n recent years there has been a revival of interest in scholarship that can reach beyond the confines of the academy. From the new "public sociologies" movement, to the debates in medicine and the natural sciences, to public humanities programs springing up around the country, it is evident that many scholars desire a stronger engagement with the world outside of the university.

The reasons for this renewed interest are not difficult to fathom. Over the past two decades the policies and practices associated with neoliberal globalization have exacerbated economic inequities and social disruptions in many parts of the globe, as well as accelerated environmental degradation worldwide. For those who work "on the ground" and can witness the ramifications of these policies firsthand, a growing sense of crisis has become pervasive. Once sharing primarily with like-minded colleagues in erudite journals and insular conferences, many academics now feel an almost desperate need to disseminate findings and collaborate with a broader community, one that stretches both across disciplines and across the traditional town/gown divides.

What forms do these collaborations take? How are scholars making the types of connections that can link disparate individuals and groups and make all of their stories relevant, interesting, and mutually supportive? Telling Young Lives is one example of this type of work. In this innovative volume Jeffrey and Dyson have exerted a strong editorial role in the creation of an accessible yet scholarly set of essays on contemporary childhood and youth.

From the very outset of the book it is apparent that the editors have a particular project in mind, one that might be distinguished from the usual youth fare. It is a project characterized by the will to communicate, and by the conviction that the best kind of communication is not a one-way affair. To this end, the volume engages not just a wider public sphere, but also a wider understanding of scholarly engagement. In each essay the story of a particular youth is framed in a way that allows this individual's words and life to come alive, to express a voice and way of being in the world, and to take a central place in the narrative. The researcher remains present and important; it is not a personal biography as cultural metonym, as in the style of some 1980s ethnographies. Rather, the voices of the youth are expressed alongside and in conversation with the narrative framing of the scholar. Thus the individual youth experiences and expressions are central to each essay, yet remain moored to a wider historical and geographical context that also tells a very particular kind of story.

There is an urgent need for work of this kind. Children and youth are among the many groups in society that have been greatly and disproportionately affected by the economic shifts of the late twentieth century. Yet even more than others, their voices are silenced and their experiences discounted. Many pundits and policy-makers view youth as adults-in-the-making rather than persons in their own right. Some researchers have followed in this vein, perceiving young people as objects of study, important only for the generalized understandings their experiences lend to a broader social science project.

To give voice to this group is to extend a kind of citizenship and at the same time to rework the meaning of citizenship. It is a political act. This volume makes that political move, and through it brings both youth and researchers into a broader, collaborative effort to reconstitute scholarship and the production of knowledge itself.

Acknowledgments

We are extremely grateful to all the young people whose stories are told in this book. Without their patience, trust, and willingness to discuss their lives, this book would not be possible. We would like to thank Katharyne Mitchell for writing a Foreword to this book, Chris Philo and Kate Swanson for their Afterword, Matt Sparke and three anonymous referees for their comments on the text, and Lisa Kleinholz for producing an index. We are also grateful to the staff at Temple University Press, especially Mick Gusinde- Duffy, for their support and encouragement.

Telling Young Lives

Craig Jeffrey and Jane Dyson

1

Introduction

Global social and economic change is rapidly altering people's experience of youth. Widespread unemployment, new health risks, and political conflict are reshaping the social landscape in which children and young people grow up. At the same time, governments, nongovernmental organizations (NGOs), and the media are centrally concerned with disciplining youth, for example, through the circulation of negative images of young people.

An important achievement of recent human geographic, anthropological, and sociological work has been to show that young people are not passive in the face of these threats to their livelihoods and self-respect; they actively and creatively shape the world around them (e.g., Bucholtz 2002; Katz 2004; Venkatesh and Kassimir 2007). This book builds on this work through considering the lives of thirteen young people living in the United Kingdom, United States, India, Germany, Tanzania, Sierra Leone, South Africa, and Bosnia-Herzegovenia. These people include nine men and four women, all but one of whom is aged between sixteen and thirty. The book examines the active ways in which these young people are responding to economic, political, and social threats. *Telling Young Lives* offers a comparative understanding of how people's experience of youth is changing and how they contest their marginalization in the political sphere.

The book is innovative in its use of individual vignettes, or "portraits," to uncover issues of youth and political change. In each of the chapters that follow, scholars use the life of a single young person to cast light on broader youth issues. We do not regard the individual as providing an unproblematic window on processes of change. Contributors do not provide "thick descriptions" (Geertz 1973), if this means adhering to the idea that a single person or scene is a microcosm of broader dynamics. Nor do scholars in this volume subscribe to the classically modern notion of a heroic individual carving out their own world (see Butler 1990). Rather, contributors share with other scholars an interest in how single lives may "reveal insights not just into the experiences and attitudes of the individuals directly concerned, but also of the wider society or social segment of which they are also part" (Arnold and Blackburn 2005: 43). To a greater extent than many other styles of scholarly writing, individual vignettes can illustrate how processes cohere to produce human outcomes, convey the textured experience of youth, and instill in readers empathy, respect, and understanding.

Our focus on narratives also reflects our interest in forms of knowledge production that depart from the standard journal article or book chapter. We asked contributors to place a premium on clarity and accessibility in the chapters that follow. The chapters do not include academic citations, specialist terms, or lengthy reviews of scholarly debates. They are written as far as possible through reference to the words, actions, and comportment of individual youth, and they often focus on relatively mundane aspects of young people's lives (see Philo and Swanson in the Afterword to this book). This emphasis on clarity and young people's expressive practice arises in part out of a desire to make the book accessible to a broad audience. But it also reflects an appreciation of the contribution of postcolonial and feminist approaches to knowledge construction and research (e.g., Madison 2005). Scholars in these fields frequently emphasize a need to break down the boundaries between the knowledge of the researcher and that of the researched (e.g., Hofman and Rosing 2007); to develop and recover knowledge that serves to counter oppression (e.g., Sangtin Writers 2006); and to recognize the unequal relationships of authority and privilege that structure all elements of research (Madison 2005). Feminist work is especially attuned to the importance of constant critical reflection on the part of the researcher regarding how one's position shapes the outcomes of research. Contributors to this volume have been centrally influenced by these approaches to knowledge production, and several of the chapters reflect on issues of reflexivity, authority, and power (see especially Chapter 12 by Gardner).

The portrait approach raises important ethical issues. We should note in this context that all of the contributors obtained the permission of their respondents to write about their lives in accordance with the ethical review boards or guidelines of their institutions. We have also taken appropriate steps to ensure the safety of the young people featured in this book. With one exception, where the young person asked for his name to be used, authors have not used respondents' real names and have obtained permission to reproduce photographs.

Ethical awareness also implies reflecting on our responsibilities to our informants. These responsibilities relate in part to providing young people with opportunities to influence how they are represented, and many of the contributors to this volume have been able to work with their respondents in the production of the portraits. Our responsibilities also involve considering how the process and dissemination of our research might shape political outcomes. Questions of how writing an individual portrait might influence processes on the ground—for example, by broadening popular understanding of marginalization or illustrating opportunities for political change—is a theme that traverses the book.

We also offer portraits of young people mindful of how individual vignettes of contemporary youth are being used by powerful institutions to support particular political agendas.[1] The World Bank's World Development Report (WDR) for 2007 begins with three vignettes of young people, which are used to bolster the arguments of the report. Distinct from these organizations, contributors to this volume refer to the politics of representation and, to a greater extent than do the World Bank and UNICEF, they foreground links between young people's lives and broader structural inequalities.

Our book also departs from many other social science studies of youth in its commitment to drawing together material from different places along the continuum from "global north" to "global south." The majority of the work published in English on youth focuses on young people in Western Europe, North America, and Australasia. As a result, studies of youth often ignore or unwittingly misrepresent the lives of young people in poorer parts of the world and fail to uncover the connections between youth in different places (Katz 2004; Holt and Holloway 2006; see also Dolby and Rizvi 2008). Against this background, our book highlights surprising similarities and striking contrasts between the strategies of young people living in varied settings. Our focus on marginalized youth provides an especially vivid picture of how social forces combine to shape the lives of individual young people. A focus on the marginalized also provides an important counterpoint to the preoccupation of business interests and the mainstream media with representing and discussing relatively privileged Western youth, who tend to be constructed only as cultural consumers.

The remainder of this introduction outlines some of the key contributions of the book to interdisciplinary and transnational understanding of people's experience of youth and young people's political strategies. We do not attempt to summarize the chapters sequentially, but rather draw out three key themes that traverse the individual portraits, introducing some of the major arguments of each chapter along the way. We begin with a discussion of people's changing experience of youth, continue by considering how youth are being imagined in different contexts, and finally we discuss young people's political engagements.

A danger of writing an introductory overview is that it squashes rich ethnographic accounts into particular boxes; we risk suggesting, for example, that X's portrait of a young person is interesting only because of its contribution to Y theme. We are also aware that many readers of this book are of a similar age to the young people featured in the volume, and that an introductory synthesis may distract from cross-learning opportunities that they find most "telling." The themes identified in this introduction should be envisaged, then, not as a wholesale review but as providing *one* possible set of starting points for comparative reflection and discussion. Chris Philo and Kate Swanson provide important alternative perspectives in the excellent Afterword that they have written for the book.

Restructuring Youth

Global changes associated with unemployment, economic restructuring, global health risks, militarization, and educational transformation have often fundamentally altered how people negotiate "transitions to adulthood" (e.g., Aitken 2001; Valentine, Skelton, and Chambers 1998; Venkatesh and Kassimir 2007). Several commentators have noted a disappearance or erosion of a phase of adolescence for the poor in parts of Asia and Africa, where rapid economic change and new health threats propel many impoverished children directly into paid work and the demands of adult roles (Verma and Saraswathi 2002; see also Robson 2004; Dolby and Rizvi 2008). Others have shown that a period of youth is being *created* in poorer parts of the world. This point emerges strongly in the first youth portrait of the volume, in which Jane Dyson discusses the life of a sixteen-year-old girl named Saka growing up in a remote part of the Indian Himalayas. Dyson shows that changes in educational and marital practices have resulted in the emergence of a new period of "youth" *(jawaani)* between childhood *(bachpan)*, which is perceived to end at puberty, and adulthood *(bare)* when young people are married. Dyson shows how Saka has been able to use her youth to create distinctive gendered cultures and experiment with new identities, even while her youth remains marked by grueling physical labor.

Dyson's chapter also shows that youth and adulthood are fluid and contested concepts whose meaning and form vary widely over space and time, a theme that has also emerged from recent scholarship on childhood (e.g., Aitken 2001; Prout and James 1997). For men, youth and adulthood are frequently defined in terms of financial independence from parents or senior mentors. But adult masculinities may also be linked to achieving noneconomic forms of respect (e.g., Demerath 1999; Willis 1977) or legal and political power (e.g., Bourgois 1995). By contrast, adult femininities are often negotiated through establishing a long-term partnership—typically through marriage—or economic independence from parents. Childbearing, biological maturity, and the acquisition of embodied skills are also important components of definitions of gendered adulthoods in a wide variety of contexts (Cole 2005).

If youth is constituted in part as the absence of adulthood, it is also clear that people associate youth with the presence of certain qualities (see also Arnett 2004). Dependence, irresponsibility, innocence, recalcitrance, and a certain restless energy are characteristics that are commonly attributed to youth in disparate contemporary settings (Bucholtz 2002), although, as we will see, the manner in which young people are defined and define themselves varies greatly through space and time.

Recent studies suggest that global and regional economic and social changes often prolong the period over which people achieve varied forms of adulthood (e.g., Weiss 2002). In a key sense youth is being detached from the biological quality of "being young". For example, structural adjustment programs in the global south and not dissimilar processes of economic restructuring in Euro-America have delayed or prevented people from acquiring financial independence from their parents and establishing separate economic and familial units. In other situations, neoliberal economic change has prevented young people from acquiring the skills, welfare goods, and social support required to manage a transition to adulthood.

These are themes that emerge strongly in Chapter 3 of this book in which Kristina Gibson describes the life of Blacc, a homeless young man in New York. Gibson identifies periods during which Blacc was able to acquire certain accoutrements of valued "adulthood," such as an independent home and regular wage. But Gibson also emphasizes Blacc's enduring inability to negotiate a hostile urban environment. In Gibson's work, youth must be understood not as a sequestered stage of relative safety, as it is in some studies in the global north (see Furlong and Cartmel 1997), but as a prolonged period of vulnerability and hardship.

The extension of youth is also a theme that surfaces in Chapter 4 in Meth's description of Vusi, a young man in his early twenties living in an informal settlement in Durban, South Africa. As a black child growing up in the Apartheid era, Vusi's education was cut short at a young age, and he was compelled to seek work in the informal economy. But, even though Vusi's transition to adulthood was in certain respects accelerated, he was also unwilling or unable to acquire many of the trappings of mature adulthood. Approaching his mid-twenties in 2005, Vusi continued to move between insecure, poorly paid jobs in the informal economy.

The picture emerging from Dyson's, Gibson's, and Meth's chapters, and those of several other chapters in this volume, is of youth as a complicated terrain of semi-autonomy in which "adult" social goods are often elusive. Young people frequently experience the acquisition of particular forms of adulthood as a partial and reversible achievement (e.g., Furlong and Cartmel 1997), and they often move back and forth between activities understood locally as "youthful" and those imagined as "adult."

Imagining Youth

Ironically, as young people are finding it more difficult in many places to acquire valued forms of adulthood, governments and the media often criticize youth for their alleged wayward, rebellious, or apathetic behavior. Of course, negative stereotypes of youth are not new. But the rise of neoliberal economic policies in many parts of the world has often been accompanied by the proliferation of discourses that criticize youth for their actions, often through reference to idealized visions of youth that young people fail to embody (McDowell 2003). Politics is often a strong theme of this negative language. Governments, media, and parents frequently imagine youth as either politically apathetic or extremist, and these discourses have intensified in the early 2000s in response to high-profile forms of youth violence in Western Europe, Latin America, South Asia, and elsewhere (Hansen 1996).

This collection highlights how young people are seeking to negotiate stereotypes of youth. This theme comes out especially powerfully in the chapters on the United Kingdom. In Chapter 5, Linda McDowell argues that depictions of working-class young men as lazy, disengaged, and violent complicate the attempts of the young man at the center of her study, Richard, to find secure work. McDowell points to the strongly gendered character of these negative depictions; young men—imagined as inherently errant and irresponsible—are said to be failing in school, spreading violent crime, and incapable of conducting service work. In Chapter 6, Peter Hopkins builds on research in Glasgow, Scotland, to demonstrate that Muslim young men of South Asian origin may suffer even more acutely from stereotypical constructions of youth in contemporary Britain. The attacks on America on September 11, 2001, combined with the bombs planted in London in July 2004 has generated a climate in which suspicion of young men in general has fused with racial and religious prejudices. The young men at the center of McDowell's and Hopkins's chapters are keenly aware of broader negative discourses and actively tried to contest these stereotypes.

An interrelated but distinct strand of commentary on contemporary youth focuses on questions of individual responsibility and tends to blame youth—at least implicitly—for their economic marginalization (cf, Katz 2004; Ruddick 2003). This strand of thinking is well represented in the World Bank's (2007) World Development Report (WDR), titled *Development and the Next Generation*. Scattered through the WDR are attempts to identify young people's individual responsibilities for their futures. For example, in the executive summary, the WDR quotes a young person in Georgia, "The majority of youth in Georgia now realize that the key factor in finding proper jobs lies in themselves" (World Bank 2007: 15). A few pages later the authors of the report conclude that in addressing the problems faced by contemporary youth, "Public spending alone will not do the trick. Policies must stimulate young people, their parents and their communities to invest in themselves" (World Bank 2007: 21). These statements are linked to the policy goal of offering young people "second chances". It is a short step from such statements to wider public and media discourses that blame young people—including those in the global south—for their poverty, deprivation, and powerlessness. Tellingly absent from the World Bank's report are the issues of power and inequality that mark the lives of the youth discussed in this volume.

In contrast to the authors of the WDR, and in line with much recent writing on children within sociology and geography (see Aitken 2001; Holt and Holloway 2006), contributors to this book situate youth practice with reference to broader structural forces. Horschelmann's portrait (Chapter 7) is based on fieldwork in Eastern Germany and nicely illustrates this strength of the book. Horschelmann describes the contradictory implications of German unification and the decline of state socialism for a young man called Sven, who was in his mid-twenties in 2006 and came from a lower-middle-class family living in Eastern Germany. The decline of state socialism has opened up new opportunities for Sven, especially the chance to participate in transnational youth cultures. But the emergence of more market-based social forms had altered the school system such that students are increasingly allocated to classes according to their ability. Moreover, Horschelmann describes how, in the rapidly changing economic scenario in Eastern Germany, even well-qualified students are not guaranteed access to secure and well-paid work. In Chapter 8, Crotty, Moreno, and Aitken expand on this theme in the context of work they have conducted in California. Their study of a working-class young man called Mike shows how neoliberal discourse enjoins young people to live responsible and autonomous lives at precisely the moment at which the removal of educational facilities and health care is undermining possibilities for social mobility. Horschelmann and Crotty, Moreno, and Aitken treat the language of "individual responsibility" not as a transparent reflection of "young people's point of view" but as an ideology shaping the lives of the young people they study. These authors also show how this ideology is built into the landscapes in which these young people live, play, and learn.

Political Geographies of Youth

The academic division of labor within geography and related disciplines has militated against sustained reflection on political geographies and anthropologies of youth, a third key theme of this book. Mainstream political geographers have shown minimal interest in young people, despite a recent opening up of this subdiscipline (Philo and Smith 2003). While several political geographies focus on young people, their status as youth and the politics of age and generation are yet to be explicitly addressed. Similarly, anthropologies of youth have tended to focus on social and cultural aspects of young people's lives to the relative exclusion of discussion of their political strategies and involvement (Bucholtz 2002).

Recent social science studies of young people that have considered youth politics often posit that there has been a transformation in the nature of young people's political engagements. In this view, there was a marked decline in class- and party-political–based activism among young people after the 1960s: involvement in party politics has decreased (Cloonan and Street 1998), young people are reluctant to vote in elections (Eisner 2004), and political mobilization based upon ideological issues is declining (Furlong and Cartmel 1997). Wallace and Kovatcheva (1998) use research in Europe to claim that all types of "formal" political action have become less common among young people. Mirroring in certain respects state and media discourses of young people as apathetic, these authors argue that young people are active only in "post-modern forms of protest— symbolic and cultural challenges to the dominant system of rules and regulations and dominant values and assumptions of good taste" (Wallace and Kovatcheva 1998: 262).

Young people in some of the settings described in this book *are* becoming disengaged from formal political action. In Chapter 9, Alex Jeffrey's portrait of Zilho, a Bosniak man in his mid-twenties living in Brcko, Bosnia, highlights this point. Jeffrey describes how the Serbian occupation of Brcko in 1992 forced Zilho and his family to migrate to areas of the surrounding countryside under Bosniak control. The introduction of international development assistance in Brcko and a cessation of Serbian violence encouraged Zilho to return to his birthplace in the late 1990s. But he returned to a physical urban landscape that had been inscribed with symbols of Serbian power and to a social landscape in which people from Serbian backgrounds monopolized the best jobs. Against this background, Zilho told Jeffrey that his future lay not in organized politics but in the types of incremental and individualized political action that Wallace and Kovatcheva regard as the purview of today's youth.

The theme of disinvestment in formal political action is also foregrounded in Chapter 10 by Danny Hoffman. Hoffman discusses a young man called Mohammed, who was in his early thirties in 2006 and lived on the edge of the city of Freetown in Sierra Leone with his wife and children. Economic and political insecurities frame Mohammed's life: the economic collapse of Sierra Leone following the introduction of structural adjustment policies in the 1980s, the proliferation of violence after the end of the Cold War, and the widespread absence of schooling and health facilities. Mohammed had responded to these insecurities, in part, through acting as a mercenary for a wealthy patron. But he was increasingly trying to distance himself from this dangerous work. Hoffman's chapter highlights young people's often precarious and shifting relationship to collective forms of organized political action.

While acknowledging how social and economic change may encourage young people to turn their back on politics—also a theme of Meth's and Nayak's accounts in this book—we wish to emphasize young people's deepening engagement in formal political action in many settings. This point often emerges in accounts of young people's involvement in brokerage work, also a theme of a wider set of youth studies (e.g., Hansen 1996, 2006). For example, in Chapter 11, Craig Jeffrey's portrait of Suresh, a Dalit (ex-untouchable) politician in north India, points to the emergence of a generation of low-caste "new politicians" who are creating a rural-urban political nexus that links them to the Indian state. Jeffrey shows that Suresh's social networking at the local level is intimately linked to the rise of a Dalit political party at the regional level, and thus that party politics remains central to youth politics in north India.

Benjamin Gardner's portrait (Chapter 12) also offers a telling counterpoint to public and scholarly discourses of youth apathy and political disenchantment. Gardner's account focuses on a young woman called Nala, who was thirty-six in 2006, but considered to be a youth in Tanzania as a result of her unmarried status. Nala was born in a Masai community characterized by strong patriarchal attitudes. Contravening the wishes of her father, Nala left home to establish an NGO—the Pastoral Women's Council—committed to improving women's position in Masai society. Nala has emerged as a key political broker between women in Tanzania and international development organizations in the global north. Gardner also points to how globalization—in this case manifested in Nala's ability to collaborate with a U.S. NGO and travel to America—has opened up new opportunities and dilemmas for Nala.

These examples of relatively formal and organized political action should not detract from the importance of the politics described by Wallace and Kovatcheva as "post-modern": everyday forms of protest that are often communicated through young people's speech, dress, and comportment. The possibility of young people using their everyday actions and cultural styles to critique broader society was a major insight generated by the Birmingham School of Contemporary Cultural Studies in the 1970s and 1980s (e.g., Hebdige 1979; Willis 1977) and is central to many of the chapters in this book. For example, issues of everyday practice run through Gibson's study of Blacc's life. Blacc's three "rules of the street"—watch out for your friends, don't appear homeless, and keep moving—all concern the everyday actions required to navigate the hostile political terrain of New York City. These practical tactics are deeply political in the sense of being geared to resisting and escaping dominant structures of power (de Certeau 1984). Nayak's discussion of a young woman, Helena, in northeast England (Chapter 13) also uncovers the importance of everyday aspects of young people's behavior—especially their speech, clothing, and demeanor—in processes of social and political change. In this account, Helena was engaged in a "reflexive biographical project of the self" (Nayak in this volume), a type of self-authoring in which she appropriated images of black culture in order to critique the racism and snobbery of some white English youth.

The importance of age and generation in processes of everyday political action is a theme that crosscuts many of the portraits. For example, Crotty, Moreno, and Aitken's chapter emphasizes the significance of Mike's shifting relationship with his brother in the process through which these siblings seek secure futures. Meanwhile, cousins emerge as important in the chapters by Gardner and Meth. Intergenerational politics are an even stronger theme. In several chapters, for example those of McDowell; Meth; and Crotty, Moreno, and Aitken, young people have been compelled to negotiate their teens in the absence of strong parental support, and often have come into conflict with their parents. In other portraits, such as those provided by A. Jeffrey and Dyson, parents have been allies in young people's struggles for security and respect. The complexities of intergenerational politics are brought out especially clearly in Chapter 14 by Skelton concerning a deaf lesbian young woman called Susannah living in the United Kingdom. Deaf themselves, Susannah's parents were strong sources of support and guidance in her early life. But she had increasingly come into conflict with her mother, who strongly disapproved of her coming out as a lesbian. In documenting this conflict, Skelton's chapter points to how intergenerational relations often constitute a social arena in which wider anxieties regarding difference and inequality are played out. She also demonstrates that these intergenerational relationships—frequently enacted within the intimate space of the home—are affected by wider political cultures, for example around sexuality and disability. Read beside the works of C. Jeffrey, Gardner, and Nayak, Skelton's chapter highlights the mutual constitution of formal politics—Politics with a big "P" (Philo and Smith 2003)—and everyday political strategies: politics with a small "p."

Negotiations between formal Politics and everyday politics are grounded in processes of spatial change. Several chapters of this volume describe how the spaces in which young people develop particular life projects are themselves transformed through youth everyday action. For example, Mohammed's work breaking rocks on the edge of Freetown was bound up in the establishment of the urban fringe as a suburb of the city (Chapter 10), and Saka's attempts to subvert gendered norms in the forest reinforced notions of the village as a space in which established notions of femininity should be respected (Chapter 2). As further examples, Blacc's constant movement may act to reinforce stereotypes of urban young men as wandering, errant, and threatening (Chapter 3) just as Nala's restless politicking helps to undermine stereotypes about "women's place in the home" in Tanzania (Chapter 12).

Similarly, processes of spatial change influence the political strategies of young people. The turbulent political violence that has characterized large parts of the Balkans since the early 1990s have markedly shaped Zilho's opportunities to express himself politically (Chapter 9). More positively, the portrait of Suresh suggests how the rise of a political party in India committed to remaking the social landscape to reflect Dalit power has offered ex-untouchable youth opportunities to develop new political cultures (Chapter 11). In both of these chapters, *spatialized networks of practice* are crucial mechanisms for young people to mitigate their exclusion and develop new forms of social mobility. In the youth political geographies offered in this volume, then, space emerges not as a static backdrop or container for young people's strategies, but as something thoroughly imbricated with their political struggles (see Massey 1994, 2005). Read together, the chapters in this book point toward the value of a spatially and culturally sensitive political economy approach to the geographies of young people, one centrally concerned with *grounding* an understanding of youth strategies in everyday and noneveryday processes of change (see Jeffrey et al. 2008).

The chapters in this volume also show that young people's strategies often involve spatial movement and migration, particularly in the context of the speeding up of global communication associated with globalization. For example, in Chapter 12, Nala has used her connections in the United States to expand the work of the NGO that she runs in Tanzania. Many of Zilho's peers in Chapter Nine have been able to make money through establishing small NGOs funded by larger international organizations. In other cases, globalization has encouraged young people to "scale up" their identities by embracing transnational cultural symbols, as Helena and Sven reveal in Chapters 13 and 7 (cf, Hansen 2006). The book therefore underlines not only thematic connections between youth cultural and political strategies, but the manner in which the lives of young people in disparate places are becoming intertwined and interdependent. Analysis of the "family resemblances" and interconnections between the struggles of dispersed young people across national boundaries should be of central concern to contemporary scholars, activists, policymakers, and young people themselves.

Note

1. UNICEF has added a "Voice of Youth" section to its Web site, which is linked to young people's digital diaries: www.unicef.org/voy/takeaction/takeaction_2692.html (accessed 04/08/08).

References

Aitken, Stuart C. (2001). *Geographies of Young People: The Morally Contested Spaces of Identity*. London: Routledge.

Arnett, Jeffrey J. (2004). *Emerging Adulthood: The Winding Road from Late Teens to Early Tweenties*. Oxford: Oxford University Press.

Arnold, David, and Stuart Blackburn. (2005). *Telling Lives*. Indiana: Indiana University Press.

Bourgois, Philippe. (1995). *In Search of Respect: Selling Crack in El Barrio*. Cambridge: Cambridge University Press.

Bucholtz, Mary. (2002). "Youth and Cultural Practice." *Annual Review of Anthropology* 31: 525–552.

Butler, Judith. (1990). *Gender and the Subversion of Identity*. New Haven: Yale University Press.

Cloonan, Martin, and John Street. (1998). "Rock the Vote: Popular Culture and Politics." *Politics* 18: 33–38.

Cole, Jennifer. (2005). "The Jaombilo of Tamative Madagascar (1992–2004): Reflections on Youth and Globalization." *Journal of Social History* 38(4): 891–913.

de Certeau, Michel(1984). *The Practice of Everyday Life*. London: Routledge.

Demerath, Peter. (1999). "The Cultural Production of Educational Utility in Pere Village, Papua New Guinea." *Comparative Education Review* 43(2): 162–192.

Dolby, Nadine, and Fazal Rizvi. (2008). *Youth Moves: Identities and Education in Global Perspective*. London: Routledge.

Eisner, Jane. (2004). *Taking Back the Vote: Getting American Youth Involved in Our Democracy*. Boston: Beacon Press.

Furlong, Andy, and Fred Cartmel. (1997). *Young People and Social Change: Individuali* Press.

Geertz, Clifford. (1973). *The Interpretation of Cultures*. New York: Basic Books.

Hansen, Thomas B. (1996). "Recuperating Masculinity: Hindu Nationalism, Violence, and the Exorcism of the Muslim 'Other.'" *Critique of Anthropology* 16(22): 137–172.

———. (2006). "Sounds of Freedom: Music, Taxis and Racial Imagination in Urban South Africa." *Public Culture* 18(1): 185–208.

Hebdige, Dick. (1979). *Subculture: The Meaning of Style*. London: Methuen.

Hofman, Nila., and Howard Rosing, eds. (2007). *Pedagogies of Praxis: Course-Based Action Research in the Social Sciences*. New York: Anker Publishing.

Holt, Louise, and Sarah Holloway. (2006). "Editorial: Theorising Other Childhoods in a Globalised World." *Children's Geographies* 4: 135–142.

Jeffrey, Craig, Patricia Jeffery, and Roger Jeffery. (2008) *Degrees Without Freedom? Education, Masculinities and Unemployment in North India*. Palo Alto, CA: Stanford University Press.

Katz, Cindi. (2004). *Growing Up Global: Economic Restructuring and Children's Everyday Lives*. Minneapolis: Minnesota University Press.

McDowell, Linda. (2003). *Redundant Masculinities? Employment Change and White Working Class Youth*. Oxford: Blackwell.

Madison, Soyini. (2005). *Critical Ethnography: Method, Ethics and Performance*. London: Sage.

Massey, Doreen. (1994). *Space, Place and Gender.* Minneapolis: Minnesota University Press.

———. (2005). *For Space.* London: Sage.

Philo, Chris, and Fiona Smith. (2003). "Guest Editorial: Political Geographies of Children and Young People." *Space and Polity* 7: 99–115.

Prout, Alan, and Allison James. (1997). "A New Paradigm for the Sociology of Childhood? Provenance, Promise and Problems." In *Constructing and Reconstructing Childhood*, ed. Allison James and Alan Prout, 7—33. London: Falmer Press.

Robson, Elsbeth. (2004). "Hidden Workers: Young Careers in Zimbabwe." *Antipode* 36(2): 227–248.

Ruddick, Susan. (2003). "The Politics of Aging: Globalization and the Politics of Youth and Childhood" *Antipode* 35(2): 334–362.

Sangtin Writers. (2006). *Playing With Fire: Feminist Thought and Activism through Seven Lives in India.* Minneapolis: Minnesota University Press.

Valentine, Gillian, Tracey Skelton, and Deborah Chambers (1998). "Cool Places: An Introduction to Youth and Youth Cultures." In *Cool Places: Geographies of Youth Cultures*, ed. Tracey Skelton and Gill Valentine, 1–33. London: Routledge.

Venkatesh, Sudhir A., and Ronald Kassimir. (2007). *Youth, Globalization and the Law.* Stanford: Stanford University Press.

Verma, Suman, and T. S. Saraswathi (2002). "Adolescence in India: Street Urchins or Silicon Valley Millionaires?" In *The World's Youth: Adolescence in Eight Regions of the Globe*, ed. Bradford B. Brown, Reed W. Larson, and T. S. Saraswathi. Cambridge: Cambridge University Press.

Wallace, Claire, and Sijka Kovatcheva. (1998). *Youth in Society: The Construction and Deconstruction of Youth in East and West Europe.* Oxford: Macmillan.

Weiss, Brad. (2002). "Thug Realism: Inhabiting Fantasy in Urban Tanzania." *Cultural Anthropology* 17(1): 93–124.

Willis, Paul. (1977). *Learning to Labour: How Working Class Kids Get Working Class Jobs.* Farnborough, UK: Saxon House.

World Bank (2007). *World Development Report 2007: Development and the Next Generation.* Washington, DC: World Bank.

Jane Dyson

2

Saka

Growing Up in the Indian Himalayas

first met Saka on a cold winter's evening in 2003 inside her family's
one-room house. The room was dark; Saka's face was only occasionally
visible by the light of the flickering cooking fire. Behind her, I could hear,
but not see, the livestock that also shared the room, the two cows, two
bulls, and a buffalo that quietly shuffled and snorted as they chewed on
their nighttime hay. Although the sun had long since set, it was considerably lighter outside. The snow of the surrounding Himalayan peaks reflected the light of the moon so that the forests on the nearby ridges were
marked out in clear silhouette.

I had just arrived in Bemni village for the first time.[1] I had made the
long trek up to the village with Saka's paternal uncle, and had subsequently
been invited to stay the night with Saka's family. My arrival that night had
brought the key male figures of the village to Saka's house. The *Sarpanch*,
the head of the village forest committee, and the de facto leader of the village, had entered the room. Despite explaining that I wanted to work with
the young people in the village, he sought to lay claim over me immediately, and loudly discussed my schedule for the next day with the assem-
bled group of men. Sixteen-year-old Saka had no place in these discussions.
She quietly continued making flat bread (roti) for our supper, slapping the
bread from hand to hand before placing it by the fire to cook. But as the
men talked, we stole smiles and glances. Early the next morning, before
the men had even emerged from their houses, Saka announced that I
would accompany her and her friends for a day's work in the forest. We

Fig 2.1   *Saka*
(Photograph by Jane Dyson)

made no mention of the Sarpanch's instructions the night before. In the growing light of that chill January day, we set off for the high reaches of the forest. It was there that I discovered a very different Saka.

Saka's home, in the village of Bemni, is situated in Chamoli District, in the far north of the Himalayan state of Uttarakhand, in north India. It is located some 40 km from the main road including a four-hour steep up-hill walk to an altitude of 2,500 m (8,200 feet). It was a large village relative to others in Chamoli District with 188 households, of which two-thirds were higher-caste Rajputs, often termed General Caste, and one-third Dalits (lower castes, also called Scheduled Castes).

Saka is from a Rajput family. She is the youngest of four children, and the only one remaining in the natal home. Her oldest brother, Vinod, had left Bemni in 1999 in search of salaried work, and in 2003 he lived in Delhi. Saka's sister was married into a nearby village and, in 2003, her younger brother stayed often with their uncle while he sought a position in the army. Saka had studied at the middle school in the neighboring village, but had dropped out in 2002 after having passed her Class Eight exams. Now she joined her parents working their 0.8 ha of land, a relatively large holding by Bemni standards.

The details of Saka's family situation point to broader aspects of social change in this part of the Himalayas. Chamoli District is an area undergoing rapid transformation. The expansion of the road network has led to the development of local markets and promoted the adoption of new cash crops. At the same time, improved access to urban centers has encouraged rural men to migrate to cities in pursuit of service employment. In the early 2000s, households were beginning to depend more heavily on cash remittances. These changes were also bound up with a sharp increase in rural people's investment in formal education: literacy rates in Chamoli District rose from 27.6 percent in 1971 to 61.1 percent in 1991, according to the Census of India. Nevertheless, there remains a dearth of rural schools, particularly in the more remote areas where roads do not yet reach. As such, the majority of the population is still prevented from obtaining a secondary school education. Moreover, the prevalence of patriarchal attitudes within rural families prevents many girls from attending school; only 27.7 percent of rural women were literate in Chamoli District in 1991.

Like the other families in Bemni and surrounding villages, Saka's family practiced a labor-intensive form of agro-pastoralist agriculture. They cultivated some crops for subsistence—particularly wheat, millet, and barley—and others for sale—especially potatoes and kidney beans. They depended heavily on the surrounding forest for pastoral use. To coordinate their arable and pastoral land use, Saka and her neighbors practiced a form of small-scale transhumance whereby they moved seasonally between three houses located in settlements at altitudes of 2,200 m, 2,500 m, and 2,700m. These small seasonal shifts offered a means of maximizing the potential of agricultural land at different altitudes.

Living conditions in Bemni were basic. None of the three settlements were served by electricity, there was no form of sanitation, and streams or scattered pumps provided water. State facilities, particularly for education, were poor; and prospects for outside employment, relatively low. The vast majority of children was educated locally and contributed to forest and fieldwork before and after the school day.

All the forest and fieldwork was accomplished through manual labor, using small handheld sickles for harvesting, and a tiny hoe for weeding. Like other young people in Bemni, Saka had been contributing to this work since the age of five. By 2003, when Saka was just sixteen years old, she had become the household's main laborer. While her father enjoyed plowing, he strenuously tried to avoid other types of work. Her mother increasingly suffered from ill health; her back and knees were continually aching, and her blood pressure was high. She looked forward to the marriage of one of her sons, when a daughter-in-law would take over her toil. But until then, Saka was responsible for the majority of the agricultural work, and particularly for the heavy labor.

Saka's days were structured around the particular agricultural needs of the season. The farming year began in March with the sowing of millet, rice, and potatoes, followed by the harvesting of wheat, barley, and pulses. The growing millet, rice, and potatoes were weeded throughout May to July and finally harvested in September and October, when the next year's wheat and barley were also sowed. Almost every day from June to October, Saka also cut fresh green grass for the nighttime feeding of livestock. Between mid-October and late-November Saka undertook a grueling five weeks cutting enough hay to last the long winter, during which the livestock spent much of the time inside being stall fed. To supplement this winter hay, Saka frequently visited oak forests from December to February to cut fresh leaves. Throughout the year, Saka spent four intensive periods of five to six weeks collecting leaf litter for use as livestock bedding. In March, June, September, and December, she made dawn trips to the high surrounding oak forests to gather huge basketfuls of leaves. Once they were soiled by the livestock, this bedding provided organic fertilizer which Saka hauled, basket by basket, to every field throughout the year. Finally, Saka also made trips to the forest, mainly in July–August and December–January, to collect firewood for cooking and heating their homes.

Saka had shown little interest or promise in her schoolwork, but she had established a reputation as a diligent and skillful worker. I remember Saka during the summer evenings returning home long after dark, climbing the steep 2 km carrying a basket of green grass that she had cut in the moonlight, having spent a lonely fourteen hours weeding the millet fields. With barely enough energy to eat, she would fall into bed at 11:00 P.M., only to be woken again before 5:00 A.M. Another abiding memory is of worrying about where Saka was during an early snow storm in November, only to see her returning from the fields having cut a huge load of winter hay, wearing just a thin cotton *salwar kameez* and laughing when she showed me how her hands were still warm. On her rare days "off," I remember Saka spending hours on washing clothes for the entire family in the freezing water of the nearby stream.

Saka said that village girls were under considerable pressure to work diligently, thereby adhering to local notions of acceptable femininity. Saka's mother was widely regarded as one of the best workers in the village—"a machine" one of her neighbors called her—and Saka was keen to acquire the same reputation for conscientious work. Saka also knew that her mother would be arranging her marriage within the next three or four years. In this part of the Himalayas, a reputation for diligence is one of the most important criteria for assessing potential brides.

In assessing the abilities and industriousness of young women, villagers in Bemni expected teenage girls to be able to use a sickle swiftly and productively, and to return from the fields and forest carrying large baskets of harvested crops or forest products. Saka's thirteen-year-old neighbor, Prema, summed up this idea when she told me: "If we carry just a little [on our backs], village people will laugh and ask, "why did such a big girl bring so little?" If I see my friend is carrying more than me, I feel anger bubbling up inside my stomach. Then I have to collect more. I don't mind if older girls have more, but I don't want girls of my age to have more than me."

In my own attempts to participate in agricultural work, I experienced the same pressure to conform to social expectations in the face of village scrutiny. At the end of a day working alongside Saka, I usually sought to carry a basket of harvested crops or forest products back from the fields or forest. Saka and many other young people, however, were aware of my relative weakness and insisted that I only carry a tiny basket usually reserved for small children. The sight of me carrying such a basket was, however, the cause for much amusement and opened me up for ridicule. I was a head taller than most adult women, and yet carried a fraction of the load that even a fourteen-year-old girl could manage. I was frequently met with laughter and comments from the villagers about the ludicrous ratio between my height and the weight I carried. Although I knew my status did not entirely depend on my ability to perform such tasks, I found myself increasingly concerned about my reputation of "incompetence."

The girls I accompanied during these trips often empathized with my concerns. Although they reassured me that, as an outsider, I was not subject to such assessment, they frequently sought to protect me from teasing. For example, on one occasion, as we neared the village on our return from the forest, Saka repeatedly urged me to allow her to carry my small basket of leaves as well as her own huge baskets, thereby sparing me from ridicule.

Although Saka was proud of her contribution to her household's livelihood, she regretted that she had little time for socializing or meeting her

FIG 2.2   *Saka cutting grass* (Photograph by Jane Dyson)

friends. She often referred to the loneliness of agricultural work and talked wistfully of her younger days. She remembered the best and most carefree period of her life being when she was eleven or twelve years old. At that time, she had spent long summer days herding cattle with a group of particularly close girls and boys. They would travel together to the grazing areas on the outskirts of the village, often on the edges of the forest. There, they would play team games, throw ropes around the branches of trees for makeshift swings, cook small meals on illegally lit fires, and sit chatting in the shade. Although they were charged with the safekeeping of their livestock, the children kept only a cursory eye on their cattle.

This period of freedom was short-lived, however. By the age of thirteen, Saka said that she had begun to understand "rules" *(niyam)* about the ways in which boys and girls were expected to behave. Boys, she said, were allowed to be lazy and rebellious. Parents hoped their sons' futures lay outside the village, in paid employment, and only half-heartedly expected them to be diligent young farm workers. Meanwhile, the girls were to become wives and mothers, attentive homemakers, and industrious farmers. They needed to be obedient, dedicated, and conscientious.

By their early teens, most girls began to worry about engaging in frivolous games in public. A thirteen-year-old neighbor of Saka's explained:

"We herd cattle and play now, and when adults pass us and see us playing, there is no problem. But when we grow up a bit, then we will be afraid of what village people think, and we won't play in front of them."

By the age of fifteen, Saka explained how she reluctantly began to separate herself from her group of special male friends. She spent less time in sociable activities such as cattle herding, when girls and boys were forced, by the limited availability of grazing areas, to occupy the same spaces. Saka understood these grazing areas to be rather risky places for young women. They were public spaces and yet their location in the hinterlands of the village meant they were on the cusp of privacy: they occupied a place from where to escape to the forest. When Saka and her friends talked of illicit affairs, lovers were always said to have met in these forests. By straddling the village and the forest, these herding areas thus offered the potential both for private liaisons and public appraisal. On the days when Saka did herd cattle, she had been careful to remain with her girlfriends and only joined mixed gender groups if the boys were members of her extended family *(rishtedar)*. She said, "I would only go with those boys I call 'brother,' and if other men or older boys came along, we would move away or stay silent."

By early 2004, aged nearly seventeen, Saka no longer took part in sociable work like herding. She understood that to do so would lead to her acquiring a bad reputation. Like her friends, Saka was aware that the honor *(izzat)* of a girl reflected on the entire village. Adult villagers had an interest in monitoring the disposition, manners, and work of young girls to ensure favorable marriage prospects of Bemni girls in the future. Saka explained, "if we don't act carefully, people would say dirty things *(gundi chiz)* about us." She was under considerable pressure from her family to maintain a good reputation: "My mother tells me all the time what to do or not to do." Her second brother, Mukesh, also monitored her behavior carefully. He and his male friends regularly discussed which of the village girls were good *(achchi)* or bad/dirty *(gundi)*. Fearful of his friends' gossip, Mukesh ordered Saka not to laugh too much or play in public, or to remain too long in the forest.

But Saka was not entirely constrained in her ability to seek space for her own fun or to escape the social norms that dictated her behavior in the public spaces of the village. During the quieter winter period, when fieldwork was scarce, Saka seized upon her forest-related work as an opportunity to spend time with friends away from adult view. Saka created spaces of fun *(maza)* through her daily trips to collect lichen in high-altitude forests.

Since 1999, when a dirt road was cut to within 8 km of Bemni, villagers had been selling lichen in the nearby market 16 km away. From there, it was sold on the Gangetic plains for the production of paint and dyes. Lichen sale prices were low during the initial years (Rs. 3–5/kg), but by 2003–2004, villagers received Rs. 35–40/kg. In 2003, one of the two main buyers for the local area estimated that each year he sent approximately forty trucks of lichen for sale in the plains, each holding about 3,000 kg.

While lichen was available throughout the year growing on the branches of mature oak trees, its collection was largely restricted to the winter months. The lull in fieldwork during winter provided time for some villagers to work outside the fields. Lichen collection remained predominantly the work of children and young people; few adults were able to spend the entire day away in order reach the distant high forests where lichen was most abundant. While the new market for the sale of lichen offered many young people the chance to make considerable contributions to their families' cash incomes, Saka valued her lichen-collection days for rather different, social goals.

Groups of between five and nine girls set off at about 7:00 A.M up the steep mountainsides to collect lichen. Once out of sight of the village, however, and having barely reached the forest, the girls would sink to the ground and rest, chat, and play. The entire morning was taken up in this way—climbing a little, stopping, perhaps collecting a little lichen, resting, and climbing some more. Later, after eating a packed lunch, the girls engaged in rough games. They teased each other about their small harvests and pretended to steal lichen from one another. Launching tackles between the trees, they dragged each other by the legs down the slippery mountainsides. The girls used their sharpened sickles in mock battles and threw armfuls of damp leaves or snow inside their friends' clothes.

The games were sometimes more personal, ridiculing the smaller girls for their unformed breasts, pulling down their tops to reveal and twist their nipples. During my first trips with Saka and her friends, they sometimes broke off from boisterous games to ask if I was shocked by their behavior or found them to be "childlike" *(jaise bachchhe)* or "dirty" *(gundi)*.

Lichen collection not only provided a chance for Saka to hark back to her childhood days, and to play around in ways that were forbidden in the village, it also offered a space for open and frank discussion. Saka and her friends talked of their changing bodies, asking about menstruation and whether they should be wearing a bra. Saka often initiated gossiping sessions that reflected her own emerging sexual desires: they focused on the subjects of men and premarital affairs, subjects that I never heard discussed by unmarried girls elsewhere in the village. They compared stories about lovers and talked about who had fallen pregnant and the details of affairs.

Saka and her friends' discussions in the forest also increasingly focused around their futures. While the previous winter Saka had been too shy to talk of marriage, by winter of 2003–2004 she began to speak of her eagerness to be married. In the relatively "private" space of the forest, Saka said that the promise of a man (with its implication of sexual pleasure) tempted her toward a situation—marriage—that was otherwise publicly dreaded. As Saka began to articulate her criteria for a suitable husband, her friends teased her about possible families into which she could be married: perhaps to a man with little land, or one living in a village on a north-facing slope where the sun never melted the winter snow.

Saka was acutely aware of the freedom that her lichen-collection days provided her. This relatively new activity provided a space for open expression that would not otherwise be available. Saka was keenly aware of the greater pressures that she would be under when married, and how this current period of "youth" is still relatively "free." She told me:

> When we go to the forest to collect dry leaves or fuel wood, we are always with young married women and they are afraid of being late because their mothers-in-law will punish them. So we have to collect the leaves quickly and can't sit and chat. But when we go for lichen, we are just girls. We only have our parents and we are not afraid of them. We don't have mothers-in-law to be afraid of, so we can do as we like. If we don't want to, we do no work for most of the day and collect a little lichen later.

Aware of the impending change that would restrict their lives even further, these unmarried girls fiercely protected these moments of carefree fun. They used a wide range of strategies to protect them.

> If we come back with very little lichen, we make up a story for everyone to tell their parents. We say we met a bear and we had to run away quickly. When we all have the same story, nobody will know what really happened.

Saka's ability to carve out these spaces of free time were largely the result of a new opportunity to market locally available resources, which reflected Bemni's recently improved accessibility to a main road. But Saka's capacity to transgress established norms of girlhood while in the forest was also a result of an ongoing social transformation in the institution of marriage. In 2003–2004, Saka and her friends were among the first generation of teenage girls in the area to spend time in their natal home. Saka's mother had received no formal education and was married at the age of twelve years. By contrast, Saka had passed her Class Eight exams and would not expect to marry until the age of eighteen. Patterns of marriage and labor were thus being transformed by the expansion of schooling.

But the growing importance of education, itself driven by the desire for off-farm secure employment, was not just a source of freedom and agency for the girls. It also increased pressure on young women to obtain educational credentials. These were important not only for boys to obtain coveted government jobs, but also for girls to guarantee a marriage to a good husband.

Despite having already left school, Saka was keenly aware of these pressures. Saka's brothers, on their return to the village, regularly chided Saka for having been a "poor student," and for not having continued her education up to at least Class Ten. Her oldest brother, Vinod, claimed to have once tested her IQ and ridiculed her supposedly low result. He said that he felt ashamed that she could barely read the letters they sent home, suggested that she would never find a suitable husband, and laughingly questioned how she would help her own children with their homework. He insisted that Saka should be educated enough to secure her own employment and remove herself from agricultural toil *(mehnat ka kaam)*.

While Saka knew that her labor supported her family, including her brothers, she said her brothers' lectures left her feeling "worthless" *(bekar)*. Saka's parents, meanwhile, sought to justify their educational strategy for Saka. Her mother, Lali, said that she had assumed that a Class Eight pass would have been adequate to marry Saka into a good rural family. Besides, having arranged her older daughter's marriage in 2002, Lali sorely needed another full-time farmer in the family; their decision to pull Saka out of school at that time was partly shaped by household labor dynamics. Nevertheless, since 2002, Lali had become aware of the growing number of rural young women from ambitious local families who had a Class Ten or even a Class Twelve qualification, and she became increasingly concerned over Saka's position in the local marriage market. Moreover, she was moved by her sons' insistence that they find Saka a family outside the remote Nandakini Valley, and marry her into a household reliant on waged-labor rather than farming. For such a marriage, however, Saka's educational credentials were almost certainly insufficient.

Saka's own opinions about her education or criteria for a husband were never sought. Indeed, she was not expected to have formed her own opinions on these matters. But, in 2004, in the privacy of the forest and surrounded by similarly concerned teenage girls, Saka had been explicit about her hopes. She was adamant she wanted a husband with lots of land, a factor she considered to be more important than her husband's ability to earn an off-farm income. This way she would be sure to create a living even if her husband was not in secure employment. Her criteria reflected her own current situation: her work on their large landholding supported her entire family, and while her oldest brother claimed to be employed in Delhi, he did not earn enough to send remittances home.

Throughout 2003, Mukesh was studiously preparing for his army entrance exams: running in the dark mornings in preparation for the physical test and memorizing general knowledge in the afternoons for the written exam. In January 2004, after several rounds of physical, medical, and written tests, Mukesh heard that he had passed and would start his nine months of training within two weeks. On the eve of his departure, Saka and Lali stayed up most of the night cooking special sweets for Mukesh. The next morning, as he hurried to leave, he bade his brief farewells to Saka with affectionate threats: "If I hear any bad stories about you [while I'm gone], I'll throw you in the river!" Saka later laughed as she imitated Mukesh, saying "If he had not been in such a rush as he left, I would have got the whole lecture!"

Saka and I then set off to the forest to collect lichen, both of us fighting back our tears as we trudged up the steep slopes in silence. A couple of hours later, when we were high up in the forest, sitting on a giant rock overlooking the village, Saka pointed out the tiny figure of her brother on his way down to the road, threading his way along the spidery paths, his long winter shadow cast across the brown fields. She was happy to witness the beginning of his journey. It seemed a very fitting send-off for a little sister to watch from high up in the forest as her brother left to join the army—the stuff of mountain songs!

I left the village three months later, in March 2004. In August 2005, I received an email from Vinod, Saka's eldest brother, in Delhi informing me that Lali's health had rapidly deteriorated. Mukesh's fortuitous acceptance into the army had entitled his family to military medical care. Taking advantage of this, Lali had been for a checkup in a military hospital whose facilities were far superior to government or private clinics nearby, which they could not, in any case, afford. Sadly, however, they discovered serious kidney failure, and Lali was immediately sent to a large army hospital in Delhi to start dialysis and prepare for a transplant. Vinod had to give up his job to look after her.

Lali's husband, Balram, had come to Delhi. His blood type and organs matched Lali's and he donated one of his kidneys. The operation took place in December 2005. Both recovered well, and after a period of convalescence, Balram returned to Bemni. But Lali will never be able to live far from a hospital, where she continues to rely on dialysis. She hates life in Delhi and yearns to return to the village, but has only been able to return once, for just three weeks, since her operation.

The extent to which Lali now relies on her children is all too clear. Vinod looks after her on a daily basis. In mid 2007, as Lali had grown a little stronger, Vinod was able to begin a part-time computing course in an attempt to train himself for more lucrative employment. Earlier in 2007, Mukesh was accepted by the United Nations Peacekeeping Force, and he was posted to the Democratic Republic of Congo. He earns Rs. 40,000 a month in this post: a small fortune for his family. His salary and the army medical facilities that Mukesh's position provides no doubt saved his mother's life. Meanwhile, Saka remains in Bemni, working the land largely on her own, growing enough food to eat and to send to Delhi. She grows ever older and remains unmarried, a situation that increasingly worries the family.

Note

1. I have used pseudonyms for the village and for all of the villagers, including Saka.

Further Reading

Dyson, J. (2008). "Harvesting Identities: Youth, Work and Gender in the Indian Himalayas." *Annals of the Association of American Geographers* 98(1): 160–179.
Mehta, M. (1996). "'Our Lives are No Different from That of our Buffaloes': Agricultural Change and Gendered Spaces in a Central Himalayan Valley." In *Feminist Political Ecology: Global Issues and Local Experiences,* ed. D. Rocheleau, B. Thomas-Slayter and E. Wangari, 180–210. London: Routledge.

Kristina Gibson

3

"All My Life, I've Bounced Around"

A Portrait of Blacc

When you take the A train from Manhattan to the eastern-most reaches of New York City, you have a one-in-three chance of ending up in Far Rockaway, the town where Blacc was born. Winding along metal rails set high above the neighborhoods, the A train takes you over a seemingly endless landscape of brick houses, rusting gas stations, and weed-filled cemeteries. Eventually the tracks split like a twisted trident, with one prong veering off toward the Atlantic Ocean and the Rockaway Peninsula. Perched on the far edge of New York City, wedged between the flat, grey waters of the ocean and the affluent suburbs of Long Island, Far Rockaway is familiar to most New Yorkers only because its name adorns the side of the A train. A world away from the car horns, taxis, and skyscrapers of Manhattan, this neighborhood is the other New York City.

The town of Far Rockaway has changed from nineteenth-century neighborhoods populated by Orthodox Jews and Irish Catholics to today's mix of working-class communities of African and Central Americans. The gentrification that transformed other neighborhoods has not made it out to Far Rockaway. The occasional decaying mansion still dots the residential streets, but a more common sight is of two-story multifamily homes, their flat facades covered in weathered wooden clapboards or cheap vinyl siding and surrounded by chain-link fences. Like many working-poor neighborhoods in New York City, Far Rockaway went through severe periods of unemployment, rising crime and drug use, community breakdown, and physical decay from the 1970s to the 1990s. When Blacc was born to a young, single mother in 1985, Far Rockaway was a graying, inner-city neighborhood, far from the city.

Street youth in New York City overwhelmingly come from a number of neighborhoods much like Far Rockaway, neighborhoods situated on the fringes of the city both geographically and economically. In New York City youth of color from the outer boroughs make up two-thirds of the street youth population. They hop subways into Manhattan to seek friends, find work, escape families and problems, and to find help. Blacc is one such youth. I present Blacc's story linearly, from his early childhood to the present day, to highlight a common trajectory of youth homelessness that includes pre-homeless conditions, socialization into street life, and engagement with social welfare. I first met Blacc at the end of a two-year, critical ethnographic study of street youth and street outreach workers in New York City. As part of this research, I spent many hours on the streets with young people and social workers, attempting to understand the everyday social forces that shaped the young people's lives, actions, and opportunities. The experience of homelessness can feel chaotic as young people bounce in and out of shelters, jobs, homes, and the streets. The layering of homeless experiences have resulted in where Blacc is today: a young man who is a successful peer youth worker and who is still facing a future as a homeless adult.

The Pre-Homeless Years

Blacc spent the first five years of his life going from one foster home to the next. "My mom . . . my biological mom was in Far Rockaway. She had my little brother and my little sister and another one on the way. It was kind of crazy for her." Blacc, along with his next youngest brother, made his way through a dozen homes in all. Blacc saw his mother from time to time during his moves between foster homes. But her appearances appeared to follow no logic. "Yeah. She used to come by regularly to give me an ass-whupping for no reason." Blacc would never live with his mother again. When he was eleven, she died of cancer. "It's kind of funny 'cause sometimes I hear her call my name or something like that. It's spooky." For Blacc, the few memories that stand out from these early years are the death of a neighbor's child and the closeness that he felt toward his own brother.

In 1990, a couple from Far Rockaway adopted Blacc along with his four siblings. They knew Blacc's mother from the neighborhood. Blacc would live with this family for the next fourteen years—starting and finishing school, making friends, learning to fight, and growing up in their home.

Despite the instability of his early childhood and growing up in a community beset with socioeconomic problems, Blacc doesn't think of himself as a troubled or troublesome kid.

> I would never take off for days at a time. It's just, I missed a night once or twice, something like that. But it wasn't like I was a delinquent. I always did go to [public] school, except for when I was misbehaving or something like that. My grades were always good in school. Then high school, I guess that's when I really started to fight. Because in junior high school I was still a punk. My friends were like, "You know we're not always going to be there for you, you need to know how to protect yourself." From that day on, I started to defend myself . . . I was pretty good at it.

Becoming a Street Kid

When Blacc was nineteen, he had a series of arguments with his adopted mother over his lifestyle and lack of employment.

> I was acting. I had just finished doing a show—The Dissenters. I wasn't working; I was just acting but I wasn't getting paid for it. Which was my mom's biggest thing: "You don't have a job, you're coming in at 1–2 o'clock in the morning. Sometimes you don't even come in; its taking up all your time." Stuff like that. So just a lot of bitching. So one Sunday, we had an argument.

After that fight his father kicked him out. "My father said, 'You have thirty minutes to pack your shit and get out of here.' Shit, okay. And that was just it. I could have begged, but I was like, 'I'm not going to beg no more to stay in his house.' So I packed my shit and I left."

Over the course of the next two years Blacc moved nearly twenty times: staying with his sister and her boyfriend's family; with a friend's family; with a second friend in a house with several roommates; in that same house after his friend burnt it down; in a studio apartment with three other people; on the subway; in a youth shelter; in an adult men's homeless shelter; back on the subway; at an overnight youth center; at a youth emergency shelter in Times Square; back to the first youth shelter; in a transitional living center for homeless boys; back to the emergency shelter; in Union Square Park; on rooftops; in empty trucks; at a gay, lesbian, bisexual, transgender, and queer (GLBTQ) youth shelter; at a gay-friendly church shelter; returning to the first GLBTQ youth shelter; and finally in a transitional living program for GLBTQ homeless youth.

In the popular media, street kids are usually portrayed as white teenagers from the suburbs living the life of urban nomads or gutter punks: sleeping under bridges or in abandoned warehouses, taking too many drugs, and losing themselves in the "mean streets" of our cities. In reality, about two-thirds of the street youth population of New York City are of color, primarily black or Hispanic, range in age from twelve to twenty-four, and are from poverty-stricken neighborhoods throughout the city. African American, bisexual, nearly six-feet tall and heavy-set, Blacc may not fit the stereotype of homeless youth, but his is the face of youth homelessness in New York City today. When I first met Blacc in 2006, he was twenty-one years old and had been on and off the streets for two years. He was working as a peer educator and outreach worker for a GLBTQ drop-in center in midtown Manhattan. I had been hired by the center to train peer youth outreach workers based on my ongoing research on adult street outreach workers. Amid the crowds of young people pouring in and out of the center during the day, Blacc stood out through his calmness. He takes his time when speaking, often measuring his words thoughtfully and carefully. "Blacc" is the name that he chose for himself when he became homeless.

There is no single route or event that leads to a life on the streets. Homelessness often evolves as a series of progressively precarious living and housing arrangements often interspersed with periods of relative safety. This was Blacc's experience, too. Young people often begin by living with extended family members. After being kicked out by his father, Blacc moved in with his sister. He told me:

> Her boyfriend is a jackass. He's a big-time thief. A very big-time thief. He used to steal cars and sell the rims. Stuff like that. [The police] raided the house and whatnot. Because he beat up a sanitation officer. Half the things that went on in the house I didn't know about because I was staying with my sister sometimes and then I wasn't staying there sometimes. Because his family was very arrogant towards me. Me and his cousin was like really, really cool. But his other family was, like, obnoxious.

Still in Far Rockaway at this point and living only a block from his parents' house, the feeling of being a slightly unwanted guest led Blacc to spend more of his time with friends and their families.

I stayed with another friend.... I celebrated Christmas at my
friend's house and that was the best Christmas I ever had. There was
no gifts. We woke up and had a water fight. It was cold as shit, but
we had a water fight. I tell people that to this day and they're like,
"How can you have a water fight on Christmas?" But what else was
there to do? You're a bunch of poor people. So you have a water
fight ... it was good. But after a while, I didn't want to intrude on
their space and then my friend started going out with this girl.

During this time, an altercation with a man who had sexually assaulted
one of Blacc's friends resulted in Blacc being arrested. After he was re-
leased from jail, he moved in with another friend. That too would only last
a short time. "He [the friend] left the house to go get some money from his
father one night. And his father called him 'gay.' Because me and him were
sharing ... like sleeping in the same room and whatnot. And his father
and was like 'chi-chi mon'—he was Jamaican. So he took out a blade and
he was cutting his father up." After this incident, Blacc's friend set fire to
the house where they were living. "Yeah, because he thought his father
was going to call the police. It was me, him, two other roommates. So he
did that craziness.... I could have been asleep when he did shit like that."

Blacc and his friends would go on living in the burnt-out shell of the
house for several nights. One of the girls who had been displaced by the fire
was able to get a small studio apartment and invited Blacc and his girlfriend to stay with her.

I was staying with a friend. Actually, she became my friend after the
friend that I was living with burnt down the house. So we was actually living in the burnt down part. Then her landlord helped her get a
studio temporarily. She was like, "You can come stay with me." So, at
the time, it was freezing cold ... there was two inches of snow on the
ground, so I was like, "Fine with me." It was me, her, her boyfriend,
and my girlfriend. So she accepted me and my girlfriend. She looked
after me. I'll never forget her name. It was Melissa. She was a struggling artist. She brought us both in. So we stayed there about a month
or two. Then he [the landlord] locked us out. He knew that me and my
girlfriend were staying there and he locked her out of the place....
But he didn't give her any warning that he was going to lock her out.

That night, Blacc and his girlfriend, along with Melissa and her boyfriend,
tried to get into a homeless shelter in Brooklyn. But because Melissa was

pregnant and didn't want to be separated from her boyfriend, the couples decided to stick together and opted for sleeping on the train instead.

They chose the A train. As one of the longest subway lines in New York, the A train is sometimes referred to as a moving hotel by the city's homeless population. From its start in Far Rockaway, the A train travels through Queens, Brooklyn, Manhattan, and finally the Bronx, before it turns around and makes its way back—nearly two hours from end to end. "That was the only one I knew at the time . . . like the back of my hand. So I was like, I'm not going to stray from it. . . . So we slept on the train that night. During the day we had separate business to take care of and we were supposed to meet up but we missed each other." Blacc searched for his other friends for several days. He went back to the first shelter and searched at a local adult Christian shelter. While he was at the Christian shelter, staff there contacted a volunteer group that aids the homeless. By then, Blacc had heard that his friends were at an adult shelter, but he thought he was too young to get into that particular shelter. The volunteer group eventually brought him to the largest youth homeless shelter in New York City.

Run by a religious charity, the Youth Shelter was founded in the late 1960s in New York City to house and care for homeless youth aged eighteen to twenty-one. In 2006, out of the 300 emergency shelter beds for homeless youth in New York City, 270 were at the Youth Shelter. Most homeless youth in New York City eventually have some contact with the Youth Shelter. Any young people without identification that are picked up by police at the city's bus or train terminals are transported to the Youth Shelter. According to Blacc, the Youth Shelter was "a hellhole." "They just was like, they're shady . . . staff don't talk to you with respect . . . you know, some shelters are better than others." The shelter's reputation for poor treatment of gay and lesbian street youth is well known among other social service providers. Out of the 10,000–20,000 homeless youth attempting to survive each year on streets of New York City, social service providers estimate that 30 percent are GLBTQ.[1] Of these, the majority are youth of color like Blacc.

Blacc stayed at the Youth Shelter for just over a month. It was winter in New York City and he was willing to put up with uncomfortable conditions in order to avoid sleeping outside and alone in the freezing cold. It was during this time that Blacc worked in both the informal (street) economy and at legal, formal economy jobs. Street youth have four primary ways of making money while homeless: sex work (prostitution), drug trade, theft, and panhandling ("spanging" or "spare-changing"). While some street youth also have jobs in the formal economy, most are minimum-wage jobs and are far below the income necessary to attain an apartment in New York City. Blacc and his friends worked the third option (theft), by "bending" metro cards. They would pick up spent metro cards, bend them in a particular way so that they would work again and then charge people cash to swipe them onto the subway:

> We would bend metro cards and swipe. We would find them on the ground. We would bend them until they worked and then we would swipe people in with the metro cards, onto the train. It's totally illegal . . . it's actually a felony now . . . it would be really crazy . . . we would go to the [station] at Times Square, on 43rd Street, right underneath the [police] precinct. So like, we really had balls. There were a couple of times that they got a rein on us, but they couldn't find anything on us. All the metro cards we had on us weren't bent. Because we would bend them as we get the customers. We were pretty good at it. Then I got out of it because I had gotten a job. I always make it a habit, that when I have a legal job, then I don't do anything else illegal. So I stopped swiping.

Blacc was kicked out of the Youth Shelter after a month because of a fight with another resident. He was then sent to the city-run adult men's homeless shelter in Brooklyn. The Men's Shelter is housed in an old armory from the late 1800s, converted in the early 1980s to house hundreds of the city's swelling adult homeless population. Rising housing costs, unemployment, and the closing of numerous state mental hospitals all fed into a population of nearly thirty thousand people seeking shelter each night in New York City. At one point the Men's Shelter would sleep nine hundred single men on the floor of its old drill hall. Eventually, dangerous conditions, theft, fighting, and drugs convinced many residents that it might be safer to sleep on the streets. The neoliberalization of the welfare state in the United States during the 1990s saw a strong shift from larger warehouse-like, city-run shelters to a proliferation of smaller, privately run shelters and transitional housing centers, usually specializing in one or two "problem" issues, such as drug abuse, mental illness, or work readiness. By the time Blacc arrived there in 2005, the Men's Shelter held just 350 beds. Drug use, fighting, and theft were still rampant. Blacc would spend nearly two months there.

Because he had already been barred from the primary under-twenty-one youth shelter in the city, Blacc had little choice but to stay in an adult shelter until his six-month suspension from the Youth Shelter was over. While there are nearly a dozen small shelters for homeless youth in New York City, most contain fewer than six beds and often have waiting lists of over one hundred young people. His other option was to hit the streets again. Conditions in adult homeless shelters are often chaotic and frightening for homeless youth.

> This guy who had HIV, he was HIV positive, one day he cut his wrists and put blood all over the place, all over people. I was like, "No, I don't want to deal with that." Yeah. I'm not going to go through my life like that. But like I said, anywhere you go, if you're homeless, you're going to find someone who's going to watch your back and you're going to watch their back. I guess that's the rules of the streets. From the men's shelter, I was on the train again with some friends that I knew from [the Youth Shelter].

According to Blacc, the first rule of the streets is that you stick with your friends. Finding and keeping your friends may mean the difference between surviving or not on the streets. Street youth, many of whom have experienced interrupted childhoods characterized by chronic broken trust, often form closely knit street families. Here each member takes on multiple roles and responsibilities. Shelters are designed to serve individual homeless youth and often break up street families.

The second rule of the streets is to not appear homeless:

> Through it all, when I was sleeping on the train, you would think that I was just a guy that fell asleep on the train. You wouldn't think I was homeless. Through my whole sleeping on the streets début and whatnot, I always took care of myself. I never looked like I was homeless. Even today, you'd never know I was homeless unless I told you. . . . People look at me. . . . I don't tell them. They can make whatever assumption they want to make.

Keeping a sense of self-respect is a Herculean task for homeless youth: "If you forget who you are, you'll end up on the streets forever." Not looking homeless is an important survival strategy for many young people. Being identified as homeless potentially draws dangerous attention from police or drug dealers and pimps, and can attract ridicule from the general public.

The third rule of the street is to keep moving. By the time Blacc was sleeping on the A train again, he had been living in a cycle from street to shelter for nearly a year. His fellow street friends offered a measure of security. And the A train was familiar territory. "I used to stay with them on the train because they didn't have a place to go. I had a bed at the Men's Shelter. I really didn't like it, but it was a bed. I would have kept the bed, if I didn't know that they were sleeping on the train. I was like, you know, 'You guys are sleeping on the train. I'll sleep on the train too.'" It is through informal networks of other homeless youth that street kids find out about shelters, jobs, places to obtain a free meal, and innumerable other pieces of survival information.

After another short stint on the A train, Blacc entered a small, non-profit youth shelter that he had heard about from other street kids. He only stayed there for two months: "I used to drink a lot. I came in drunk. . . . So I got discharged." From the small youth shelter, Blacc spent a week in an emergency shelter in the Bronx before heading back to Manhattan and his friends, some of whom were sleeping in Times Square:

> We used to hang out up there. Cop a squat [hang out] by the ticket booth. We wouldn't go to sleep until the streets were dying down. . . . there was always something to do, somewhere to go. . . . We would just like hang out, talk to people, flirt . . . all kinds of things. It was just me and my friend Offwhite. . . . We called him Offwhite because he was this Jewish kid and he was, like, really, really black. He smoked weed and everything. [Offwhite] knew this guy "Ace." . . . He used to make sure that me and Offwhite had something to eat and stuff like that. When you're homeless, you always have to find somebody . . . and you always have to look out after each other. You know what I'm saying?

After a while, Blacc decided to try the Youth Shelter again. "Well, I went back last year. . . . I had to have a job in order to get back in. So I had this job, but they said 'No.'" The staff instead referred Blacc to a transitional living program for homeless youth in Brooklyn. He would only stay for a few months: "The kids there were, like, crazy. . . . I got discharged from there for fighting. I had a fight with this kid. Over gang matters and what-not. I used to have anger problems. Now I can leave it. He was Blood. I'm Crip. He touched something he wasn't supposed to touch and we started scrapping. It's a boundary matter." From the transitional living program both Blacc and the other youth he fought with were discharged and sent to the same emergency overnight shelter in the Bronx where Blacc had been before. "So after a while, I spoke to him. . . . I'm not one who is going to hold a grudge. We talked, 'get over it.' . . . So we was man enough to put it behind us. Like I said, when you're on the street, somebody is going to have to take care of you or you're going to have to take care of somebody . . . so we had that little buddy system going on and it actually worked out pretty good."

Unfortunately for Blacc, the six-month suspension that he received from the transitional living program would be up four months after his twenty-first birthday, the age at which he must leave the program: "I didn't want to sit there and waste my time if I was going to age out in two months." The emergency shelter in the Bronx once again tried to get Blacc back into the adult shelter system. "They thought I was in the Men's Shelter because they give you a referral to the Men's Shelter and I was like 'Okay, I'll go.' But in all actuality, I was sleeping on the train . . . because when I did go to the Men's Shelter . . . it was like . . . hell."

Blacc stayed in a number of places in addition to the A train. He tried living in and around Union Square, sleeping on benches and picnic tables, but there was too much drug dealing and police presence:

When there was a lot of drug use going on back there . . . I guess [the police] scoped it out . . . then they shut things down . . . like, you know, "You can't sleep here" and it's like 11:30 P.M. We would just move over to where the tables and benches are and sleep there. But most of the nights I would stay up and watch the skateboarders do their tricks, 'cause that's what interests me. And I would stay on Twenty-fifth Street, in one of the project buildings near Tenth Avenue. I had some skateboarder friends . . . you know, we used to go over there, get drunk, whatever. I think that's the biggest thing you do when you're homeless . . . go with the coolest things. It seemed like the coolest thing. You stay drunk to run away from problems. Not really because you have the money, but to get away from problems. Then I met up with another friend that was sleeping in the project buildings. . . . I stayed in there. Up at the roof. . . . It was just cold and there wasn't enough room for two people. Nothing that I would do again. . . . Then I was going to sleep in the U-Haul trucks. Which most homeless kids used to do. . . . It's just a parking garage where the U-Hauls used to park their trucks. But since a lot of kids would sleep there, it was locked. They moved them to a different location. I had slept in the U-Hauls before. So I figured that I could do it again. But then I went to Kat's [Joint] to use the bathroom, and they asked me was I in here for intake, and I was like "Yeah!"

Housed in an old protestant church on Manhattan's west side, Kat's Joint was the first GLBTQ youth shelter opened in New York City. On any given night, about a dozen youth people will crash in the back room of the church. "It's a sauna. It gets awfully hot in there. It's a very crazy environment. It could be a very cool environment. It depends on how you are and how you interact with other youth. It's just a big open space, full of cabinets . . . there aren't really beds . . . we sleep on cots. But in the summer most of the kids sleep on the floor and whatnot. It's more comfortable."

After a few months at Kat's Joint, Blacc was transferred to an affiliated center in another church in Queens. However, the Queens shelter was closed after only a few short months. It was shut down quickly and quietly, taking social workers by surprise. Several weeks after the shelter had closed there was still confusion over why it had closed and if it would ever reopen. In the meantime, Blacc went back to Kat's Joint, which was now overcrowded, housing both their regular residents and the youth coming from the closed shelter. Blacc had been back at Kat's Joint for about a month at the time that I met him in the summer of 2006.

Finding a Way Off the Streets

When I met Blacc through my work training peer outreach counselors, he had been working at GLBTQ drop-in center for a few months. Housed in a grey stone, twelve-story office building in midtown Manhattan, the drop-in center offers counseling and social services for young GLBTQ homeless. The majority of the center's clients are young black men from the ages of thirteen to twenty-three. Part of Blacc's job at the center is to watch the front door on the nights the youth have dances and social events, making sure that none of the members are harassed entering or leaving the building. Blacc's other job is to go out and talk with other street kids, telling them about the services of the center and handing out free condoms. Peer outreach seems to come naturally for Blacc—he's been looking out for other homeless youth for years. The various jobs around the center are also giving him space to take a step back from his life, from his homeless self. Being on the streets has been a hard transition to adulthood for Blacc: "I've learned how to be a hell of a lot more independent. I've learned the city more. . . . You learn a lot . . . but I miss my bed. I miss a bed. Out of all the things that I miss, I miss going home . . . all the things that you take for granted when you're there."

But Blacc doesn't envision himself going home: "I think about living other places. I do want to leave New York for good. And I think about where I would go. Because I don't want to go where I have to start this bullshit all over again. . . . Homeless is not fun at all. Its very hard." Blacc sees himself getting off the streets, but maybe not in New York: "I might come back every year or something like that, but I've gotta get out of New York for a while. Just for a little while. New York is just too hard." Blacc is hoping that a construction job outside of New York might offer the dual benefits of employment and getting him out of the city for a while.

A month after this conversation, Blacc was kicked out of Kat's Joint for fighting with a staff member. A social worker related the incident to me later:

> Basically, a staff member assaulted a client. He pushed him out of an office, hard enough to throw him against the wall of the adjoining hallway. This client was a friend of Blacc's. When Blacc confronted the staff member, the staff member became irate, screaming insults at Blacc. The staff member told Blacc that he had to leave for the night. When Blacc turned to leave, the staff member continued to yell and insult Blacc, following him out into the vestibule. At this point, Blacc turned and threw a cup of apple juice onto the staff member.

The end result was that Blacc was suspended for a week. Blacc was eventually allowed back into Kat's Joint, but within weeks would be transferred to a long-term transitional living program for GLBTQ youth in Harlem. In this program, Blacc is sharing a small apartment with several other young people.

It is tempting to try and summarize Blacc's experiences into a few pithy metaphors about the "mean streets" and the hopelessness of fighting your way through a system that seems designed for failure. The strengths that are rewarded on the street are rarely the qualities rewarded in the shelter system. Fighting and laying low, independence and sticking together seem like contradictory strategies for surviving the streets, yet homeless youth manage to negotiate these tactics with a fluid grace, shifting goals and expectations to manage what few opportunities they encounter to improve their lives here and now. The lives of street kids are all too often disruptive, violent, fast, boring, fragile, and short. It is important to remember that Blacc's story and the stories of others like him are ongoing. There are estimated to be 1.5 million homeless and runaway youth in the United States, yet these young people remain a nearly invisible and all-but-forgotten population. Blacc hopes that his story will begin to change that.

Note

1. See Empire State Coalition of Youth and Family Services, "The New York City 2007 Homeless Youth Survey," www.empirestatecoalition.org.

Further Reading

Hagan, John, and Bill McCarthy. (1998). *Mean Streets: Youth Crime and Homelessness.* Cambridge: Cambridge University Press.

Karabanow, Jeff. (2004). *Being Young and Homeless: Understanding How Youth Enter and Exit Street Life.* New York: Peter Lang.

Lewnes, Alexia. (2001). *Misplaced: New York City's Street Kids.* New York: Xenium Press.

Paula Meth

4

Vusi Majola

"Walking Until the Shoes Is Finished"

Vusi was one of twenty men who participated in my "Men, Violence, and Methodology" research project carried out in Durban, South Africa, during 2006–2007 by my research assistant Sibongile Maphumulo. Vusi's story told below is an assemblage of a detailed and emotive solicited diary he wrote over a four-week period, an extensive life history interview, and a series of photographs he took to illustrate his diary entries. His words are delivered through Maphumulo's translative voice and his story told through my narrative voice.

Two themes run through Vusi's life story. The first is a prolonging of "youth" as a life stage at the same time as an acceleration of youth's transition to adulthood. Youthful traits, such as hedonistic living and economic dependency, persist well into adulthood. But much decision making, familial and sexual relationships, economic survival, and exposure to political brutalities demand adult maturity. A second theme is the persistence of a tenacious willingness to survive and also to enjoy life in the face of the daily overt dangers facing young people. These dangers range from violence to the high risk of HIV infection.

Vusi's story must be understood against the background of his economic, social, and political context. One significant aspect of this context is the provenance of Zulu culture, which is traditionally fiercely patriarchal and hierarchical. The everyday lives of young men and women in Durban are explicitly shaped by this pervading political reality. But changing circumstances now mean that youth at times resist age hierarchies. Vusi's ideas about women, parenting, and marriage provide us with an example of these continuities and changes.

The rise of the African National Congress (ANC) also shapes Vusi's story. Durban is a stronghold for the ANC, which has a history of violent clashes with a regional black opposition party, the IFP (Inkatha Freedom Party). Being politically neutral was never really an option for young black South Africans, who perceived apartheid to be their ultimate enemy. Resistance to apartheid came at a price: children's education, home lives, safety, and employment prospects were disrupted. But resistance also produced an inspired and explicitly political personal identity for millions of young South Africans. Vusi's story illustrates this contradiction and exposes the everyday realities of post-apartheid South Africa, where freedom, hope, and expectation are pitted against painfully slow rates of service delivery, debilitating unemployment, frightening levels of HIV infection, and high rates of crime. I turn now to Vusi's story to explore the remarkable and unremarkable life of a resident of one of Durban's informal settlements.

Growing Up in Apartheid South Africa

Vusi was born in the township of Clermont in Durban in the late 1970s. As a child he lived with both of his parents, and while they worked he was cared for by his paternal grandmother. When Vusi was fifteen, his parents divorced and he remained living with his father. His mother moved to live with her natal family in the rural area of Ndwedwe. Vusi was one of five children but the only son born to his parents. After the divorce, his father remarried a woman with four of her own children, extending Vusi's siblings to eight. Vusi's decision to photograph his stepsisters (Figure 4.1) illustrates his comfort with his stepfamily. But the photograph also reveals his father's patriarchal attitudes toward women and sexuality; Vusi explained that his oldest stepsister was not present because "she is pregnant and my father [was] chasing her [away from] home."

Vusi described his relationship with his stepmother positively: "It is good because she treat us as [her] own child." He said that his relations with his family were strong. Vusi appeared relatively forgiving about his parents' divorce and stated the cause blandly without passing judgment: "I'm not exactly sure but I think it was because of my father was drinking a lots. He was use to shout [at] my mother if he [was] drunk."

Vusi's experience of school education during apartheid was complicated by political upheaval and an inadequate educational system. His description of his school in KwaMashu (Durban) as "bad" and "chaotic"

FIG 4.1   *Vusi's stepsisters*
(Photograph by Paula Meth)

typified township schools during the 1980s and 1990s, as anti-apartheid activism and state-fuelled civil violence reached its climax. Vusi illustrated this by elaborating on a terrifying incident at his school in 1990: "It . . . was the time of political violence and the principal of that school was died. There were people come to school and shot the principal. . . . We were in classroom and the principal was died in his office. We were heard the gun and we come out and saw the two men running with the guns." As a result of this incident, and general political upheaval, Vusi changed schools frequently, moving to live with family in rural Ndwedwe, which was relatively peaceful. His resultant education was patchy and fragmented as he explained: "I learn in Clermont from first year to standard four [penultimate year of primary school, approximately aged 10], standard five in Kwa-Mashu, six and seven in Ndwedwe, in standard eight I [went] back to Clermont and standard nine [penultimate year of high school] in Clermont."

The township of Clermont—Vusi's residence as a child—was renowned for its political activism and an abundance of political leaders lived in the area. Vusi, an ANC supporter, described the area as predominately ANC controlled and alluded to violent strategies on the part of the ANC to maintain this dominance: "There were three other political parties but the people who were supporting other party the ANC was kill them by burning their houses or putting the wheel [on] the neck and pour petrol and burn. People were die while they crying." Vusi confirmed that these acts "happened in front of me" and his memories were that the violence was random and brutal: "They didn't choose, if they come in your house they killed all the family members."

Like many township youth in South Africa, Vusi was drawn into politics at a young age by fellow residents in his area. He recalled being told about the work of Mandela "[what] he done and that things was motivate us to be part of the politics. We were want freedom and another thing you know the songs of politics was encouraging us to participate." Vusi's grandmother was a member of the ANC Women's League, a powerful body at that time, but Vusi joined the ANC in the face of his parents' overt dislike of politics. He explained that, despite their concerns, his parents did not prevent him joining the ANC because "every one was joining political parties [especially] in youth, they [i.e., local political activists] didn't like persons who were neutral. We were living together in the camp and I was going home if I need clothes to change or food." Training in ANC camps accelerated young people's exposure to adult experiences, as children became familiar with modes of killing and tactics of resistance. Campaigning also exposed Vusi to brutality at an early age and he described witnessing the death of his friend Jabulani when he was fourteen years old: "Even now I can't forget that incident and I don't know how I [was] safe from that."

Vusi's memories of apartheid referred specifically to racist practices and discrimination. For example, Vusi said that, "In 1989, I remember if you go to beach there [was a] swimming pool [where it was] written that it's for 'White only' and the place for entertainment such as clubs for example Capital Red Club was for 'White only.' . . . In the post offices or banks the White persons didn't stand in the queue because they got [more] power than us." But his memories were also more brutal and revealed high levels of state-sponsored violence on the part of the apartheid government as well as the particular vulnerability of young black men. "If we were sitting in groups as youth along the road the police were come and beat us with the cane for nothing. Other people were arrested and even now their families didn't know . . . where were died because the police didn't tell them. The police take them and didn't come back." Vusi also mentioned strategies used by the state and the privileged white minority to maintain spatial and political separation in his discussions of white housing, which had "security who were standing there [at the] gate were tall and carrying guns." Urban space was not public space during apartheid—or at least not for the majority public—and Vusi's memories of passing through the city center revealed the difficulties faced by a young black man during this time: "If you walking at night in town the police were searching you and beat you, sometimes you [had to] walk because . . . the transport is finished [i.e., the buses or taxis were no longer running]. After 1994 everything has changed."

Political Campaigning and Living Informally

Vusi lived in Cato Crest, a large informal area within the redevelopment settlement of Cato Manor in inner Durban. His father built the property—which is made out of durable materials but lacks key services—in the late 1980s. His father subsequently moved to the nearby area of Manor Gardens (formerly a middle-class white suburb). Vusi moved into the Cato Crest house from Clermont township in 2003 in order "to watch my father's house and look [for] the job in town and it's near to walk [to town]." Watching his father's house also required Vusi to act as a resident landlord: his father rents out three rooms of the property to tenants. This practice of "shack farming" is common in informal settlements. Vusi photographed his home for this project (Figure 4.2) and its relative formality and generous dimensions corroborates its use as rental accommodations.

Life in Cato Crest held mixed fortunes for Vusi, and he had conflicting opinions about the suitability and appeal of the area. Sociability was a positive feature of living informally and he explained that "the first time I was miss my place where I grow up because I left my friends there [indeed he emphasizes his initial loneliness later] . . . but now I don't miss it because I got many friends in this area." This sociability came at a price. Informal settlements are typically composed of residents from a wide range

FIG 4.2   *Vusi's home in Cato Crest* (Photograph by Paula Meth)

Fig 4.3   *"December 25" Thokozan's place of death* (Photograph by Paula Meth)

of backgrounds and destinations. The resultant social incohesion is often cited by residents and analysts as the cause of the excessive rates of crime in the area, and Vusi shared this opinion: "[t]he crime of this area is abusing us. People who are staying here are not the same and [they are] coming from different places. We didn't know people who are staying here." All twenty of my research participants provided stories of violence. Vusi offered a particularly anguished account of criminal violence which he further supported by photographing the place where his friend, Thokozani's, body was found (Figure 4.3).

Vusi said:

On the 25 December 2005 we were all happy friends and neighbors because [it was] Christmas. My friend [Thokozani] left me at home and he said he [was] going to stop 5 [a taxi and bus stop] and he will [be] back soon. It was around 7 [in the] evening, but it was not dark because it [was] summer. The criminals come to him and robbed [from] him a cell phone, wallet and remov[ed his] tackies [trainers, sneakers] which were Nike. What is painful [is that] they tied him with the rope in the neck and cut the neck. We find a message next day early in the morning, he is dead. We wake up and go there. We find him lying in the dirty water. In this area there is water walking [flowing] around the house because people have no place to throw [dispose of] water. He was lying [in] that water. People of that place—stop 5—were covering him with the white cloth. They kill him between those houses of that place. What was abusing us [was that] the police was take time to come and we were looking [Thokozani] lying like that.... If I pass through to this place something is happening in my mind if I [remember] that day [Thokozani was] lying in the bad place.

Thokozani's murder illustrates the dangers facing youth within this settlement and it is also illustrative of the breadth of emotional experiences that young people are forced to manage. In his attempt to make sense of the many other accounts of crime and violence in Cato Crest, Vusi referred to the material realities of the informal settlement which he argued facilitated the proliferation of crime. For example, he explained that, "It is different to where I come from because [in] informal settlements; [it is] crowded, dark, police didn't have access to walk around because of the shacks and dirty place. Actually I was fear to walk at night because of the noise of the guns in this place." Pathways and transportation routes were frequently cited by Vusi as sites of conflict and crime, illustrating the day-to-day difficulties for residents attempting to conduct their business. Indeed, his decision to photograph a bridge was telling; almost all the other men in the project mentioned and photographed bridges as key sites of vulnerability. Vusi used his photograph (Figure 4.4) to illustrate his story of a mugging incident he suffered while crossing the bridge when walking home one night with two women. Two men took ZAR37 from him—all he had—and he said "I [did] not fight back. I gave him what I've got."[1]

As revealed in the account of Thokozani's murder and evident in Figure 4.4, sanitation facilities are limited in Cato Crest, and the issue of water pollution plagued Vusi's diary entries.

There is water flowing passing at the back of my house. That water is dirty and bad smell. It is worse during the weekend [when] many people [are] doing washing. People were washing even the nappy [diaper] of the child. That water is abusing me because if it [is a] hot day I can't stay in my home because of that smell. I couldn't open the window [it] creates more mosquitoes. That channel of water is flowing passing to my house. They didn't have any place to throw water.... Even now that water still smells.

FIG 4.4   *The bridge of the incident* (Photograph by Paula Meth)

Although all squatter settlements lack basic facilities, those in Durban and its surroundings are particularly vulnerable as a result of the climate and geological landscape. Tropical rainstorms and an intensely hilly topography make the stability of informal housing in the city a challenge, and Cato Manor as an area was no exception.

In 2001 December there was a raining hard. If you staying in the informal settlements is bad if it raining. We were abus[ed] because our house were raining. It is not a proper house. If it rain while you not in your house you find many things wet and even the place to sleep such as bed if you have. That house abusing us [especially] the man because you have to climb in the roof to close [seal] where is leaking. That rain in December most of the houses were falling down. If it is raining hard [you] cannot sleep because sometimes that houses falling down [around] you while you sleep.

Vusi was involved in the upgrading of Cato Crest by virtue of his involvement in campaigning for the ANC. As the dominant political party in the area, the ANC was considered responsible for upgrading and renewal, and various developments within Cato Manor were cited as flagship projects of the ANC's leadership. Vusi was fiercely against opposition parties in the area and he suggested that the goal of formalizing the area was not necessarily shared by all residents. "Those other parties are against to the developments which take place in this area. They are enjoying that life of *mjondolo* [shacks] because some of them have business such as renting house and running tuck shop [small general store]. They know if we destroy those informal settlements their businesses should be gone." His anger was fuelled further by his personal stake in the developments: "I am hoping"—he said, to receive an "RDP [Reconstruction and Development Program—the ANC's 1994 manifesto program] house, two rooms and bathroom." Vusi's anxieties over how politics might impede this dream were clear: "Today [this] afternoon that other party was abusing people who are working as construction in this area. The [constructors are] building houses for development. What is painful to me is that, my new house is one of [those] houses [that] are disturb to be finished. We are going to ask the police to protect that construction."

Vusi's views on politics were not wholly positive. He explained that he worked as a volunteer campaigning for the ANC. He worked with a female Member of Parliament (MP) who approached him to volunteer. But he justified his acceptance of this request by then damning politics in general: "I was like to [I wanted to] do it because I took the decision to stop in that thing for politics. My future was destroyed by the politics and if you are in politics you walk until the shoes is finished, so I'm tired. There is no boss in the ANC even Thabo Mbeki is not a boss to us." He reinforced this view in his interview as he said "I didn't like now the politics. . . . The thing is that I hate to talk too much. In politics you have to talk lies every time and laughed even too hard [laugh heartily] to do that because you need the votes. There is no truth in politics. We convinced people by lies. For example many people are come to me and ask where the promises are. . . . I tell them the thing is coming slowly [they] must wait and they would get that houses." His calls for patience appear to also be attempts at self-persuasion given that he, too, was awaiting housing to be delivered by his very own party.

Vusi's description of "walking until the shoes is finished" is poignant and reveals a certain apathy toward political life and exhaustion with politics. He never broached the contradiction of suppressing his own patriarchal beliefs while working for a female MP, arguably an issue for many ANC supporters who publicly promoted women's rights but privately embraced the dominance of men. He continued to invest substantial energy in supporting the ANC locally and he pointed to various events and tasks in which he participated on behalf of his party. For example, Vusi explained that: "We launched all the structures such as [the] women's league, youth league and we also changed the council and the committee because the old committees [had] done the fraud in terms of developments." His commitment to local politics illustrated his proactive approach to improving his community's future, despite the dangers that this entailed. He spoke repeatedly of his fear of opposition parties and concerns over personal safety. He stated that "the other political parties believe in violence if something happened or if there is a misunderst[anding]. The political party I fear most is IFP because . . . they like to kill other parties."

> On the 10 February 2006 I was coming from my other home which is located in Manor Gardens. . . . When I [got] back to my shack I saw a crowd of people in [bus or taxi] stop 15 but I didn't fear because always [on] Friday [one] happen[s] to find many people in the road. I was walk when I turn to my house, I hear someone calling me and [say] "Stop there." I stop because I saw the lights of the torch and I was thought maybe was a police. When they near to me I saw that [the] people was the political party which is against us. They surrounding me and asking many questions. They were frighten me and want to beat me. I explain to them I coming from home. They said to me they want to decrease crime in this area because they beat criminals who are walking at night. I was fear and thought maybe they would kill me because they know me [and that] I belong to other political party. I was fear and trembling even at home.

"I Am Not Good in Relationships": Vusi as Boyfriend

Vusi had a strong sense of self and firm ideas about the position and rights of men. Reflecting broader patriarchal norms within Zulu society, Vusi believed that men should occupy a more powerful position in society than women. He justified this sentiment by referring to a particular model of gender politics within the home: "I think the men are more power[ful] than women because the end word at home is for men." Evidently, Vusi's gendered politics of male dominance centred around the home. Despite this, he was curiously hesitant to create this power base himself. He explained how he was delaying marriage and settling down because of his desire to be independent, or at least free from the curtailment presented by a wife: "I'm not ready to stay with [a] woman and I want to get married at the age of 36." This explanation is particularly significant given that he already had a seven-year-old daughter named Duduzile with his girlfriend, Nomusa, who both lived in the township of Clermont. Despite stating that he enjoyed visiting them and also underlining his deep love for Nomusa, his need for freedom overrode his immediate desires for parental and matrimonial responsibility. He explained:

> I know my self and I know my girlfriend, I don't like to talk too much [argue] or got headache because I [have been] drinking, I like to spen[d] time in entertainment place such as night clubs. I don't want any person to be boss [to] me. If I marry her now, she will complain if I come later [at night] at home and I think is better to get married later. At this time even [if] I come [home] in the morning no one was questioning me, it is nice. Maybe at the age of 35–36 I will be tired to go to night club.

Vusi's desire for maintaining a youthful and free lifestyle was clear and he was explicitly enthusiastic about nightclubs. He said: "I enjoy watching people dancing in night club and even if you depressed you laugh a lot there." He also admitted to meeting women on his nights out, explaining "The girlfriend I find in *shebeen* [informal drinking place] is not a serious thing [relationship] it just for that time only." Vusi was adamant about the sincerity of his love for Nomusa and also for Flora, his "other girlfriend" who lived in Johannesburg but visited Durban on her holidays. Maintaining a relationship with Flora required careful management of his "other girlfriends."

> [Flora] as she [is] working in Johannesburg if she is [on] holiday she was to stay with me all the time and I didn't have a chance to check other girlfriend. . . . My other girlfriends were complaining if [Flora] is here because I didn't have a time for them. All they know [is] that I got [Flora] who is my first girlfriend. She is staying to other province [Johannesburg] and if she here I give her all my love.

Vusi was unable to make a connection between his own behavior—pursuing and maintaining multiple relationships—and the behavior of those he regarded as "dishonest women." He stated that "I believe in love and respect and I didn't trust women except [Nomusa] because she is honest to me." Vusi spoke of how Nomusa once found him with another of his

girlfriends. Vusi said that he managed to convince Nomusa of his innocence: "I told her the lies because I was fear to tell her the truth." When
asked if she was suspicious about other women he explained that, "She sus-
pects but she [isn't] sure because if she phoned me she use to ask 'who are
with you' and [she] ask [me] to tell her I love [her] so that [she] will be sure
I'm alone." He then went on to tell a story about another of his girlfriends,
who was covertly seeing a friend of his while seeing him: "There was another girl who loved my friend . . . [my friend and I] were not aware of that
and she was not aware that [Phumlani] was my friend. She was shocked to
find that." Vusi explained how he found out about the girl's deception:
"Other my friend was told me that we sharing one girlfriend with my
friend." Vusi dealt with the situation man to man and arranged to meet
Phumlani. "We talk nicely and we were making that girl a fool. . . . We
were not interested but we were playing with her, actually we gave the les-
son to not love two men in the same area."

Vusi said that his relations with women were all sexual: "The only girlfriends I didn't sleep with . . . are that one I had at the young age, and it
was not serious love." The high levels of HIV infection in the KwaZulu
Natal region made it important for Vusi to act responsibly in relation to the
disease. He explained that, "Yes, I make sure to protect myself to getting
disease. . . . I'm afraid about this illness because it's eating the body slowly
and people talking whatever they like while you still alive." Although his
final concern revealed his anxiety about public perception of HIV status,
his comments about a fellow resident illustrated his sensitivity about the
illness: "There is one lady who was told us about her status. She was brave
to share with us. Her body was getting thin now. Her mind was not working properly because of the stress."

Vusi's multiple relationships could be viewed as a cultural norm and
embedded within a sense of "woman as property." In his diary, Vusi wrote:

On the 31 December 2005, while we were preparing to enter in
2006. My friend and I [have] got girlfriend[s] who are working in
Johannesburg. My cell phone rang and is my girlfriend [Flora] asked
me to come and celebrate together New Year. She invites me to visit
[her] at her home. She is staying in two rooms. I took my water
bottle to put my nice drink [i.e., alcohol] to it and go. I was already
drunk on that time. When I walk in the road I smell meat and hear
loud music. Everybody was happy [from] house to house. I join
[Flora's] family to celebrate together. . . . [Flora] is not a person who
drinks but she said she will try only wine just for today.

We were eating meat and also different kind of food. When around 12, we were celebrating with the [crackers], music, dancing. I make a call to [Sipho] because one girl was asking . . . where is he. [Sipho] come and joined us. He was carrying a bottle of premium Klipdrift™ [brandy]. In this household the old sister of [Flora] and [Jabu] know us well and she love us. We were sitting outside [Flora], [Jabu], [Sipho] and me. It was my suggestion to sit outside because of the other boys was [walking] up and down here [the street]. In this area if that household got girls, many boys like to go there. I was avoiding [preventing] them to come. Sister's [Flora] was giving us food and drinks. It was nice that day because of listening music and dancing. [Flora] was drunk and I asked her to go and sleep so that she will be able to [go] with us to a beach in the morning. She goes to sleep around 3 in the morning. When she sleeps, she said that bed is surrounding [spinning] because she drink for the first time. She was holding me. I was holding her until she fall sleep. [Sipho] and I we carry on with drinking. [Jabu] was also sleep on that time. We were sitting with sister's [Flora]. [Jabu] was forgetting to close the door, the time she going to sleep. When we drink there were two boys come to join us. We were drink with them and they said to us they going to his home. After a few minutes we hear [Flora] was crying when we [got to] . . . where they sleep we find that two boys trying to rape them. Luckily they failed to remove the clothes. *That boy was naughty because they know that girls are belonging to us, may be they didn't respect us.* We beat them strongly and they running [my emphasis].

As this diary entry shows, Vusi and Sipho's immediate concerns in the case of attempted rape were over the possession of their property and their own respectability. This response indicates the persistence of traditional interpretations of both male-male and male-female relationships. They also point to the possession and protection of women as a mark of maturity for young men.

Vusi's resistance to settling down, illustrated by his keenness to avoid having a wife who will "boss" and "complain," was predicated on his ideas of his own relative youthfulness. Yet, he also considered very seriously the importance of marriage: "Yes, because I want my child [to] grow up under the supervision of the two parents. I didn't like my child experienced what I had experienced, I'm old but I still need my both parents." Vusi made no mention of the possible financial burden he may face because of the Zulu

FIG 4.5   *Vusi's daughter Duduzile*
(Photograph by Paula Meth)

custom of paying *lobola* [bride wealth] for a wife, but he was pragmatic about his choice of wife, and recognized the possibility that marriage with Nomusa or Flora might not succeed.[2] In this case he had a back-up plan: "I have one girlfriend at this time and I phoned her if I need her in my house. She use to come and do the washing for me and she is my second choice if I failed to marry [Flora]. I love her because she is a humble person and she loves me so much. The name of my girlfriend is [Zani] and she also living in Cato Crest. If [Nomusa] phoned me while I with that girlfriend, I didn't cut off her call and I will speak to her as [if] I'm alone because I respect her to all what I have done."

In recognizing the importance of marriage and the role of Nomusa as wife and mother, Vusi carried a concern about his own failings as a bread-winner, particularly in relation to the upkeep of his daughter, Dudzile, whom he photographed for this project (Figure 4.5): "To be a father is a not nice if you are not working because you can't afford to buy what [that] child need."

Indeed, reflecting his fragmented education and the high levels of un-employment in South Africa, Vusi's employment history was patchy. Hav-ing worked as a part-time gardener, road worker, and for the armed forces in the past, he is currently employed on a contract basis in road construc-tion again. Given his lack of permanent employment he has, at times, had to rely on his father and sister to support him financially. He explained that his father provided him with groceries and his sister with clothing. He said that he preferred not to rely on his relatives: "I think [it] is better . . . if I'm working I'm not a problem for them." Recognizing himself as a potential burden he also pointed out that "I feel sad to say thank all the time and sometimes they buy for me a clothes which I don't like it but I can't say anything because they helping me. I'm old I need to buy clothes I like. My sister is helping me a lots but she is talking too much [commenting or complaining] if she gave me something." Vusi's perception of age and concomitant expectation emerged here again, but this time his reliance on his family was deemed inappropriate because he was too "old."

We are left then with a complex portrait of Vusi's life. He portrayed a cavalier management of his finances, admitting, "Yes I spent a lot in the club. Sometimes you use money without budgeting." This, his attitude to women and marriage, and his love of nightclubbing reveal his self-styled youthfulness. But this contrasts starkly with his political commitment and sense of himself as a man in need of employment and financial independence. He told Sibongile during their interview, "My dream [is] to have a nice house, car and [to be] married," and he specified further that he had dreamed of a career as a lawyer or a premier soccer league player. He mourned the passing of time and the loss of these opportunities: "I feel sad because my dreams were not succeed and now I'm getting old." Vusi's dreams, and the striking contrast they present between aspirations and social realities, make for a fitting conclusion:

> When I was trying to walk I feel my right foot [was] heavy. I didn't notice that those criminals were shot me on the leg. . . . That incident was abusing me in [my] mind because [in] those days I was waiting to go to do trials with the Lamontville Golden Arrow which is the soccer team playing in Premier Soccer League. When I [came] back from hospital I was walking with the stick. My bone was broken the time they shot me. My chance was lost on that way.

Notes

1. This is equivalent to about UK£2.5, or US$4.6 (as of April, 2008).

2. Vusi switched between Flora and Nomusa in his interview narrative, although he later explained that they are two separate women.

Further Reading

Beall, J., A. Todes, and H. Maxwell. (2004). "Gender and Urban Development in Cato Manor." In *Urban Reconstruction in the Developing World: Learning through an International Best Practice,* ed. P. Robinson, J. McCarthy, and C. Forster, 309–332. Johannesburg, South Africa: Heinemann.

Campbell, C. (1992). "Learning to Kill? Masculinity, the Family and Violence in Natal." *Journal of Southern African Studies* 18(3): 614–628.

Morrell, R., ed. (2001). *Changing Men in Southern Africa.* London: Zed Books. (See chapters by Xaba, Morrell, and Wood and Jewkes in particular.)

Linda McDowell

5

Young, White, Male, and Working Class

A Portrait of Richard

had arranged to meet Richard outside a McDonald's in the Meadowhall shopping center in Sheffield, England: a large mall designed as the simulacrum of a Tuscan hill town. It was a cool blustery day and Richard phoned me to say his shift was late clocking off. As I waited for him, I watched a stream of young people pass by, with and without friends, some pushing buggies, all of them looking harassed. I thought about the life chances of young people growing up in a de-industrializing northern city where life was still hard for the working class. I was there waiting for Richard as part of a comparative and longitudinal study about how young, unskilled, white men with few educational credentials found work and organized their lives, at a time when the British government seemed unable to see such young men except in stereotypical terms: as "yobs" (anti-social youth, typically male) and hooligans, or less pejoratively as "lads," out for a laugh at best, intent on damage at worst, and in need of control. Richard was about to turn seventeen that spring, but he looked younger: a slightly built, nervous young man with bags of energy. I had come to Sheffield to talk to him and some of his friends who were among a group of young men who had recently passed out of a "failing" school in that city. I wanted to find out whether media images of troubled lads, outperformed at school by girls, competing for jobs in the "feminized" service sector, and worried about their masculine identity had any resonance with young men in Sheffield.

As we move into the twenty-first century, it has begun to seem as if the rhetoric of gender inequality that dominated the final decades of the twentieth century has been reversed. Increasingly the problems of inequality and underachievement in the United Kingdom (and in other service- dominated economies such as Australia and the United States) seem to be those of young men rather than of girls and young women. There are three strands to the argument. The first area where boys are represented as underachievers, even as failures, is in school leaving exams. In the United Kingdom, each August when school-leaving-exam results are published, the relative underachievement by boys compared to the success rates among girls typically is headline news. The gender gap is actually quite small—less than 10 percent—and a growing number of school leavers of both sexes are achieving good results. But girls do better than boys on average and are now becoming dominant among university students—not that Richard and his peers would ever see the inside of a university. In fact, the problem of low attainment is not a gender issue per se but rather one of connections between gender, class, and ethnicity. It is white, working class-boys and boys of African and Caribbean origins who continue to perform poorly, not boys in general. Middle-class youths attending "good" schools continue to gain excellent results and are moving into post-compulsory education in increasing numbers.

The reasons for the poor performance of some working-class boys, instead of being located in an explanation that emphasizes low expectations, poverty, or racism, are instead commonly located in the second strand of current debates about the "problem with boys." These young men, it is argued, are not reaching their potential at school because they are lads or yobs, only interested in having a good time and disturbing the peace of more respectable citizens in the process. Members of the Labour Government in Britain, and their advisors, have argued that the type of yobbish culture exhibited on soccer terraces and in urban public spaces coincides with the laddish culture of schools and a more general lack of respect. After a series of measures designed to control or punish yobs (fines, curfews, etc.), Jack Straw, then the Home Office Minister, announced in 2000 the extension of so-called zero-tolerance "anti-social behaviour orders" (ASBOs) under which the courts were to be given new powers to jail anyone who is persistently disorderly but not convicted of a specific crime. As commentator Ros Coward noted, this was "bogeyman politics, spinning working class men as hate figures."[1] But the spinning has continued. The Home Office's 2003 White Paper "Respect and Responsibility–Taking a Stand Against Anti-Social Behaviour"brought some of the disparate strands of earlier measures together and extended the mechanisms for the state control of children and young people.[2] ASBOs, first introduced in a 1998 act, astonishingly were now to be served against children as young as ten, and fixed-penalty notices for children aged sixteen and seventeen were also extended. Individual Support Orders which require children and young people to attend organized activities to address the causes of their offending and antisocial behavior were also introduced.

While the White Paper seemed to attribute to those committing nuisances or behaving antisocially a considerable degree of responsibility for their own actions, it was also noted that "[p]arents have a critical role in teaching their children the difference between right and wrong, and giving them the confidence to grow up to feel proud of themselves, their families, their friends and their community. Respect is all-important, and this is missing in families that behave dysfunctionally."[3] In 2005, a Respect Unit was established within the Home Office and a "respect czar" appointed to push forward the respect agenda. In policy terms then, working-class young men are defined both as failures, unable to make the transition from school to useful adulthood, in part because of their family background, and as dysfunctional, disaffected, even protocriminals, alienated from the mainstream institutions of society and in need of resocialization.

There is a third strand to these arguments about the growing "problem with boys." This lies in structural economic change, especially in the decline of manufacturing and the growing concentration of employment in poorly paid, bottom-end, service-sector jobs in advanced industrial economies such as the United Kingdom. This materialist explanation is, however, neglected by the current British government. Twenty-five-years ago working-class men who left school as soon as they could were able to find reasonably secure and relatively well-paid work in the manufacturing sector. Today their sons are more likely to have to look for work in the service sector, where casualized and insecure work is poorly remunerated, especially for young workers who are a significant part of the labor force in catering, fast food, and the retail sector. Working in these types of "Mc-jobs" brings little respect to young men and low wages. Under-eighteen-year-olds, for example, were excluded from the provisions of minimum-wage legislation until 2006 and are now eligible for a special low rate, whereas eighteen- to twenty-one-year-olds are eligible only for the youth rate. The full minimum wage (£5.35 in 2006) is payable only to workers aged twenty-two and above.

Furthermore, work in the service sector demands a particular sort of embodied performance in which clean and well-presented employees have to provide a polite and deferential service to customers and clients. Older forms of acceptable "macho" behavior among working-class men that used to be a key feature of male manual employment, as well as contemporary "laddish," aggressive, or "in your face" versions of masculinity common among working-class boys, are now a disadvantage in the labor market, where self presentation, punctuality, attitude, and demeanor to customers and superiors are important. Attributes such as deference and docility— more commonly associated with socially constructed views of femininity— are now the most highly valued skills in these bottom-end service sector jobs. If male socialization in schools and in the locality continues to emphasize traditional male ways of doing things, young men may find themselves increasingly excluded from the only labor-market opportunities open to them in their locality. The youth labor market is also particularly susceptible to economic downturns, and the association between urban unrest in British cities in 1981, 1991, and 2001 and high rates of unemployment among young men, especially in inner London and in deindustrializing cities in the north, is noticeable.

This combination of these educational and economic changes has led many commentators to identify a "crisis of masculinity" among young men. But what do young men themselves think of this idea? Are male school leavers increasingly disadvantaged in the service sector? And is the version of laddish masculinity presented as such a problem in policy debates the only option open to them in the transition from school to adult worker? These were the sorts of questions I explored with Richard and his friends.[4] What they told me both confirmed and challenged current views of working-class "lads." On some occasions, and in some parts of their daily lives, they conformed to stereotypical views of lads or yobs but most of them also held down jobs, albeit low-paid work in the service sector, and had clear ideas about masculine responsibilities. What saddened me was how clearly these youths were both aware of and internalized majority views of themselves as "a waste of space" (Chris, Cambridge), despite, as I show below, their commitment to "traditional" values such as the work ethic and domestic responsibility. All twenty-three of them may have accepted their designation as a lad, but they explicitly rejected the label yob, drawing a clear line between enjoying yourself and going too far. "I may get drunk but I don't go out looking for trouble" (Darren, Sheffield). I have chosen Richard from Sheffield to speak for his cohort.

Richard grew up on a peripheral local-authority housing estate in Sheffield, originally built in the interwar period. He went to a school with a poor academic reputation and where a high proportion of pupils were eligible for free school meals (a key indicator of poverty). Another boy, seeing me waiting for Richard one day, told me that Richard's family was "a right rough one, a real rough Dad." His father, who had worked in the steel industry in his teens and twenties, had been unemployed for almost a decade at the time I first met Richard. However, his mother was a nurse and the major breadwinner in the family, which consequently was not among the very poorest households in Sheffield.

> Me Dad's like one of those housekeepers. While she's at work he cleans up and irons and that. He were always in trouble when he were young. Never did owt [anything] right. But now he knows. He tells me "it used to be different in them days, now you want to keep your head to the ground and keep working." Cos if he could turn time back he would. That's it. He did get a few jobs when he were young. He worked in a steel factory but he's not worked for years.

His father's lack of work seemed to be a key reason why Richard felt so strongly himself about holding down a job, although he felt sorry for his father rather than regarding him as less manly for taking on the traditional female role in the household.

Richard took his father's advice to heart and on leaving school he determined to look for and hold on to a job. In some ways it is perhaps surprising that Richard became such a committed worker, although he changed jobs rather often. His school career had not been a promising one, involving absences, truancy, exclusions, and aggression. He had been excluded several times for bad behavior, including physical violence.

> I have had some fights at school, cos when you get mad you just like flip. . . . I don't like fighting. I can't stand it, but when it comes to it you got no choice. It's better than just standing there and getting beaten up. I just, if someone came up to me and just punched me one, I'd say, "why did you do that?" But if he kept doing it and doing it, I'd get mad and just knock his head off.

Despite this, and other stories he told me about minor vandalism, Richard felt that he was unjustifiably labelled as a troublemaker by the school authorities: "Well, it's not always me. I don't always start it but I always get the blame." He also had a pattern of truancy.

> Year 7 to 9 [aged eleven to thirteen] I had about 100 percent attendance. Year 10 I went a bit more sloggy [playing truant], and this year I'm worse but I'm just trying to put up with it. It's like I was off and on. I didn't truant. I just stayed at home. I told me mum I were

ill but I weren't. And then the attendance officer came and I had to go back.

Interestingly, Richard's explanation for his behavior lay in gender differences—in both boys' attitudes and differential treatment of girls by teachers—paralleling some of the academic debates about why working-class boys "fail."

Well, boys want attention from girls and that why they mess about. And so teachers like girls more because they think girls behave more and boys mess about, like, that's because they pay more attention to girls so boys mess about to get attention. . . . So then boys start getting a bit stressed and that and getting upset and mess about more and the teachers get mad with them. That's why boys get excluded and then they just don't come anymore.

He rejected single-sex groups as a possible solution—"Well, that just wouldn't feel right, would it?"—although he recognized that, "they [boys] might do better in lessons though cos there wouldn't be so much showing off." Instead, he had a more radical suggestion for helping boys to improve in school: "I think year 9 [pupils aged thirteen and fourteen] you should have a bit of a break and then come back. It [getting fed up and playing truant] happens to everyone cos there's so many years of school. So you start stopping off [not attending]." Richard had also been in trouble locally as well as at school. He had been cautioned by the police for stealing: "I were nicking [stealing] stuff and I got done off by the coppers [the police]," and he had once been arrested for climbing on the school roof during the summer closure period.

As soon as he was sixteen—in March of year 11—Richard started looking for waged work, ready to leave school if he found employment.

I'm hoping for retail and that. I did work experience at the Co-op this year. I've been for quite a lot of interviews so far. Madhouse in Meadowhall, they sell clothes, like designer clothes, but they said, "We can't take you on cos you've not left school yet." I showed them me plastic card [a national insurance card issued to all sixteen-year-olds] but they said, "We still can't take you on cos we need GCSEs and you haven't done them yet."[5] He goes, "Come back after you've done your GCSEs and we'll sort summat [something] out." They'll keep me on a list while I'm waiting.

He went back to school, but his aim was to find a job as soon as possible after leaving in early June, and to live at home, saving money for socializing. Although Richard had had some work experience when still at school, it was short-lived and promised little for his future working life as a deferential service-sector worker.

> I did do a Saturday job but it didn't last long. I think I went twice but they treated me like crap that's why I didn't like it. I were working in this grocery store and he starts swearing at me, so I swore back and just walked off. But he still paid me. I made sure he did. I weren't going to work for nowt [nothing].

Richard did enter the retail sector, initially as a shop assistant in Sports Soccer, a chain store selling relatively low-priced sports clothing and shoes. He had started there in May before he officially left school, going in during the final term just to sit his final exams.[6] In the eight months between taking this job and the second time I talked to Richard in Sheffield, he had changed his job twice. He left Sports Soccer in July for a better-paying but similar job in Burtons, a menswear chain, but found the atmosphere stuffy and had left after only two days. His next job, which he had applied for at the same time as Burtons, was in McDonald's. All three of these jobs were in the Meadowhall shopping center, which was a short bus ride or thirty minutes' walk from Richard's home. He had found them by scanning advertisements placed on a board in the center and used no other method of job search. Talking about his decision to leave Sports Soccer, Richard said:

> I were getting bored wi'it, it just weren't good and it's better money thear [there] [at McDonald's] and when it's better you just want to move, you know what I mean, go somewhere else where it's better. I've only been thear seven month and I'm training already, which teks up to two year to do, so I am hoping to pick up a floor manager's job in a year or two.

In this second interview Richard was largely positive about his working life at McDonald's. As he told me, the money was good for his age: "I'm on about £900 a month" but the shift work was a problem sometimes:

> They like me on early, but at 6 when I have to get up, I'm really hurting. It very bad, reet annoying. I work 6 while [until] 2, but it can be

3, even 4 when I finish and sometimes 10–5 or 11–6, or you do a closing. I ain't done one yet cos I am not 18, but you start at 5 and do while 3, but you get a free taxi home.

He enjoyed the company of his workmates, positively describing their division of labor in classic Fordist terms: "We all work in a circle as a team. So to do like a Big Mac or something, there's one on table dresses t'Big Mac, passes the bun on to grill, and another takes it off so its reet quick, like a formation cos it only takes 30 seconds to get like five or six Macs off." These types of fast-food jobs epitomize the assembly-line structure of deskilled service jobs, so highly routinized and scripted that they leave no scope for individual initiative. Even so Richard told me, "I'll try and make a career of it." But he also told me in the next breath that, "I'm looking for other good jobs out thear. . . . I don't want to waste my life staying in one place." However, by the time of the third interview almost six months later, the monotony and sheer hard work of McDonald's had made him more dissatisfied even though he had progressed to become a member of the training squad and played a part in training new floor staff. He was registered for a vocational qualification based on workplace experience: "I'm learning the till [cash register] cos I'm doing an NVQ [National Vocational Qualifaction] there, I'm training already which takes up to two years to do, so I'm hoping to pick up floor manager in a year or two." He had also become eligible for holiday pay, although he still had no formal contract of employment to his knowledge. But he had begun to find the hours demanding and the surveillance demeaning:

> I just work when they ask me. I often do 45 hours a week. And they watch you, there's people watching you work all the time, passing information on to the manager. And they push people around, management does that. . . . People often don't last long here. They leave after about two months because they can't handle it. It's like slave labor.

Richard had arranged an interview in TopMan (a men's clothing retailer) for the following Saturday after I spoke to him in person for the third and final time. "Maybe it's better work, it's cleaner and not as hard in a shop."

Behind his commitment to employment, though, lay a different dream and one that Richard also actively pursued, although with little chance of success. His dream was to record a song he had written, hopefully initiating a career change.

RICHARD: Yeah I have started me own band up and made a song called "Heaven." It took me about a year to learn to play the guitar.

LINDA: So your band?

RICHARD: Yeah, a two-piece guitar they call it. We play in pubs and things at the moment, in . . . The Stanmore over in Nethershire [a nearby estate] but we didn't get a commission there. He said we were too 80s rock but it were good, we weren't too bad. We've got a copyright on it from CBS records. I sent the song but they sent it back. They sent a letter back and said it was going to take about a year and we went, "yeah" [disbelievingly]. I mean they are just pushing us away cos they don't like. And we ain't heard nowt [nothing] since but we've still got copyright so no one can nick [steal] it and sell it, and it costs us eight quid a year, I think just for copyright.

I was impressed by Richard's initiative in sending the song to CBS and asked him how he had done it.

I found it on the internet. I went to www.survive.music.com and I sent an email to CBS and they said, "Can we have a demonstration on tape and the lyrics and that?" so I goes, "Way, this is a bit weird this, in case someone nicks it" so I went down me'sen [myself], down near . . . erm . . . I think it were Essex, down in Essex. I went down there. It's not far from London, that is it. I just didn't want to leave it there in case any one nicked it, cos I am suspicious like that and he went, "No, no, no one will nick it. Trust us." So I went down to Essex and I went in with tape and that and played it. I were only thear about 40 minutes and he went, "It's all right, it's all right. We'll assess it." And I got a letter and he said it is too 80s rock. Like the pub said. But it's all right and that, I am getting on and that.

Travelling to Essex alone was brave and out of character. Most of Richard's life took place in a tightly defined locality. He worked a few minutes from home, went out locally most of the time—drinking in local pubs (although he was underage)—and only on special occasions venturing into the city center [downtown Sheffield] to go to a club. "We went to Club Wow at Christmas. I'm not 18 yet but I still get in; the best way is just to walk in." He had only once been abroad, for a family holiday in May before he finally left school and started work.

I told you, didn't I, that we went to Gran Canary? . . . We got there
and the pool was just totally in bits, they were building it while we
were thear, so that turned the holiday off a bit. Everywhere we went
people come up to us and went, "Want to buy this, want to buy
that?" and we kept walking off and that. Too many people coming
up to you and bugging you all the time. I just got right fed up with
that and we were going to come home a week early but we didn't
cos you have to pay to come back, so we didn't.

While Friday nights were nights out with his friends, he usually reserved Saturday evenings for his girlfriend: "I go out with our lass, me girlfriend." He told me the story of how he met her.

RICHARD: I went in House of Fraser looking for stuff and she went,
"What are you looking for?" I said "Oh, I'm looking for a birthday
present for me mum" and I walked away and I just looked at her
and she went, "Are you all right?" and I went "Yeah, yeah" and
she said "What's your name?" and I said "Richard" and I walked
away and she nipped me arse [laughing] so I just turned round,
and I went to the toilet—they have got a toilet there—and I got
this thing and I went to the till, paying for it and she got this
receipt and she passed me her phone number with the receipt.
And I went "Oh aye, thanks for the phone number" and that.

LINDA: And then you rang her, did you?

RICHARD: Yeah and we went out, we just started going out with
each other.

To explore Richard's views about the relative life chances of young
men and young women, I asked Richard a series of questions about the local labor market, about sexism and racism, and about his own life chances
compared to those of his father. While he was unhesitatingly sexist, with a
clear opinion of the suitability of different jobs for men and for women
and of the naturalness of the gender division of labor, he did not hold racist opinions. Indeed he was thoughtful in response to several questions
about race. First I asked him about his friends at school:

I don't mix with the Asian boys much. I am not racist or owt [any-
thing], but I just don't mix with them, except a couple. And there's
like the black kids. I talk to them all the time. But most of me

friends are white. It's because where I've grown up, cos round here there were never no Asian kids or black kids. At school, they do stay separate, cos it's like you were growing up with black people, you'd probably be hanging around with black people and if you grow up with whites you hang around with whites, that why. But that's why secondary schools bring all people together, to try and talk, to stop racism like . . . I think that's good.

By the time he was working at McDonald's, Richard had met a more diverse group of people. "I've got loads of friends, and we all go out together. They are from all over the place, from Italy to Afghanistan, girls as well as lads. We all muck in together. There's no trouble."

I asked him to describe himself to me in the third meeting. "I'm talkative, one of the lads. That means you like having a laugh, tekking [taking] piss out of each other, laughing at each other." But he also emphasized that he was hardworking and reliable, a view that his work history certainly supports. For him, life was a careful negotiation between a rambunctious, laddish social life and an adherence to the protestant work ethic. Richard was also thoughtful in his responses to a series of questions about the current position of young men. He thought that life was equally stressful for both young men and for young women but that it was up to individuals how they handled it.

I know the papers are full of problems for boys and I do think about that, everyone thinks about that. I think that in a way everyone has got a hard time in life and you just get through it the best you can without too much stress. Well, everyone has got to go through stress, without stress it wouldn't be a life but the best way is to leave all that behind and just go for the future. I mean it's just like being sexist in a way, the paper saying that.

In a moving final comment he said: "Me dad has had a hard life, a bad life; it were reet [right] bad but I'll do better. I've had a good life, although I have wasted parts of it. I'd like to go back and reconnect but I can't exactly do that so I'll just leave the past and hope for the best for the future."

Richard was not quite eighteen years old at the time he made this comment. I found it unbearably sad to think that he accepted that he had made mistakes but could not see a way to "reconnect." He seemed to have already given up on the option of returning to school or taking some form of further education and was resigned to a life dominated by low-wage labor.

I kept in contact with him for some time afterward, talking by phone. The penultimate time he talked to me he had just started a small window-cleaning firm with his brother and a friend; not quite the life of a singing star but he was full of optimism for a future as an entrepreneur and small-business man, relishing the chance to work on his own terms. Unfortunately, only twelve weeks later, the firm had failed, the coworkers had fallen out, and Richard was once again looking for a job in a retail outlet in Meadowhall.

Notes

1. Ros Coward, "Slurring the Proles," *The Guardian*, July 4, 2000, p. 20.
2. "Respect and Responsibility—Taking a Stand Against Anti-Social Behaviour" (London: Home Office, March 2003).
3. "Respect and Responsibility," p. 8.
4. I talked to ten young white men in Cambridge and thirteen in Sheffield from working-class backgrounds. The work was funded by the Joseph Rowntree Foundation as part of a wider study of young people's lives in twenty-first-century Britain. This research, conducted in 1999, was based on a comparative case study of two schools on working-class, suburban housing estates—one in each city. The cities were chosen to reflect a long-time service-based and a deindustrializing economy respectively. The schools were selected on the basis of several indicators of poor performance. Young, white men in the final year of compulsory schooling (aged fifteen to sixteen) classified as low achievers were invited to participate in a longitudinal study which involved interviewing them three times as they left school, searched for work, and entered the labor market. I personally undertook all interviews in "neutral" locations (pubs, cafes, parks, shopping centers etc) which were recorded and transcribed before analysis. I met them twice more over the next year, asking them about their hopes and aspirations, job prospects, view of their "local community" and neighbourhood, as well as their everyday lives.

When reporting the testimonies of these young men I decided to reproduce their speech as accurately as possible, not correcting their expressions or grammar and, in the case of the Sheffield participants, their regional dialect words. I hope this decision is not regarded as patronizing.

5. General Certificates in Secondary Education—these are the leaving examinations taken by British schoolchildren in May and June of their final year of compulsory education, when aged fifteen or sixteen.
6. Richard took only four subjects—math, religious education, English literature, and English language—and achieved only low grades (two Es and two Fs) which are too low to qualify him to move on to advanced-level courses or further education. This very low level of achievement does not reflect his abilities, in my view. He was an articulate and thoughtful interviewee, as this chapter shows, but his "devil-may-care" attitude at school meant he did no academic work whatsoever.

Further Reading

Bourgois, Philippe. (1995). *In Search of Respect: Selling Crack in El Barrio.* Cambridge: Cambridge University Press.

Finnegan, William. (1998). *Cold New World: Growing Up in a Harder Country.* London: Picador, 1998.

McDowell, L. (2003). *Redundant Masculinities? Employment Change and White Working Class Youth.* Oxford: Blackwell.

Newman, Katherine. (1999). *There's No Shame in My Game: The Working Poor in the Inner City.* New York: Vintage and Russell Sage Foundation.

Peter Hopkins

6

Young, Male, Scottish, and Muslim

A Portrait of Kabir

Everyday Practice

Kabir and I first arranged to meet on 12 December 2002 at the central mosque in Edinburgh, close to the University of Edinburgh where he was enrolled as a student. I had contacted the mosque to request their assistance in finding potential participants for a research project I was conducting on the geographies, identities, and everyday lives of young Muslim men living in Scotland. Kabir was one of the young men who made contact with me after hearing about the project. At the time of our first discussion he was eighteen years old. Kabir's father was born in Kenya, the son of an Indian Muslim family, who moved to Pakistan before marrying Kabir's mother, a Pakistani Muslim woman, in 1978 and moving to Glasgow. Kabir's older brother was born in 1980 and Kabir was born in 1984. Kabir is a reasonably tall, slim, bearded young man. I was particularly struck by the depth of the conversation we had at the first meeting, which lasted almost two hours. On completion of the research project, I arranged to meet Kabir in September 2005. I hoped that this would give him the opportunity to read over a summary of the findings of the research project, talk through his views about the study, and perhaps reflect on the ways his everyday experience had or had not changed since our previous conversation. In this chapter, I reflect on Kabir's everyday practices and how these are mediated by his sense of Scottishness and global issues relating to his religious faith. Research participants were recruited for participation in focus groups and interviews in Glasgow and Edinburgh where discussions focused on communities, Scotland and Scottishness, being a young man, and being a Muslim.

From the conversations I had with Kabir, it became clear that there were important anchor points to his negotiations of his everyday practices. I asked him if he could tell me a little about his everyday life and he said:

> A typical day is, you know, obviously trying to wake up in the middle of the night for the . . . prayer which is the early morning prayer, the dawn prayer . . . then obviously, for me, would be university and then even during the day, sort of lunch time or whatever, I would come to the mosque. . . . The good thing is the mosque is in good proximity here in Edinburgh campus, so I'd come here for the prayer, em, then I'd go back to my class. It depends on the timetable. So that's kind of what I do . . . in the evening, relax or study or do whatever work. For me, a lot of time is spent on the Internet. I do a lot of work on there, my Islamic work as well, and then probably the Isha prayer, which is the night prayer, I would perform probably just before going to sleep. That's kind of the routine.

Here Kabir highlights the importance of three key dimensions of his everyday life: performing his religious duties, attending university, and doing community work or what he refers to as his "Islamic work."

Before commencing his studies at the University of Edinburgh, Kabir lived in Glasgow with his parents and one of his brothers in a large detached house. His father was employed as a secondary-school teacher and his mother was a social worker. His older brother ran his own business and his younger brother had recently started university. Kabir completed all of his compulsory schooling in Glasgow, and upon leaving school had gained the highest marks possible with five Highers at grade A and three Advanced Highers at grade A.[1] Kabir had a relatively middle-class background. The majority of the young men involved in this project experienced a middle-class upbringing, and Kabir's views and experiences were relatively typical of the other young men involved in the research.

Islam was a central focus of Kabir's everyday life. Kabir conceptualized Islam as believing in "one God, the creator, who created, sustains, and covers the universe and to whom everything will be returned, and that to whom people will be accountable for their actions." Kabir continued: "Islam is a code for life; it's a way of life. It's not just a religion, it's not just a set of beliefs and rituals, it's about the way you live your life, if you see what I mean." Islam is more than just "staying in the mosque"; it entails "spreading that message in whatever way you can." Kabir saw the Koran as source of "guidance and instruction" for his everyday life, an important part of which should include "the five daily prayers: before sunrise, one of them is at noon time, one is sort of late afternoon, one is at sunset, and one is . . . at night time." Kabir continued:

> I mentioned the five daily prayers, fasting, pilgrimage to Mecca in Saudi Arabia, giving *Zakat* which is the poor due, giving some money from your savings every year is obligatory, as well as recommended to do it all the time.[2] These are just some of the duties, as well as some things that are forbidden, you know, that is to say, don't commit adultery, don't drink alcohol, or corrupt your mind in such ways, don't steal, don't murder . . . these kind of things are things we're instructed not to do.

Kabir was clear about the potential rewards associated with being committed to his religion: "God will reward us with Paradise and if we don't, then, he'll punish us with Hell." However, these obligations were not regarded as cumbersome: "You can be a good Muslim and participate in society and be a young, cool person and be happy." His religious faith was therefore a key component of his everyday life and practice.

Related to Kabir's commitment to his religion, he also talked about the community work he was involved in, noting that he was "very proud to be an activist." He worked with various organizations and societies through university as well as through different regional and national Islamic organizations. Before our second meeting, in particular, he was busy taking phone calls and clarifying arrangements. During our interviews, he regularly discussed organizing "conferences, large talks, and organized camps"; "representing Muslims and providing services"; "catering for the needs of Muslim students"; as well as working on campaigning issues such as a very large demonstration in conjunction with Stop the War Coalition. Kabir's everyday practices were thus closely connected to various key international events. He was motivated by social justice and political concerns and wanted to "see an honest portrayal of Islam and Muslims" in the press. Thus, as well as visiting the mosque for prayer and fulfilling other religious duties, Kabir spent time going to meetings on various days of the week. He noted:

> Meetings are one of the main things in my life to be honest. So there is home, there is university, there is mosque, and there is meetings, and there is peer group, yes, a lot of that is meetings and it might be in the mosque. I don't tend to have very much time to maybe go out for sports and things like that so that isn't really much a part of my life. Nothing against it, I just don't tend to get the time to have pure leisure. I don't tend to have that too much.

Alongside his university studies, community work, and religious duties, Kabir talked with much fondness about his family and friends, and said that he kept in touch with politics through watching television, reading newspapers, and surfing the internet.

Related to Kabir's engagement with various forms of media, he noted his frustration at the ways in which Islam and Muslims are misrepresented and demonized in the various media, such as in newspaper and magazine images and on television news coverage. Seeking to challenge stereotypical understandings of his identities, Kabir criticized the language used in such discourses:

> If you ask me some questions . . . if you decide on a definition of fundamentalist, I may well be one. If you decide on a definition of extremist, I might well be one, if you decide on a definition of radical, I might well be one. So, if I'm a radical, extremist, fundamentalist, does this mean I am [one] - according to the profile of what a radical, fundamentalist, extremist is supposed to be? Or could you be surprised about the actual projects I am involved in, that I actually work in the media, I actually help the police? . . . you know, but I am maybe a radical, extremist, fundamentalist. . . . You know, these words are just political, they don't have any meaning whatsoever . . . no linguistic value whatsoever, they just have maligning value.

This brief insight into the comings and goings of Kabir's everyday life demonstrates his commitment to his education and religion and his passion for helping other people, alongside the racism and intolerance he has to face on a daily basis. This account of the life and times of a young Scottish Muslim man is far removed from the stereotypes of aggressive young

Muslim men who are labeled as members of the "Asian gang," in conflict with their parents' generation and disturbing the moral order of the street.

Scottishness

During our discussions Kabir and I regularly talked about issues relating to his connections and affiliations with Scotland and Scottishness, as well as his personal views about politics. These discussions demonstrated his depth of insight into his various identities, the ways they were perceived by others, and how they were changing over space and time. Moreover, Kabir's opinions and views challenged simplistic understandings about young people being disengaged from politics; he articulated a sophisticated and nuanced understanding of the political situation in which he found himself.

Kabir was very aware that there are people who, for racist and exclusionary reasons, see him as not being Scottish. However, as Kabir saw himself as someone "who contributes to Scottish society"—a society that "he loves"—for "someone to say that something about me is not Scottish— that I am less Scottish than someone else—is deeply offensive." As Kabir reminded me, he was born in Scotland, speaks with a Scottish accent, and "was holding Scotland's flag" when he was one of a delegation who visited the European Parliament. "How many of those people have done anything for Scotland of that nature?"

Research about Scottish national identities has tended to adopt a simplistic approach that seeks to measure a person's Scottish national identity in comparison with their sense of possessing a British national identity. This approach forces people to prioritize their identities and ignores the processes that might give rise to a person's sense of national identity. Recently, more attention has been given to the ways in which people narrate their identities, and tell a story about the identity groups to which they may or may not belong. Following this approach, Kabir saw himself possessing multiple identities:

> I say that I am Scottish Muslim, but what I mean is that these are multiple identities, they are not clashing identities. They are faces that you have, or they have their use at some time. I mean you could face completely that way, to completely that way, or you can have in between, and there are all different levels. It is about context and what is appropriate in a particular time. . . . I have never ever felt that, for whatever reasons, you need to prioritize one over the other. . . . I mean for me, linguistically, I am giving primacy to

Islam if I say I am a Scottish Muslim because Muslim is my identity and Scottish is the adjective attached to it.

Kabir clarified that these multiple identities, contrary to popular opinion, are not in conflict with each other. He noted, "I wouldn't say there's
anything about me that's not Scottish but I would say that there are things
about me that are other than just purely Scottish." Furthermore, he also
felt that, in many respects, his Islamic and Scottish identities reflected different aspects of himself as a person:

> I'm a Scottish Muslim because I'm Scottish and I was born in Scot-
> land. So it's my culture, it's my background; it's my home. Muslim
> is my goal. Being Muslim is my philosophy or my belief system. It
> doesn't contradict my nationality in any way because they deal with
> different questions, you know. It's like being . . . a blue square: it's
> blue and it's a square. Its being a square doesn't interfere with it be-
> ing blue. Its being blue doesn't interfere with it being a square.
> They're just nothing to do with each other but they complement
> each other and they make a complete blue square. If it wasn't blue
> it wouldn't be a blue square, if you see what I mean. So being a Scot-
> tish Muslim, you know, both of them go together and they make
> me who I am. They're part of what I am. They're not even complete
> of what I am because it doesn't describe my character or personal-
> ity but they don't contradict each other in any way.

Discussing this at the second meeting with Kabir, he queried "I mean,
why do some people ask if you are British first or Muslim first?" Emphasizing the importance of context and time, Kabir clarified that another way of
looking at his Scottish and Muslim identities might be to compare himself
to a "vegetarian poet." "I mean, if someone is a vegetarian poet, at a dinner
party he might say he is vegetarian, and in a literary circle, he might say he
is a poet. He wouldn't introduce himself as the other thing at a dinner—
'oh no, I'm a poet'—he wouldn't say that, but primarily that is what he is."

Reflecting on his location in post-devolution urban Scotland, Kabir
clarified that he is content to see himself as both Scottish and British, although he links questions of nationalism primarily to Scottishness:

> I mean, I don't have a big thing about saying I'm Scottish rather
> than British. I'm happy to be both. I don't have any problems with
> being Scottish and British. What I don't accept is when somebody

would say I'm English because I'm not English. Not that I have anything against being English, but I'm not.

As people narrate their identities, they often reflect on what they are
not as well as what they are. Here, Kabir was clear about not being English
and wanted to distance himself from an English identity. Similarly, he re-
sisted being associated with people, "such as English football hooligans,"
when he mentioned "I would rather say that I am Scottish, because I would
rather not be identified with some of the other types of British people."
However, for Kabir, "being Scottish entails being British. I mean there may
be some people who are staunchly nationalistic [Scottish nationalist] and
against being identified in that way, okay, fine. But at the moment, with
the basic setup of the country, you can't help being British if you are Scottish. You can't do anything about it because that is the way the system is."

The numbers of people who are politically active—choose to vote, join
political parties, campaign for political parties—in the United Kingdom has
declined substantially in recent years. According to much of the literature in
the social sciences, the reasons for such a decline must be sought in young
people's unwillingness to engage in politics when compared to their parents' generation. Instead, young people are stereotyped as disengaged, apathetic, and inert, and disinterested in their political futures. Some scholars
have responded to this idea by suggesting that young people are engaging
with the political in different ways. According to this argument, the problem is not young people's disengagement from politics but is instead the
narrow definition of the political adopted by researchers. Kabir's opinions,
views, and actions contradict both of these suggestions. As a young man, he
is politically aware, active in politics, and knowledgeable and understand-
able about the political maneuverings of those elected to represent him.

As someone who was "not really impressed by the idea of Scottish independence," Kabir "probably wouldn't have voted for SNP [Scottish National Party]." Although he had been "quite impressed" with some of the
MSPs (Members of the Scottish Parliament), in particular from the SNP, as
a result of their stance "when it comes to war and the situation in the
Middle East," he felt that "being part of the UK is better than separating."
Although independence is not to Kabir's taste, he suggested that "Scotland
has its own flavour, you know, compared to the rest of the UK" and that
"Scottish people have their own kind of sense of humour, em, their own
way of looking at life, they take things more lightly." Alongside suggestions
of Scotland being different from England, Kabir also articulated his political awareness of the British context and was particularly motivated by

issues relating to the Iraq war. He was very frustrated by the approach adopted by the Labour Party and a number of its members, and he stressed his support for members of parliament who stood down in opposition to the pro-war stance of his party. Kabir noted: "I would certainly say that Tony Blair is my leader and I would say that this is a disastrous situation that we are in, and we as British society deserve better than that." He continued: "So I see Blair as being a very hideous man. I do not view all of government in the same way. I do not view all of the Labour Party in the same way."

In our discussions about Scottish and British politics, I also asked Kabir about his views with regard to the BNP (British National Party) which, in recent years, has advanced their far-right agenda by promoting an anti-Muslim campaign. Kabir said that he had "always regarded them with contempt for their stance on race," as he saw them as being responsible for urban unrest in England's northern cities due to the way they "stir up tensions," "whip up hatred," and act as a "trigger for the riots." Kabir was aware of how the BNP changed from "simply talking about Asians, to turning specifically on the Muslims" and noted how he had visited their website and found "pure hatred." However, Kabir also observed how the BNP had "not been very successful in Scotland." Kabir was aware of the ways in which the BNP had advanced their racist and Islamophobic agenda by strategically realigning the focus of their campaign in response to local issues and global events.

Global Muslim Danger

There have been a number of events in the last decade that are often regarded as "global" in character and have had particularly stark consequences for Muslims living in different parts of the world. The terrorist attacks in New York on 11 September 2001 and the underground bombings in London on 7 July 2005, alongside the "war on terror" advanced by the Bush and Blair regimes, have changed the lives of many people. For Kabir, these events had resulted in an increasing mistrust for people who follow the Islamic faith: "especially since September 11th, more and more people have taken the opportunity to express their hatred of Islam" and "there's a rising tide of Islamophobia." September 11th "was the biggest turning point for British Muslims and the Muslim world." Kabir suggested that, "after such incidents, there is a period of time when things get worse in terms of the public, and then, over time, it just abates." After the London bombings, Kabir found that "things have been really quite bad in terms of the feeling out there and it is still quite bad, but it is abating I think." After each of these events, Kabir found that his sense of his everyday emotional vulnerabilities intensified. Talking about the days after 11 September 2001, he said:

I felt upset, maybe I felt angry probably, and a little bit worried and insecure about what might happen to our community. You know, you worry about what may happen to your own family, and I was walking down the street after [9/11] and I just didn't feel very safe walking around, and it was a terrible feeling where you somehow feel guilty for something that you shouldn't feel guilty about. It's as if, you know, I was thinking, somehow, oh yeah, somehow I'm to blame for all this, which of course I'm not.

These feelings of anger, insecurity, and fear sometimes led Kabir to alter his everyday movements and use of the city: "I mean, they [these events] shouldn't make us change our habits, but they do. So really, that's what the worrying thing is when these things happen that they change your pattern of behaviour."

Following these events, Kabir talked about his everyday experiences of racism and discrimination; the insecurity, fear, and anxiety sensed by his community; and the abuse encountered by his peers and family. Mosque buildings were attacked, a friend of Kabir's sister was spat at in the underground, and so he was increasingly careful, tactful, and anxious about how he negotiated his everyday life. These experiences led Kabir to question whether he could defend his religious faith and he suggested that many Muslims had to face up to important and difficult questions: "If you had to defend yourself, I mean, defend yourself and proverbially defend your corner; do you know the first thing about Islam? Can you explain to somebody that you're not a terrorist, that Islam doesn't encourage terrorism? Can you explain that? Do you have sufficient knowledge?"

During discussions with Kabir, it also became clear that racism, discrimination, and Islamophobia were a part of his everyday life. He referred to being "shouted at" regularly in the street, and during our second discussion noted that "even yesterday someone was shouting 'black bastard, black bastard.'" Kabir responded to these remarks: "And you know I just use a trump card, I don't really care, I just shout back, 'What are you,' not because he is black, just like "what are you" to be shouting abuse at anyone else, but you know, as I walk away, my legs feel a little wobbly and I feel a bit not at ease and it affects you no matter how small it is."

These experiences of intolerance were, according to Kabir, down to "racism" and "ignorance." However, he also perceived them to be about "racism and Islamophobia" which he regarded as being overlapping but distinct phenomena. He therefore disagreed with those opposed to legislating against Islamophobic attacks or faith-hate attacks because "basically they are just race-hate attacks masquerading as faith-hate." However, he also stated that race is socially constructed. He said that he doesn't "believe in race as any kind of absolute concept. Logically speaking, it doesn't hold much water." Not only did Kabir distinguish between racism and Islamophobia, but he saw his experiences as being gendered: "It is men who are behind the London and New York bombings, so in some ways I feel more under scrutiny than women would be." Kabir also recalled his feelings and experiences when visiting London:

> I mean I was in London a few times over the summer, and yeah, I felt really badly at ease on the underground, and in fact, I did get stopped and searched as well, which was interesting ... and it is just the kind of feeling that you have always got to be aware about how you look and, I run a lot to the train because I am always late. I always run and I always have my bag—sometimes I have another bag, sometimes *The Guardian*[3]—I don't really think that is what terrorists read but anyway—but I am conscious of that at that same time. I mean people looking at me running, how do I not look like a terrorist? I mean there is no real way, if I look like a terrorist that is it, I do.

The particular situations that Kabir encountered following the terrorist attacks in New York, London, and Madrid were particularly challenging because they all resulted in the promotion of an ideology that perceived Islam and Muslims as a threat to the moral order of civilized society. However, Kabir's experience of these events and processes were especially intense due to his belief in the *umma*: "The global community umma is essential, a very important concept for Muslims. We can't deny its existence. We're told in the Koran that Muslims are one brotherhood, one *umma*. So we have to remain united, em, look out for each other."

Kabir noted that "the prophet Mohammed said that you should help your brother" and he explained that the significance of the *umma* is intensified when "it comes to suffering of people." But Kabir argued that Muslims involved in terrorist activities do not belong to the umma:

> But what I can judge is whether they are part of our community—the Muslim community—and I say emphatically that they are not part of

the community because, number one, they are not representative of what the community as whole, with all of its diversity, has a general idea of what it wants to be doing . . . which is not destruction, it is construction. Number two, because they have done it without any consultation, whether with religious scholars, whether with political analysts and strategists in this country . . . they have done something that has resulted in catastrophe for the Muslims in this country, so how can I say that they are part of our community? I can't. I can say that they are Muslims but I don't say that they are part of our community. So that is the way I kind of encapsulated things that . . . I mean I still very much believe in the concept of *umma*, I still believe very much in the concept of a community, a mini *umma,* if you like, of this country.

Kabir therefore felt empowered by the *umma* and suggested that there is also a strong universal bond and connection between Muslims living across Scotland, referring to this as a "mini *umma*." Young Muslim men like Kabir felt threatened because the Muslim *umma* is under attack, fearful for their safety as they negotiate the potentially racist streets of Scotland's cities, and angry about the ways in which their religion is constantly under attack. He noted that, for many, "Muslim is a negative word. . . . You know people talk about Islam and the media; it is just—there is never really any basic analysis of what is Islam. I think if you were to ask most people for a definition of what is Islam, they will not have a clue, and if you were just to do a simple word-association game, say cat, dog, swing, park, Islam, Violence—I think that would be the first word." These issues angered Kabir and he believed that many Muslims were similarly frustrated: "Yeah, so why are Muslims angry? Is it fear? I think in some sense, you know, they fear that if one country gets bombed, the next country gets bombed, what is going to happen to the Muslim *umma*, what is going to happen to us, what is going to happen to our religion?" In many ways then, Kabir is in a challenging situation as he continues to try to represent his religious faith in a positive light and fulfill religious requirements, while managing experiences of racism and ignorance.

Kabir's engagements with Scottishness and global issues connected with his religious identity. But his personal identities and political futures are rooted in the lived and material cultures that are positioned close by: his sense of self and community are critically shaped by the scales "closest in": the markings on his body, the placing of the mosque, the character of the street, for example. By his late-twenties, Kabir hoped to "be married . . . hopefully with probably children, still living in the UK, having a quite secure job, probably something to do with research and physics and lecturing." He also hopes to still be "involved in sort of community work and spreading the word as I put it, you know."

Notes

1. Highers are examinations that pupils attending Scottish schools normally take at the end of their fifth year of secondary education. Advanced Highers are of a similar standard to the English A-Level and are normally examined at the end of the sixth year of secondary education.

2. As Kabir notes, Zakat is one of the five pillars of Islam and requires Muslims to give a proportion of their wealth to the poor and needy.

3. *The Guardian* is a left-leaning British newspaper.

Further Reading

Hopkins, Peter E. (2004). "Young Muslim Men in Scotland: Inclusions and Exclusions." *Children's Geographies* 2(2): 257–272.

Hopkins, Peter E. (2007). "Global Events, National Politics, Local Lives: Young Muslim Men in Scotland." *Environment and Planning A* 39(5): 1119–1133.

Hopkins, Peter E. (2007). "'Blue Squares,' 'Proper' Muslims and Transnational Networks: Narratives of National and Religious Identities amongst Young Muslim Men living in Scotland." *Ethnicities* 7(1): 61–81.

Kathrin Horschelmann

7

Politics, Lifestyle, and Identity

The Story of Sven, Eastern Germany

Sven was a fifteen-year-old boy who participated in a research project conducted by myself and Nadine Schäfer in the eastern German city of Leipzig (Saxony) in 2003.[1] He was one of five participants in a group we interviewed over a period of five weeks. The group met once a week and discussed a range of issues centred on globalization, identity, and youth culture. We explored how important friends, family, and locality were in the young people's lives, how their leisure interests connected with global flows of culture, and to what extent their current cultural activities intersected with concerns about future opportunities for education and careers. In order to make the research as accessible as possible and to explore the benefits of both verbal and nonverbal forms of expression, we included a range of qualitative methodologies. In addition to focus-group interviews, we asked participants to conduct a brief questionnaire-based survey with one another, to complete a week's diary, to take photographs of their everyday lives, and to draw mental maps of places that were important to them. The groups also produced posters reflecting the outcomes of the research. These were exhibited to the public in a cultural institute at the end of the year.

The methods we chose allowed participants to answer questions about globalization and everyday life in significant depth. The time taken for group discussions made it possible for participants to reflect on their answers as well as on the visual materials they produced. The group setting meant that we could observe processes of interaction and opinion formation between young people as they occurred. While this influenced their responses, it enabled discussions that were led less by the researcher than by dynamics in the group. It also allowed our participants to set their own priorities.

Young people in Western Europe are often described as more lifestyle oriented, less bound by traditional values and communities and having more choice over their future life-options than previous generations. This greater choice is seen to lead to heightened individual freedom, but also to greater risks, as responsibility for the choices one makes increases while fewer welfare provisions and more flexible labor markets produce new uncertainties. For young people in Leipzig many of these developments were noticeable, but for different reasons and with greater severity.

The main cause of an increase in lifestyle options and insecurities was the end of state-socialism in 1989. Since the so-called Peaceful Revolution, new freedoms of political opinion, religion, travel, and consumption have led to a multiplication of lifestyles and a move toward more varied, global youth cultures. At the same time, the education system has been over-hauled radically from a comprehensive system that gave students equal opportunities independent of class to a new, tiered system that divides students by their ability from an early age.[2] Students and their parents now have to choose between two differently graded senior high schools from the age of eleven to twelve. The lower- to intermediary-level schools are called *Realschule,* while the higher-level schools, which lead to university- access qualifications, are called *Gymnasium.* At the *Realschule,* students are graded further by their ability. Some obtain a basic certificate at the age of fourteen, while others go on to gain a higher grade at the age of sixteen, which qualifies them for vocational training or to move onto a university- access course *(Abitur).* Although there are possibilities for students to move between school levels, their original choice often determines their future training and career paths. "Choice" more accurately translates as "responsibility" and is restricted by young people's social backgrounds.

After their school education, young people enter a strongly regulated educational market, in which they typically either complete an apprentice-ship or gain a university degree. Despite these relatively clear options, un-certainty abounds, either because students have to wait for a long time before they can get an apprenticeship or because they do not fulfill the re-quirements for a university degree of their choice. Students with a basic certificate and those without any school-leaving certificate frequently take a "job-preparation course," while those with an apprenticeship or on a uni-versity course struggle with low salaries or low stipends and may take on additional jobs to supplement their income. Parental resources make a big difference to students' options. In eastern Germany, the situation is made even more difficult by a tight job market with a related shortage of apprenticeships. At the time of conducting our interviews, school leavers in Saxony were offered a cash bonus if they took up an apprenticeship in the neighboring western German state of Bavaria; the state's answer to young people's restricted training and job opportunities was to encourage them to leave. Not surprisingly, most of the participants in our project underlined the need to be "mobile" to gain employment. Their "choice" of career options may have increased relative to their parents, but structural conditions of the labor market imposed severe restrictions and shifted the emphasis to flexibility, mobility, and individual responsibility for training.

The difficult employment situation and political upheavals also had effects on young people's parents. Higher unemployment and lower salaries than in western Germany meant that parents often lacked the financial resources required to support their children's move along uncertain career paths, and they also struggled to provide guidance. The socioeconomic uncertainties have been reflected in higher divorce rates, lower birth rates, and an increase in the age of marriage. Many children thus grow up in single-parent and divorced families. They usually only have one sibling.

Sven's story brings together many of the issues that concerned our participants. While his experiences of growing up and his plans for the future differed markedly from those of his parents, he shared with them the sense of rupture and uncertainty that the move from a state-socialist to a market society had entailed. His own life was already one of great change, as his parents were divorced and he had moved with his mother from a suburban village to a central part of Leipzig. Sven was an only child and did not have a close relationship with his mother's new partner. He also never mentioned his father in our interviews.

Just before we started our interviews, Sven had found out that his mother might lose her job as an administrator of a private firm. This introduced a further element of insecurity into his life, especially as the family had no major savings to fall back on. The political and economic conditions in eastern Germany before 1989 had made it difficult for people to accrue enough private capital to secure themselves against economic problems. For young people like Sven, this meant that there was greater urgency to find employment and less opportunity for experimenting with different lifestyles and careers backed up by parental financial support than for young people from wealthier backgrounds.

We met Sven as part of a mixed-gender group (three thirteen-year-old girls, two fifteen-year-old boys), who regularly attended a youth center in the east of Leipzig for a course in ceramic modeling. He had joined the course after visiting the center with his school class. While the other members of the group had a very busy, meticulously organized schedule for their leisure time and had consciously chosen to participate in a number of artistic courses, Sven occupied a somewhat unusual position, having joined the course on a whim rather than as part of a larger project of self-development. He also came from a medium-grade high school, a *Realschule* rather than a *Gymnasium*. Reflecting these differences, Sven played shifting roles in group interviews, sometimes showing greater maturity than others while at other times not being able to comment on issues that interested the rest of the group. Sven only had a year left at school and was thus already far more focused on his future career than the girls, while Tom, the other boy in the group, intended to stay in school longer to gain the university-access qualification (Abitur). Tom was protected from having to make the immediate career choices that confronted Sven.

The topic of hobbies and friendships were prominent in our discussions with Sven. Apart from the ceramics course, his leisure time was spent in a fairly unplanned and loosely structured way:

> On Wednesdays I do ceramics, so that fills the day more or less after school. I don't tend to go out much in the evenings. Unless I do something in the afternoon, I don't go out. I only really do that on weekends, when I go and meet people in the evening. And on Thursdays, I take my extra maths lessons, because I am really not good in maths. Apart from that, I always have time to do whatever I want.

Meeting friends to play football [soccer] and to "hang out" were important aspects of Sven's daily life. He disliked anything that was too rigidly organized and required regular attendance:

> I would really like to do more sports, like skiing, but somehow the days are just too short, because first you go to school, then you want to relax a bit, then somebody may call me to go out, and so the day just goes by. I mean, I do some sports, like playing football, but nothing serious. Like I'm not in a football club, because I don't have the time and I would probably just forget to go. We have a football pitch next to my house, but I'd rather just play with my friends, not in a serious club. I don't think I would be good enough for that and I really don't like being forced to do it.

Despite his preference for unplanned leisure activities, Sven was strongly committed to his friends and explained how important it was for him to be part of a community. Since moving to a new part of town, finding new friends had been difficult for him, and, as an only child, he missed the company of friends his own age. He traveled extensively across the city to meet friends, but was worried about losing touch with them and not being able to establish new friendships.

> I used to live in Gholis and, well, I preferred that to where I live now. I mean, I still know people from school, but not from my neighbourhood, whereas in Gholis, I could leave the house and meet people. I could talk to them and didn't have to rely on friends from school. We also used to have a kind of meeting place, where all the young people gathered, but that's gone now and since then, I have only bumped into people occasionally in the city. The place where we used to meet was a playground, where you could sit for ages and chat or play football. We mostly used to just sit there and chat or walk around a bit, if the playground was closed.

Moving to the city from the suburbs had made Sven feel quite isolated and alone. His example shows not only the importance of friendships for emotional well-being but also how much confidence it takes to make new acquaintances:

> I think it is hard meeting new friends. You just don't have the confidence to go up to a group of people and say, "Hi, I am Sven, would you like to be friends with me?" It's too embarrassing. Usually it's more like one of your mates from school knows somebody and so you get to know his friends. But I would not go up to somebody, unless they come up to me and we decided to do something together. I just wouldn't go up to somebody and say, "Hi, would you like to be my friend."

Sven's mental map (Figure 7.1) gives a vivid impression of his efforts to maintain connections with his previous friends. It also indicates how committed he was to other family members and shows how much of his daily life was spent on the move:

> On the map, you can see where I live and where my granny lives. Her house is in Paunsdorf, not far from the Paunsdorf Shopping Center. My friend Sarah lives in the house next to hers. She is a very good friend of mine from school. Over here, I have included Munich

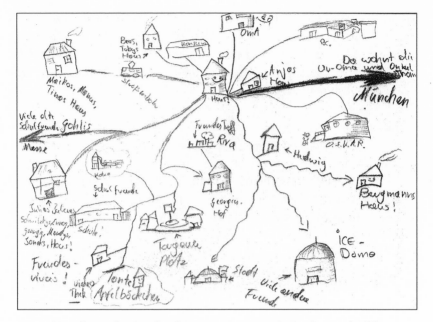

FIG 7.1   *Mental map showing the places most important in Sven's everyday life*
(Photograph by Kathrin Horschelmann)

because that's where my great-grandma lives and my uncle Matthis
with his girlfriend. Then there is the club, "Oskar," and the house
where my friend lives, in Taucha. I've also drawn the ice-cream par-
lor where I sometimes meet my friends, and the city, that's where I
meet people sometimes in the afternoon, on Torgauer Platz. The
"Riva," that is where we play football and then here are the houses of
a few more of my friends. If I want to see them, I have to take the
tram because they live in Gholis. Aunt "Apfelbäckchen," that's where
I take my extra maths lessons. And then I have a few friends who
live near her. I've also included the video shop, where I go to get my
games. And this is where we meet in the summer, at the playground.
"Hedwig" is a youth club I used to go to, but I don't anymore.

In the photographs (Figure 7.2–7.6), friends outside of school figured
little. The most important pictures were of Sven's mother, his guinea pigs,
his room, and his computer. All of these were centered in the home, but
the computer connected Sven with the wider world:

I have a room of my own, as you can see in the photos. I've tidied
up especially! There is my computer and the "Giga-Wall," which I

Fig 7.2   *Sven's room* (Photograph by Kathrin Horschelmann)

Fig 7.3   *His computer connects Sven with the wider world*
(Photograph by Kathrin Horschelmann)

FIG 7.4   *The 'Giga-Wall'* (Photograph by Kathrin Horschelmann)

FIG 7.5   *Sven's guinea pigs* (Photograph by Kathrin Horschelmann)

Fɪɢ 7.6   *Sven and his mother recently moved into a flat in the house opposite*
(Photograph by Kathrin Hörschelmann)

made after going to an IT show in Düsseldorf. I took some photos there and won that T-shirt. Then here are my beloved guinea-pigs. And this is where I live. The "Konsum" shop is in the background and you can look onto the roof of the "China-Bistro."

Though not a favorite site, school loomed large in all of our participants' lives. School took up the majority of their time during the week, starting at about 7:00 A.M. and finishing between 1:00 and 3:00 P.M., depending on age. Sven photographed his school (Figure 7.7) several times over, not because he liked it much, but because it was an important part of his day and because he needed it "to get a job some day."

Having lost many friends through moving, and without extensive extracurricular commitments, Sven spent much of his leisure time playing computer and video games or watching television. But he also enjoyed reading and had enough command of the English language to read Harry Potter in its original language. Sven's one great passion was computer and video games. He invested much effort, creativity, and money in playing them, and this came before other activities such as sports:

I have my own PC and I love playing games on that or on the Internet. But I never play for long. Only for, like, half an hour or so at a

FIG 7.7   *The middle-school where Sven is completing his formal education*
(Photograph by Kathrin Horschelmann)

time. My favorite games are the "shooting" ones. The other ones are too expensive. I've tried to teach my mum how to do it, but she doesn't get it. So I play "Sims" and "Settler" with her. I also like strategy games and role-play. Got this one game from the video shop that I've copied, though I probably shouldn't admit that.

Over time, he had become highly knowledgeable and learned enough English through playing games and using the computer to access websites and other information that is not available in German. While most students in the German school system will learn English as their first foreign language, actively using English in his spare time improved Sven's competence considerably and will make it easier for him to gain employment in the professional sector, where fluency in English is almost always a prerequisite. It will also make it easier for him to move to a foreign country for education or employment, should local conditions become too difficult.

Sven spent most of his money on computer-related goods, games, and magazines, but the pocket money he got was limited (five to ten Euros) and, although he had access to savings, he researched major purchases carefully and hated to waste money on ephemeral things, such as fashion:

If I really want something, I can buy it because I have five hundred Euros in my savings account. And I can access that with my cash card. But I wouldn't want to spend that money on restyling myself. That would be such a waste. I mean, I have everything I need and I don't need a new style. If I really want something, I usually do a bit of research first, especially if it's for my computer. I want to know that it's good quality and whether there is anything else I might need for it. But if it's fine and it is exactly what I need, then I'll go and buy it. I don't spend much money during the week. Maybe five to ten Euros, like for food in the school canteen or for the odd computer magazine.

Our interviews with Sven pointed to tricky negotiations and efforts involved in everyday performances of gender. Sven loved his ceramics course, which was mainly taken by girls. It was his only regular extracurricular activity. Yet in our interviews he appeared reluctant to discuss this hobby and he stressed instead his involvement in activities coded locally as "male": football, skiing, snowboarding, and technical aspects of computing:

Apart from the ceramics course, I don't do anything in a club now. In my spare time, I like to go skiing, rowing, cycling, and snowboarding. I would love to do more snowboarding. That's really cool. And I like playing on the Internet.

Girls like to go shopping, whereas boys are much more interested in computers, like how they are built. Most girls just want to know how a game works. So they use it more in order to play, whereas boys want to know what's inside the computer. Boys are far more interested in the practical stuff.

Sven talked at length about his own clothing style, his body shape, and his hairstyle but identified not being interested in one's appearance (or not seeming to be interested) as an important masculine trait:

I think it's embarrassing for a man to be into his appearance, to be using anti-aging face creams for instance. Because men are supposed to express something more like: we are "hard-men," we are better than women, we are not vain. And if a man changes his hairstyle, he isn't going to draw everybody's attention to it.

I recently bought myself a pair of G-Star trousers. They were awfully expensive, but I can't wear them. They just don't look good on me. I have quite a small frame, so I'd rather wear something a bit larger. Changing my hair color would be fun. I really don't like brown anymore. I was born blond, but that's got darker over the years. I wouldn't mind going back to blond, but I'm too lazy to go and buy the hair dye. It's also too embarrassing.

Sven's love of guinea pigs might also be seen as uncharacteristic for a young man seeking to underline his masculinity. But across all of our interview groups and independent of age or gender, we found that participants had pets that they cared very much about and were happy to photograph and describe with great affection. After family and friends, pets offered an important emotional anchoring point in their lives.

Another issue that Sven raised in relation to differences between men and women was that of careers. Being in a group dominated by girls, he shifted between asserting gender differences and recognizing possibilities for their transgression. When we asked him what jobs he associated with men, he struggled to find examples:"What's a real man's job? Maybe a plasterer. Although I don't want to say that I agree with the old stereotype that women belong to the kitchen and men go to work. Maybe boxing or football, they are more manly occupations. Okay, so some women also play football, but it's more of a men's sport. You don't get a women's premier league, do you?" Sven stressed that having a respectable job was a prerequisite for living well. Employment determined whether he could find a girlfriend and was essential to his masculinity:

> Having a job is important for self-esteem. You want to be respected. If you meet a woman and she asks what you are doing for a living, then you don't want to tell her that you are unemployed. If you do, you might as well forget it. You have to be able to say, "I work in this or that profession," and it has to be something good. I mean, she's not likely to move in together with a guy who lives off social benefit.

We met Sven at a crucial stage in his education: one year before taking his final exams. As a good student from a *Realschule*, he had to decide whether to apply for vocational training next or, depending on his results, to move to a higher-grade school (Abitur) to gain the university-access qualification. Sven was doubtful that his results would be good enough to be accepted for an Abitur-course, but he was ambitious and keen to learn a respected trade with good future prospects. His main concern was to find an apprenticeship, which is still a requirement for most skilled occupations in Germany. It offers a viable alternative to university education and a clear career path with prospects to gain the qualification of "master" *(Meister)* in a particular craft or trade area after further training and experience. Even for students who qualify to go to university, apprenticeships are an attractive option, since they enable them to earn an income while relatively young and to develop a reputable career. Sven's mother's threatened redundancy heightened the importance of his being able to obtain an independent income:

> I am very worried about being unemployed. My mum is probably going to lose her job. It's not definite yet, but it means we've had to think about what it would mean. So my mum's been very stressed lately and she keeps saying that we have to save, save, save. She says, because she may not have a job in a few weeks' time, we have to learn to live within our means. We'll have to live more modestly, but we'll probably get used to it.

Like many of his peers, including those from higher-grade schools, Sven worried about the shortage of jobs and of apprenticeships that has been a persistent problem in eastern Germany since unification and the end of the Cold War. Although Leipzig has lower rates of unemployment than most other cities and regions in eastern Germany, our research participants were pessimistic about local career opportunities. Most were prepared to move to western parts of the country and saw it as their responsibility to be mobile and hard-working enough to find an apprenticeship or job. Sven was less convinced about this individualistic approach, recognizing that "trying hard enough" offered no guarantee of a job in an unstable labor market. Nonetheless, he was prepared to move to a different part of Germany in order to realize his goal of becoming a cook:

> Everybody says that it's hard to get a job in the east and that you can't earn as much here as in the west. So I would go to the west, either to get an apprenticeship there or to work there. If they have enough jobs, why shouldn't I go there?"

Sven also worried that getting good results at school was no longer enough to secure a job. He invested extra time and effort in improving his results in maths through after-school classes and considered gaining additional skills:

> I worry about getting a job. You have to really think hard about what you want to do and what you might need to get there. Maybe

you still need to get a university degree or you need to go to a vocational college, get a better qualification. An employer will probably go for the person with the extra qualification, not just a school certificate, but something extra, and definitely not the person without a school certificate.

Just how important a fulfilling career is for young people like Sven became clear when he talked about his desires for the future:

> You should never do what you like for a living because you'll probably then stop liking it. For me, there are jobs I would hate to do, jobs I wouldn't mind doing, and jobs I would love to do, but which are probably impossible to get. So, for instance I would not want to work as a cleaner or a rubbish collector or any other devalued job like that. I wouldn't mind working as a chef. Being a star would be my dream, but that's unlikely. I mean, some people manage it, but it's hard.

Instead of the shifting, fragmented lifestyles that are often highlighted in youth research, Sven's goals in life centered on predictability, stability, and "traditional" values. He wanted to be in a steady relationship, own a house, have enough money to live comfortably, and have children. "Flexibility" thus became a means to an end, not an end in itself:

> We did this game in the ceramics course: What would your dream life be? I made a dice and on each side I put something that's important to me. So there is getting a job, having a girlfriend, earning money, then a house, two kids and, again, the girlfriend. Well, and me. On the upper side I drew a laughing face and on the opposite side a crying face, which stands for all the things that have not come true.

Contrary to common concerns about radical right-wing tendencies of jobless youths, Sven did not translate his worries about unemployment into a search for scapegoats. This became particularly clear in his discussion of music. Moral panics about youth subcultures commonly lead adults to overlook the possibilities of particular musical and subcultural trends becoming a resource for countering racism and intolerance rather than reinforcing it. For Sven, music was more than a casual interest. He associated himself with the hip-hop scene as a lifestyle that embodied and expressed antiracist political views:

I would say that I belong to the hip-hop scene and I dress like that too. The low-cut trousers and jumpers [sweaters], then those shoes, either trainers or skater boots. There's a great shop in town, where they have a whole section of just hip-hop clothing. By wearing those clothes, I want to make a statement. I want to stand up to my beliefs, like not hating foreigners. For me, it is not important where somebody is from. We are all human.

A lot of people in my class like hip-hop, no difference between girls and boys. You can tell straight away by the clothes they are wearing, like the skater clothes, that's usually hip-hop. And those clothes, with hip-hop they are not just a fashion statement, they are about a whole lifestyle, a whole way of life. Like, not to be right-wing, to help others, especially foreigners. So you can't just shift from one fashion to the next. A hip-hop fan would never go and beat up a foreigner. I mean, of course it's possible that you get into an argument. But you would not hate foreigners in general. You would never say that all Turks are criminals, for instance, just because you got into a fight with one of them.

Despite his strong political views, Sven described hip-hop as a moderate form of youth culture and distinguished himself from more "extreme" lifestyles like those of punks and goths. Hip-hop was about belonging to a majority group, an "in-crowd." It offered a safe middle ground between being trendy and too different or individualistic. In many ways this mirrored Sven's concerns about the loss of friendships and his interest in pursuing a stable, respected career. Belonging to a mainstream group might well have helped him to alleviate some of the uncertainties of his life:

Punks and goths also have their own lifestyles. In a way, punk is one level up from hip-hop. I wouldn't want to be a punk. It's more extreme than hip-hop. And the goths, well, you can't really describe them. They're somewhere in between, loving darkness and sleeping in coffins and so on. And if you see somebody walking around with bell-cut trousers, then you know it's a techno-fan, because that's really not in fashion anymore, so you would only wear it if you were really into techno.

What Sven liked about hip-hop and rap was their directness and the way they addressed injustices and politics explicitly:

Most of the time, the texts of songs don't mean much, apart from Eminem perhaps with his "Cleaning out my closet." I don't know how you would translate that into German. With rap or hip-hop you get more serious texts, not like techno. It is more critical, even political. They try to say what makes them angry about the way people live and they try to express that in rap.

Sven did not comment on the ways in which hip-hop often replicates sexist stereotypes, is commercialized, and has become a fashion for white youths who do not associate themselves with its politics. For him, being a hip-hopper was about commitment to tolerance and antiracism and a way of distinguishing himself clearly from neo-Nazi youths. Sven had little interest in party politics, but his lifestyle was powerfully politicized.

Sven's story differs from common perceptions of how young people in eastern Germany tackle the contradictions of their lives. Being concerned about the difficult job situation in and around Leipzig, Sven neither accepted that the solution to problems such as unemployment was purely individualistic (trying harder), nor did he look for easy targets—such as immigrants—to blame. His story shows some of the ways in which young people create meaningful lives for themselves in difficult and uncertain circumstances.

Notes

1. This project was funded by an ESRC Small Research Grant, number R000223955.

2. Privileges and disadvantages in the socialist education system depended on political commitment. Opportunities existed for higher-ability students to progress to university, but those with strong religious beliefs and dissident political views were severely restricted in their choice of education and profession.

Further Reading

Bundeszentrale für Politische Bildung. (2005). *Die soziale Situation in Deutschland.* Available at www.bpb.de/wissen/MCBEV2,0,Arbeitslosigkeit_in_den_Bundesl%E4ndern. html (accessed November 15, 2006).

Cieslik, M., and G. Pollock, eds. (2002). *Young People in Risk Society: The Restructuring of Youth Identities and Transitions in Late Modernity.* Aldershot: Ashgate Publishing.

Evans, K. (2002). "Taking Control of their Lives? Agency in Young Adult Transitions in England and the New Germany." *Journal of Youth Studies* 5(3): 245–269.

Lehman, W. (2004). "'For Some Reason I Get a Little Scared': Structure, Agency, and Risk in School-Work Transitions." *Journal of Youth Studies* 7(4): 379–396.

Sean Crotty, Christopher Moreno,
and Stuart Aitken

8

"Each and Every Single Story About Me ... There's Like a Huge Twist to It"

Growing Up at Risk in the United States
—A Portrait of Mike

Home supervision is . . . no friends over . . . you can't go
outside, no telephone use, and no Internet. The mom is
supposed to be the supervision over that. Like she decides
if you get terminated [reported for violating home supervision rules] or not but, like, the home-supe officer is
supposed to come over, like, every day and . . . check in on
you. . . . [Once] I had a friend over when the actual officer
came over. . . . Everything was cool. I'm glad I didn't get
locked up [sent back to Juvenile Hall]. These stories are so,
like, complicated because there are so many twists to them.
Like, each and every single story about me being locked up,
there's like a huge twist to it.

—MIKE, IN RESPONSE TO STUART'S QUESTION ABOUT HIS
EXPERIENCES WITH HOME SUPERVISION

Mike is seventeen. He is handsome, with a sharp wit and a sense of
humor that can light up a room. Mike's mother, Debbie, was a
drug addict when he was born and for the first eight years of his
life. His father left when Mike was two years old and he has not seen him
since. Debbie is now in her ninth year of recovery from twenty-four years
of alcohol and methamphetamine addiction. As young children, Mike and
his older brother suffered from severe neglect, and when adults were present there was often physical and emotional abuse. The family moved from
place to place in California, most often residing in environments characterized by gangs, prostitution, and addiction. At times the family was homeless.

Mike has been incarcerated in Juvenile Hall three times, primarily for stealing and vagrancy but also for behavioral problems at school, and on one occasion at the behest of his mother who believed that the experience would change his life.

Mike's story is a series of twists and contradictions. The story is resolutely embedded in his family's local context and the larger influences (e.g., school, neighborhood redevelopment projects, neoliberal economic transformations) that mold those contexts. The first twist came with his mother's recovery from alcohol and drug abuse. With recovery, Debbie took responsibility for herself and her family and, as part of this responsibility, she became involved in neighborhood and community affairs. For the past eight years, Mike has lived in El Cajon, California, in an apartment complex that his mother manages. The apartment complex is sandwiched between a gentrifying downtown, a state courthouse, and residential neighborhoods marked by drug dealers and gangs. Drug free due in large part to Debbie's efforts, their apartment complex is, in many ways, a haven of hope carved out of an otherwise forgotten and derelict landscape. Mike and his brother are part of those changes. Mike is a devoted son and, to the degree afforded a seventeen-year-old of meager means in today's neoliberal consumer-oriented society, a responsible member of the local community of which he is part. Mike's story is not one of unmitigated redemption, but one of energy, passion, and hopefulness.

In some ways, Mike's story mirrors neoliberal ideals that speak to the creation of citizens who are autonomous, free, and responsible for their choices. And this suggests another twist: the state encourages people to develop this kind of citizenship while rolling back the means for people like Debbie and Mike to achieve success. We argue that Mike and Debbie are in this place of responsibility and hope in spite of neoliberal agendas that diminish state support for their welfare. This, of course, is a contested and problematic "illness-and-remedy" that constitutes contemporary neoliberal globalization. Economies and systems of governing and education are not the only things to be restructured under neoliberalism: important twists occur when parents and children undergo a form of restructuring of their own as they resist, adapt to, and rework the changing circumstances of their daily lives. Reworkings at the individual and family scale then unleash a number of complex, contradictory, and unexpected changes that may, in turn, affect the economies and systems of governing and education. As a consequence, the outcomes of neoliberal economic restructuring are not always anticipated. The imaginative twists in Mike's history and geography (and his daily life) do not reflect the contemporary promise of neoliberal education: a student who is globally competitive. Rather they suggest the ways that Debbie takes responsibility for herself and her small part of El Cajon, and the ways that Mike supports that responsibility.

This chapter is about some of these contradictory and unexpected twists as they relate to the evolving context of Mike's life. In what follows we outline a typical day in Mike's life and use moments in that day to contextualize his past and his local geography. Through this discussion, we consider the ways that social and environmental changes taking place under neoliberal restructuring affect Mike's life.

A large part of Mike's daily life is colored by his criminal record and the time he spent in Juvenile Hall. Mike is nonetheless working hard in school with particular focus on a welding class that he hopes will provide him with employment skills. Currently, he is intent on finding a part-time job at a local mall so that he can help out his family financially. Mike acknowledges a network of friends and extended family who care for him. He thinks about his future and uses resources at hand, including a local mentorship program called Boys to Men, which helps him with issues of trust and responsibility. Sean has acted as Mike's mentor in this program for several years, and it is through this relationship that we came to know Mike and his family. The information presented in the following discussion is drawn from several sources. Background information and observations of Mike's engagement with his family, local community, and school are drawn from Sean's weekly interactions with Mike and his family. The remainder of the data presented is drawn from a short series of semistructured interviews with Mike and Debbie.

A Day in the Life of Mike

Getting Started: 7:30 A.M., October 2006

Mike wakes up for school. He looks down from his bunk and thinks about dropping a flying elbow on his older brother sleeping below. In many ways this thought is Mike's response to his claustrophobia and lack of privacy, but it is also a playful jab at his older brother with whom he has struggled through, and survived, many painful experiences. Mike's bedroom is a contested space: on a daily basis each brother tests boundaries of dominance and independence. The brothers' relationship with each other is one of tough love, often moving back and forth between play fighting and actual fighting. Mike wipes the rest of the sleep from his eyes and considers his brother's pregnant fiancée, also sleeping below. He decides against the flying elbow. Mike and his brother have shared this room for ten years, and the fiancée adds a new twist to their struggles.

During Debbie's drug-using days, Mike and his brother shared the experience of parental neglect. In many ways, they raised each other, fumbling to understand the derelict and abusive world around them and their place in it. Mike often comes across as the one who took responsibility for the family, a position he still energetically pursues. One of the dramatic changes for both brothers was Debbie's recovery and her daily amends to her sons through a program of responsibility that taught her to embrace a mother's role. In this emotional space of parental engagement and presence, the boys began to compete for her attention. Debbie puts it this way: "So now I finally had some attention and love to give [after beginning rehab] you know? They both wanted it so badly that I think Mike stepped aside and let [his brother] have it because he saw that [he] needed it more."

Mike hops down from the top bunk, lands silently, and quickly gets dressed for school. Debbie has already left for work. Mike has taken care of himself for quite some time so it is no special hardship for him to fix breakfast and get ready for school. During his first nine years he was never really *seen* by his mother, particularly not at this time of day. Debbie speaks about the lengths to which Mike, as a toddler, would go during her period of drug addiction: "You know I would take some down time and just crash . . . and I would get up and he would have gotten into the fridge and everything was just everywhere. One day it was the freezer, the next day it was the fridge, the next day it was the bathroom cabinet. It was his way of saying, "Hey mom, I am here, I am hungry." When Mike gained his mother's attention, there were few contexts and fewer boundaries. She placed no effective restrictions on his movements. Mike had a lot of energy, and he would misbehave in hopes that she might notice him. With a wry smile, he notes that: "My mom's rules were 'Be home . . . whenever you want to. . . . I don't care. . . . I'm not watching you. . . . You're hyper . . . I can't keep up with you . . . leave me alone . . . shut the door.' Yeah that was my life . . . for five years, all the way to, like, twelve."

Mike makes breakfast, grabs his books and cigarettes, and is off on what he calls his "Chevro-leg" to school. He will not be late for school today.

School Begins: 8:15 A.M., October 2006

Mike just got to school. From a past replete with truancy this may be viewed as an achievement. He has attended El Cajon Summit High School for three years, but has only completed 32 of the 200+ course credits required to graduate. He is a seventeen-year-old freshman, a distinction of which he is not proud. Even if he takes the maximum number of classes from this point on, Mike cannot graduate before he is twenty years old. Like all U.S. schools, Summit High is marked by the 2002 Education Reform Act dubbed "No Child Left Behind." Not only did Mike get left behind, he never really got started within the context of this ambitious and problematic legislation. The Reform Act created schools dedicated to teaching complex skills so that children could compete in a rapidly changing world. It was a strategic move toward the constitution of citizens as responsible, globally connected, and competitive, and away from locally based strategies that constitute citizens as responsive, locally present, and participating. The ironic twist is that Mike today fits wonderfully into the second format, and yet he is forced to be a full-time student as part of his probation. He is unlikely to graduate but, at the very least, a good attendance record at school plays a role in keeping him out of Juvenile Hall. Mike has been on probation for the better part of four years, and much of his concern with school is to not violate this probation. Given his past behavioral problems he takes the minimum number of mandated classes so that he can keep out of trouble. For the most part, his attitude toward education centers on his desire for employment:

> In my opinion I do not think school is necessary for life. It's really not! It is just a waste of time. Like sure, it is cool to be smart, you know? And, uh, to have knowledge upon certain subjects or whatever your relative interests are. So, um . . . it is really a waste of time because you could be out there learning like, say, all you really need to do is work in life. . . . You need basic math to run a cash register. That's it! If you are going to a job where you're going to be a cashier why not just study to be a cashier for a while? Just get the basics down. Just math. That's all it is.

Mike is concerned about future job prospects when he leaves school without graduating. With vocational jobs in mind, he is enthusiastic about his welding class. Class does not start for forty-five minutes, but Mike arrived early so he would have extra time to practice. He likes welding because upon completion he can test for a welding certification with NASSCO (National Steel and Shipbuilding Company) shipyards on San Diego Bay. Mike believes that a well-paying welding job could finance a trip to Japan where he hopes to indulge his real passion: martial arts.

I really need to catch up . . . as I was telling you. And I do have plans for college, I do. Um, I want to uh . . . what I really want to do, is I want to move out to Japan to take martial arts . . . Ninjitsu. The art of ninja. . . . That's um, I'm really kind of astonished by being like, invisible, to the naked eye. Cause, like I mean, I've always had a passion for martial arts, I have.

Given his past history with local police and probation officers, is it little wonder that Mike likes the idea of being invisible. Mike often mentions his knowledge of local alleys and drainage ditches in which he can travel throughout his neighborhood quickly and often without detection.

Mike's morning schedule is filled out by weight lifting and biology. His official class schedule is from 9:00 A.M. to 1:15 P.M. and includes an hour for lunch. Perceiving them as redundant for his job prospects, Mike hates most of his classes. He particularly dislikes weight-lifting class because he thinks the gym teacher is constantly trying to "whip his ass."

Weighty Burdens at 10:30 A.M.

Mike's weight-lifting teacher is picking on him for doing shoulder presses incorrectly. The teacher tells Mike that there is no way that he will pass weight lifting because his T-shirt is not a standardized El Cajon Summit gym shirt. Mike couldn't wear his EL Cajon shirt because it is dirty. He did not have time to wash it last night because his family's washer and dryer were in use the previous evening by his brother. Mike is marked as a problem student by his gym teacher and others. This is largely due to his past behavior, probation status, and a diagnosis of Attention Deficit Hyperactivity Disorder (ADHD).

Mike has found strength and confidence in the last few years. He is a remarkably protective young man with an intense sense of justice. Many of his teachers seem to miss this. Their opinion of Mike was shaped two years ago when he was fourteen and, as Mike puts it, "I just didn't give a fuck . . . because I used to be really hyper, um, didn't really like to listen, really defying . . . [chuckling]. A lot of defiance going on when I was younger. Didn't really care." Mike has changed a lot since then.

On the Way to Juvenile Hall: Flashback to 6:00 P.M., July 2004

Mike was fifteen the first time he went to juvenile detention. His first serious offense was stealing sets of motorcycle tools from a local dealership.

Under normal circumstances, Mike would not have been locked up for a first offense, but his mother told the police to come down hard on him. Therapy and counseling mandated by the federal court system helped her to stop using drugs eight years earlier and, when Mike got in trouble, she hoped that he could benefit from a similar rehabilitation program. Diminishing state funding for juvenile-detention programs, however, created another twist:

> I needed help with [Mike] and I was hoping that probation was it. . . . It turned out that the state did not have enough money for the probation program to be run effectively so the next stop was Juvenile Hall . . . with no programs. There is no counseling, therapy, nothing in Juvenile Hall. They go to a school and that is the most dangerous place because there is no guards. What kind of an environment is that? They can either choose to go to class and risk getting beat up or they can go back to their cell and do nothing.

The state of California has had varying levels of control over Mike's life since that time, and the legal requirements of his home supervision and probation have impacted his decision making since his last trip to Juvenile Hall. Without the therapy and emotional counseling that was integral to his mother's successful rehabilitation from drugs, alcohol, and the lifestyle that accompanied those vices, Mike's only motivation for improved behavior after his first trip to Juvenile Hall was to avoid a return trip:

> Juvenile Hall [is] not the place to be for me . . . the only thing everybody does in there is sleep all day . . . until calisthenics or til rec time. . . . Um, other than that, I mean like really I was just reading, working out in my room all the time. Um, that's pretty much all you can do in there. But that's really what I [emphasis on I] was doing in there, not all you can do, because people find other stuff . . . negative stuff, to do. I was really working on getting my time over and done with so I can just uh, [chuckles] move on with my life. 'Cause, I'm not gonna lie, I was crying every night in there because I was worried for my mom. 'Cause at the time she was having heart problems and back problems. And uh . . . a lot of traumatic stuff went on. . . . Those were hard times in my life . . . really hard times, that I had to face. And that's when I decided that I had to uh, get involved with something that was positive, an influence on my life.

A further negative influence on his life during those hard times was substance abuse. Mike began experimenting with marijuana and alcohol before his first trip to Juvenile Hall. During his probationary period Mike was drug tested periodically. He had to stop using marijuana in order to avoid being locked up again. Mike said that the emotional circumstances of his school and home life left him wanting to get high, but drug testing forced him to rule out any drug that would stay in his system for more than a few days. Mike discovered methamphetamines, what his mother, Debbie, describes as an, "easy transition for a kid who had been on Ridalin."

Mike's Group: Noon on October 26, 2006

Mike is on his lunch break at school. He really enjoys this part of the day. He has considerable social and leadership skills. Mike and his buddy George are talking and watching over their "group," which meets every day during their lunch break in a grassy area between two rows of buildings. The following interview excerpt suggests some of Mike's abilities:

> I usually warn them before we end up fighting. I mean like, I don't really get into fights at school much, like, here and so on the streets just because . . . 'cause some people are dicks like that. That was my whole reason for being known. Especially like, in my "group." I was known. And uh, a lot of the people in my group have problems with each other, in the group also. So like, I'm always the one to kind of mediate it, you know? Like, to resolve it I'll be like, "No, come here." And I'll seriously get serious about it. I'll be like, "You guys need to quit arguing or bickering or whatever you guys are doing" because I get sick and tired of the principal and shit . . . walking down there personally. Bam, bam, bam, bam [sound of the principal quickly identifying multiple misbehaving members of the group] . . . grabbing somebody by their collar and being like, "We're going to the office." Because like, a lot of people are always like, cussing and yelling, and throwing trash on the ground.

At this moment, the school's principal walks up to Mike to advise him that his group needs to keep their area clean and "act right" or the school will wall off their grassy lunch area with a fifteen-foot chain-link fence. Mike tells the principal that it is under control. His group won't be leaving any trash around on his watch.

"That's a big one that I've been taking care of recently. People were throwing trash all over the ground. So I went through and I've told everybody . . . 'Don't litter on the ground. If I see you do it, believe me, I will kick you out of the group.' Because I have the power to do it."

From the principal's admonition, Mike senses the threat of Juvenile Hall and curbs acting out on his anger, but he nonetheless feels the injustice of the ways disabled students at his high school are treated:

"I think its, like, really fucked up at my school, um, how fucking [stupid], they have all those uh, mentally challenged and disabled people fucking cleaning up our trash! Its really fucked up that, like, some people just can't pick up after themselves."

Mike is keenly aware of the activities of learning-disabled students because of his ADHD. He visits the disabled students' office regularly to talk to his advisor about problems in class or his Individual Education Program (IEP). IEP is designed to custom fit a learning program to the specific needs of students with disabilities. In the past, Mike got in trouble for not sharing common goals with his educators and not performing as they wished in the classroom:

That's why I'm placed in special ed, because I have . . . everybody has their own needs, and mine are like, I want to say, its just really different because in special ed everybody thinks it's like, "Ooh, everybody in special ed are like retards." It's not like that. The only reason people are in special ed is because of the IEP. So I'm placed in it because I have trouble focusing in a larger environment. I work better as an individual!

Testing Out: 12:45 P.M. (Memories of a Year Ago)

Mike is in biology class. Today is the last test of the quarter and the teacher's assistant just gave him a severe reprimand because there was too much talking in class yesterday. Mike wants to explode. He can't contain his anger so he decides it is better to leave the classroom than to say something that will get him another referral. A year ago, his campus advisor threatened to call his probation officer and have him sent back to Juvenile Hall for mouthing off in class. Mike fell victim to a panic attack, couldn't breathe, and eventually passed out:

That last time I . . . was on probation. When I had the anxiety attack at school, I was on my last day. And I remember this clearly. It was on a Friday. My last day of being on probation. And my advocate threatened to call and have my uh ... my probation officer lock me up ... and uh, the thought of it, I just started losing breath. I started breathing heavily. I couldn't ... like it felt like I couldn't breathe. I started to sweat ... and a lot of it I don't remember cause I think, I think I fainted ... actually. Because it just got so bad I just started breaking out and ... breaking out and crying. And I just didn't want to go back because I care too much about my family.

Back in biology class, Mike misses the last test completely. His grade is high enough that he will still pass the quarter, but his decision to leave class and not take the test in order to avoid an argument with the teacher's assistant will drop his final grade from an A to a C. From the point of view of probation, it is more important for Mike to stay out of trouble than achieve good grades. The teacher's assistant knows that Mike has special needs in the classroom but ignores that and continues to ridicule him sarcastically during the rest of the class period.

Mike is constantly in motion, often defining himself through his fearless gymnastic abilities: "I've been bouncing off the walls since I was born. I think I was doing summersaults at age two." Before the beginning of this school year Mike stopped taking stimulant medications prescribed to control his ADHD. Debbie is a firm believer that American children are over-prescribed with drugs such as Prozac and Ridalin as a form of behavior modification: "I am so glad he is off meds, what an awakening it has been for him. You know I thought he needed them, but you know, that was to help me not him. . . . I did not know it at the time, I thought he needed it. All it did was help me. In this last year he is doing better in school than he ever has."

Since deciding to stop taking prescription drugs to treat his ADHD, Mike has improved his attendance record and received higher marks than at any other point in his high-school career. Mike has received fewer citations for misbehavior at school this term as well. These changes have not always come easily, and Mike has suffered setbacks. He does still receive misbehavior citations on occasion, but Mike has managed to modify his behavior in class, and without the drugs on which he thought he was dependent. The unfortunate reality of Mike's situation is that, despite these measurable improvements, he remains impossibly behind. If he continued at his current, improved pace he would require three additional years to graduate. Mike's course-credit situation has a real effect on the way he engages with his own education. He takes as many vocational courses as possible, with the hopes that those skills will help him find employment after

his eighteenth birthday. He also takes some classes that are meant to prepare him for the high-school equivalency test which he will be taking in
the next few years. The key point, however, is that for the remainder of
Mike's high school education, his grades and credits are virtually meaning-
less in the formal sense. He must motivate himself to learn for reasons beyond simply getting good grades or accumulating credits.

Back Flips: 2:30 P.M., October 2006

Mike is preparing to pick up his little sister from school. He has been home
for only twenty minutes even though he has been out of school for more
than an hour. Mike's walk home takes a while because he knows a lot of
people in the neighborhood and loves to talk. His street is the one safe
space for him in an area that is bordered by spaces he does not consider
safe: gangs prevail at the western end of his block and to the east is a
four-lane road on which four drunk-driving accidents have occurred in the
past six months. While walking home from a friend's house one time,
Mike was nearly hit by one of those drunk drivers before the car flipped
and crashed into the wall of a bank building.

Mike's preferred path home from school is defined by his desire to
avoid a downtown redevelopment project just one block from his home,
near El Cajon's Historic Main Street redevelopment project. The public spaces
along this street were privatized as part of the redevelopment and are patrolled by private security guards known as "ambassadors." The redevelopment includes the creation of new park space, in which youth activities are
highly regulated. The new park prohibits skating, skateboarding, biking,
and, most importantly for Mike, climbing. As such the new park space is a
space reserved for adult recreation; driving to the vintage car show or attending a wine tasting in the park is okay, but skateboarding in the park and
doing summersaults down the hill are considered public safety hazards.

Later that afternoon Mike goes to a small park down the street from
his house. Because he is, for the most part, unwelcome in the security-
patrolled parks in his neighborhood, Mike seeks out other spaces in which
to hang out and play. There is a small park on the corner of his block that
has been saved as part of the historic preservation effort tied to the downtown redevelopment. This park is not patrolled by private security forces
so Mike is able to play in the manner he likes. One of his favorite pastimes
is perfecting his back flip from an artistically painted electrical box at the
edge of the park. A police car drives by and slows down. This is still a
monitored space.

In the past Mike's energy in alternative play spaces led to incarceration. While hanging out in an undeveloped field near his home, one of Mike's cousins started burying matches in old bales of hay. The hay caught fire and the fire brought the attention of local authorities. When the police officers and firemen arrived at the scene, they found a telescope that Mike and his friend had stolen from a backyard earlier in the day. Initially Mike was held responsible for stealing the telescope and starting the fire because he stayed to try and extinguish the fire, long after his friend had fled the scene. Not wishing to return to Juvenile Hall, particularly for a crime he did not commit [starting the fire], Mike chose to tell the police where they could find his cousin.

> I was in and out of the smoke, so when the fire trucks get there, I'm there and I tell them the whole story. And, you know, I wasn't gonna let it go down on me, so I told them exactly where my cousin lived. I didn't want to be a snitch or anything like that but . . . shit, I could've been like . . . in really big trouble for that. [Stuart: Mmm-hmm.] And I was like, that's not gonna be on me. So I told them where he lived at the time and . . . they went and got him and he confessed after I was locked up . . . confessed that it was all him. So the D.A. [district attorney] tried to, like, bring it back on me, they wouldn't let me off because of arson.

For young men in postindustrial societies, tension often plays out in increasingly controlled environments and in places where their activities are increasingly under surveillance. Fear brands some children as "at risk others" in neoliberal urban environments where their mere presence is viewed as a blockage to the flow of capital in spaces of consumption. In these monitored spaces of consumption, young men are viewed in much the same way as drug addicts, homeless, street vendors, or day laborers who seemingly violate the clean, manufactured landscapes of consumption that are the hallmark of urban renewal. Public places are legitimately transformed with long-term security and surveillance. Many so-called "at risk" young men are left behind in the in between, out-of-control spaces that are not yet part of gentrification. The privatization of public space in conjunction with youth curfews and anti-youth public space regulations that prohibit certain forms of children's play all serve to precriminalize children, or at least provide police and private security forces with the legal resources to remove young people from spaces where they are disrupting the flow of commerce.

Twists: 7:00 P.M., February 2006

Another way that Mike has found alternative spaces for play is through the Boys to Men mentoring program. Mentoring programs such as this one grew out of a 1980s men's movement that sought to redress a perceived "crisis of masculinity" as adult men realized that they were emotionally disconnected from other men (as well as from women and the domestic realm). The growth of this men's movement does not reflect a desire to get back to the patriarchal roots of masculinity, but was rather a journey into deeper emotional and personal connections boys and men could share and create with one another. Men's weekend retreats, training, circles, and encounter groups grew in popularity through the 1990s and out of one of these evolved Boys to Men, which specifically targets at-risk boys aged fourteen to eighteen.

The Boys to Men program holds weekly picnics at Mission Bay Park as well as weekend camping retreats in the mountains north of San Diego. These picnics and retreats offer Mike and other young men the opportunity to escape the confines of their normal routine and the stress, pressure, and fears that are often a part of young men's lives. The role of the program in Mike's life should not be overstated; unlike state-mandated mentoring programs, he can choose whether to participate in each activity. Moreover, the boys hold each other accountable and sometimes challenge choices:

> I lit up a cigarette, thinking like, "I get to smoke at the Boys-to-Men meetings" . . . I mean I'm sure they're against it but, you know, they're there to uh, provide help and understand what's going on, and uh, it's been a lot of that so far. . . . So I get off the bus, light a cigarette, he says "Put it out," so I put it out, and he says, "Now get down from there." And one thing just led to another and he's like, "Do you want to leave?" and I was like, "Whatever man, I don't care." . . . but uh, that weekend was uh, I got like, a lot of trust out of it, and a lot of stuff off my shoulders. A lot of burdens. . . . I have to say. I look back on it now and I'm just like . . . "wow."

Boys to Men is similar to other mentoring programs in that each boy is assigned a single mentor with whom he spends a few hours a week. Boys to Men differs from other programs because the young men are encouraged to forge deeper emotional connections with *all* members of the larger organization. The larger community of mentors and journeymen all provide emotional support for each other, which facilitates the creation of much larger support networks for the young men involved in the program. Through his interaction with Boys to Men, Mike has developed a network of friends and mentors that extends far beyond the confines of his home, school, and neighborhood.

Looking Forward through the Past: 8:00 P.M., October 2006

Sean is Mike's Boys to Men mentor. He often goes to the Sunday picnics with Mike and he was part of his training weekend back in February 2006. This October evening Sean is conducting an exit interview with Mike for this book. Last week, Christopher interviewed Debbie and the week before that Mike sat down for an interview with Stuart and Sean in an office at San Diego State University. That interview was Mike's first time visiting a university campus. This particular evening Mike is talking about his future. His life is locally circumscribed by a Southern Californian economy that is currently doing exceedingly well. But El Cajon is still primarily a relatively low-income, blue-collar town. The robust regional economy means that there are opportunities for skilled welders in small industries in this town, but white-collar and professional jobs are scarce. Mike dreams of making money to fund the visit to Japan. He wants to go to college, and he got a glimpse of what that kind of life might entail when he first met Stuart on the San Diego State campus.

Tonight Sean asks a lot of questions about Mike's dreams for the future, and it is clear that he is a little uncomfortable talking about his plans and potential. Normally, Mike does not think too much about the future. His life is not distant or global, it is in a very real sense locally circumscribed. Even though he knows he will not graduate in the traditional sense, he just wants to *finish* school. That's his only focus. From his mother's recovery, he learned that life is taken a day at a time. Mike has been part of that recovery and has seen how that has changed their apartment complex, creating a relatively safe place. That said, the final twist for Mike as he talks to Sean about his day is about how little he is concerned about safety:

> MIKE: Right, well it's not so much safe. Its just more, quiet you know? Like more, like I want someplace that's. . . . I don't really care if it's safe or not. Of course, I mean my safety is a matter of my own life, you know? But I think that safety wouldn't really be the main key because there's so many people in the world, I

mean what are the chances that it's, it might just happen to be
you . . . that one time? Or that second time that you're just walking down the street and something might happen? You know?
It's really high . . . odds. You know? I mean I'm sure there's still
some probability that it could happen. I mean I just don't want
it to be really, really safe, like "Hey there's no guns allowed in
this certain area what-so-ever" cause you get checked hardcore,
by like the stations or something. I don't know. I mean . . .

SEAN: you wouldn't want to be like . . . uh, have to get searched a lot?

MIKE: I mean there's not really any place that's safe either? Am I
right? Like no place is really safe?

SEAN: Well it depends. Some places are safer than others.

MIKE: Well like . . . the courthouse, or maybe a police station. . . .

SEAN: Yeah, well. . . . That depends who you are!! [laughing] But do
you think that your neighborhood in El Cajon is safe?

MIKE: Nah. . . . My block. My little street, Park is officially safe
[chuckling].

Neoliberal Twists and a Future of Hope

Mike's story illustrates the difficulty of growing up as a youth in the United
States today. Certainly, Mike has faced challenges and circumstances that
not all American youth experience. His childhood was marked by parental
neglect and abuse, incarceration, and personal drug use. But many of his
daily struggles are common to a great number of American youth. By his
own account, the events and stories of his life have all involved surprises
and twists. Some of these twists were forced by changing institutional
structures. Mike's mother asked the authorities to come down hard on him
after his first run-in with the law, with hopes that he would benefit from
the same type of emotional counseling that had been so vital to her own
rehabilitation. Unfortunately for Mike the state withdrew funding for
counseling during probation, so he was sent to Juvenile Hall instead: clearly
a twist that neither he nor Debbie expected or desired. Education and the
school experience were completely twisted for Mike while he was on probation, during which time his attendance and behavior became more important than his learning or academic achievement.

In other instances it is clear that Mike has taken an active role in "twist-
ing" his own circumstances to make the most of his situation. Mike has
found ways to develop himself and prepare for his future while he is at
school. He focuses on classes that will provide him with vocational training

that may help him find a well-paying job without his high school diploma and classes that will help prepare him for his high school equivalency exams. He also uses his time at school to develop his own leadership skills, as evident in his role as leader and mediator of disputes in his lunch group. Mike and Debbie also managed to twist their circumstances to connect Mike to the Boys to Men program which provides the emotional support that was not a part of his state-sponsored rehabilitation program.

It seems to us that Mike has begun to develop emotional connections and resources that will serve him well in his future. He has developed a network of friends and supporters who know him as being much more than a troubled, at-risk youth. They know the young man who sees the flaws in an educational and legal system within which he is forced to live. They know the young man who bounces off the walls and does flips out of trees, and love him for it. They know the young man who cares for his family so much he was paralyzed with anxiety and sadness when he was locked up and could not be there to protect them. Mike's future is yet to be decided. Things have already begun to change. Mike is going out for the wrestling team this week. He and his mother have few secrets from one another. Debbie is looking forward to being a grandmother, and Mike is contemplating the responsibility of being an uncle. And Mike is going to have his own space. His brother and fiancée are moving into another apartment in the same complex. Mike will have his own room for the first time in his life. Only twenty-two days to go. He's counting.

Further Reading

Aitken, Stuart C. (2001). *Geographies of Young People: The Morally Contested Spaces of Identity*. London: Routledge.

Harvey, David. (2005). *A Brief History of Neoliberalism*. Oxford: Oxford University Press.

Venkatesh, Sudhir Alladi, and Ronald Kassimir, eds. (2007). *Youth, Globalization, and the Law*. Stanford, CA: Stanford University Press.

Alex Jeffrey

9

Zilho's Journeys

Displacement and Return in Bosnia-Herzegovina

From a glance at the urban landscape of central Brčko, a town in northern Bosnia-Herzegovina (hereafter Bosnia), there is little physical sign that it was a site of conflict a little more than ten years ago. On warm summer evenings children play on miniature motorized cars on the pedestrianized main street, groups of young people sit in the many cafes that line the pavements, and live music drifts out of the doors of the large Hotel Posavina. It is on the veranda of the hotel in 2003 that I sat talking to Petar Mihajlović, a youth representative of the nationalist Serb Democratic Party (SDS), about the destruction of Brčko between 1992 and 1995. As we ate ice cream and watched people on the pavements below, he gave a frank assessment of the roots of the previous decade's conflict, citing the intrinsic ethnic differences of the peoples of Bosnia. Leaning forward conspiratorially Petar came to his conclusion: "You see Alex, we just don't like being mixed."[1]

This nationalistic idea—that the Bosnian population should be divided between its three main constituent ethnicities (Bosnian Muslim or Bosniak, Croat, and Serb)—has been central to recent Bosnian politics and to the life of a young man I have come to know well, Zilho Mahić. I first met Zilho in late 1999 in Brčko; he was working for an environmental nongovernmental organization (NGO) and I was working for a small charity promoting multiethnic reconciliation among young people. Confident and funny, Zilho was an anomaly in the NGO sector in the town at this time since he was a young Bosniak who was willing to commute from his displaced home in the nearby village of Gornji Rahić to work in the center of

Brčko. I met Zilho a number of times over the following four years and conducted a series of interviews, in particular in 2003 when I returned to Brčko to undertake doctoral fieldwork examining the role of NGOs in the democratization of the district. This research employed a range of qualitative methodologies, in particular sixty-seven extended interviews with members of NGOs, political parties, the international community, and the local state. In addition, I participated in the daily routines of NGOs, attending seminars and meetings, and helping with day-to-day project work. Over this period of research Zilho experienced many changes: he married his girlfriend Edina, returned to Brčko and rebuilt their pre-war home, and he was promoted to a full-time project worker with the environmental NGO. Over the course of our conversations, Zilho painted a vivid picture of his youth in Brčko and articulated many hopes for his and his family's future.

Like many other young people I spoke to over the course of the doctoral research, Zilho divided his life into two distinct periods: before and after the 1992–1995 conflict. He was born in the early 1980s into a wealthy secular Bosniak family and lived in a prosperous residential district in the town. Both his parents were employed in local state-owned companies. Zilho's father worked in a machinery plant and his mother was employed in a textiles factory. During the 1960s and 1970s, when Zilho's parents were growing up, secure and well-paid manufacturing jobs were plentiful in Brčko. The town is situated on the River Sava and its port and surrounding agricultural land made the town a valuable location for the production and transportation of goods and food. Zilho said that his parents provided a traditional Yugoslav upbringing: "The two of them were raised after the Second World War and knew only about the Tito period and communism." The pillar of the socialist rule of Josep Broz Tito from 1947 to his death in 1980 was the cultivation of "*bratstvo i jedinstvo*" ("brotherhood and unity") among the ethnonational groups within Yugoslavia—a practice of social, cultural, and economic engineering that included rapid industrialization and the creation of shared memorials and public rituals. These Yugoslav cultural traditions are reflected in Zilho's childhood: he was a member of his local "Tito's pioneers" group, he played in goal for the youth soccer team *Brčko Jedinstvo* (Brčko United), and he remembers his father as an active member of his neighborhood's *Mjesna Zajednica* ("Local Community," the lowest strata of the Yugoslav socialist state architecture). Zilho used these events and memories as evidence of the insignificance of ethnonational identity when he was growing up, remarking "I didn't even know I was a Bosniak until 1992."

The reaction of Zilho's family to the outbreak of war in Brčko demonstrates the uncertainty and disbelief that typified the broader public response to the violent disintegration of Yugoslavia. Following the declaration of Bosnian independence in March 1992, Serb nationalists tried to create the Republika Srpska (RS), a monoethnic territory within Bosnia. The town of Brčko was a key target within this territorial project, since it connected the two halves of the nascent RS. Prior to the conflict, the population of Brčko municipality was made up of the three main ethnonational groups in Bosnia. Following a series of Serb military maneuvers in 1992, the Bosniak and Croat populations were expelled from the town, and many fled to the rural areas which were still under Bosnian federal government control.

Zilho's father first heard of the possibility of Serbian military action through Serb colleagues at the factory, who warned him to leave Brčko. Zilho said: "We never felt that could happen in our town, amongst our friends." But the *Jugoslavenska Narodna Armija* (Yugoslav People's Army or JNA), which had recently become exclusively Serbian, had a large barracks in the center of Brčko allowing for the gradual militarization of the town over early 1992. In April the conflict escalated, leading to the expulsion of Bosniak families and a series of war crimes against the Bosniak population. At this time Zilho's family had the chance to take refuge in Germany. But Zilho explained that he and his mother returned to Brčko two months after fleeing to Germany "because my mom was not aware of what was going on; she thought that the conflict would disappear in a couple of days. This did not happen. I stayed in fear and terror for eight months." He continued:

Finally the Red Cross managed to exchange Mom and myself for two Serb soldiers. I remember lots of white vehicles and the UNHCR [United Nations High Commission for Refugees] were also there. I remember arrival in Gornji Rahić on 29 November, 1992. That was a small rural place where I had never been before, even though it's 12 km away from my town. But when I saw my dad and brother, everything changed and I did not care what is going on. For me, it was important to be with my parents. Living in 83 m squared flat before the war, makes you be a child of that environment. In Rahić, eighteen kids and fifteen older people lived in 13 m squared. "Wow," I said, "How can we survive here?" I asked my dad. He was laughing, I remember. Day to day, I consumed various food, I would not call this normal human food today, and used imitations of toys for children like sock balls, etc. . . . The important thing for me in that period was that my close family did not die or get injured.

The war continued for three more years. Zilho and his family lived in cramped conditions in Gornji Rahić, surviving on NGO handouts and relief from the UNHCR. Many of Zilho's friends were sent to stay abroad, particularly in countries with close economic and cultural relations to Yugoslavia, such as Germany and Austria. But Zilho stayed in Gornji Rahić and finished school at the age of seventeen. Following the end of school, Zilho took odd jobs in Gornji Rahic making ends meet by serving tables in local cafes and keeping goal for Brčko United, an exiled version of the town's former team. Zilho also tried to improve his English-language skills "by watching satellite TV." His contact with numerous international NGOs and intergovernmental organizations in Gornji Rahić had taught Zilho the importance of English.

In December 1995, international efforts at resolving the Bosnian conflict intensified. The U.S. government hosted discussions at a U.S. air-force base in Dayton, Ohio, which resulted in a proposal to divide Bosnia into two substate "entities": the Muslim Croat Federation and the RS. But the representatives of neither of these two new entities could countenance losing control of Brčko, since it linked the two halves of the RS while providing the only access to the Sava River for the Muslim Croat Federation. This territorial dispute resulted in a stalemate. At the final stages of negotiations, however, Slobodan Milošević, the president of Yugoslavia who was representing Serb interests, agreed to place the municipality into international arbitration until its future could be decided. For four years no further agreement was made, leaving the town governed by the RS and the remaining countryside under the sovereignty of the Muslim Croat Federation. The Serb nationalist political parties that dominated local and national politics in Bosnia between 1995 and 1999 introduced new street signs, religious rituals, and public memorials designed to discourage Bosniak refugees from returning to the city.

In March 1999 an international arbitral panel announced the creation of a single multiethnic territory—Brčko District—which would lie within both the Muslim Croat Federation and the RS. The agreement also increased the powers of the international community in Brčko, principally represented by the Office of the High Representative (OHR). At the head of the OHR was the U.S.-appointed district supervisor, whose first task after the announcement of district status was to appoint an interim multiethnic municipal government reflecting all ethnicities in Brčko at the 1991 Yugoslav census.

The political changes that accompanied the establishment of the Brčko District in March 1999 encouraged Bosnian refugees to return to Brčko. OHR unified the political institutions of Brčko District into a single government. The district supervisor also attempted to reduce the influence of nationalistic political parties through the appointment of a multiethnic government and assembly. The antagonisms between individual government members often created deadlock. But this was not a barrier to institutional reform, since the terms of the district status granted the supervisor the authority to pass any legislation deemed necessary for the unification of the district. Thus, despite considerable local opposition, the supervisor managed to create integrated institutions in Brčko, such as a multiethnic education system and a unified police force.

Zilho cited this new political climate in Brčko as a significant factor in his family's decision to return to the town. But he doubted that the new district status had changed the political orientation of the town. "Brčko is still the Republika Srspska!" he exclaimed on a number of occasions, justifying his belief by demonstrating that mobile phone reception in the town was restricted to RS phone operators and television news bulletins were still broadcast by RS local news companies. Zilho's family's decision to return to Brčko was not based solely on political considerations; the creation of Brčko District had also brought new employment opportunities. The resolution of Brčko's status had stimulated an influx of international development assistance, such as a US$3.1m United Nations Development Program designed to regenerate the economy. In addition, international companies began to tentatively reinvest in the area, and funding for international NGOs increased. Zilho felt he was well placed to secure employment in these new international initiatives, in particular on account of his English- language skills, and he was hoping to obtain employment as a translator. But he explained that employment opportunities were more limited than he had expected: "Returning in Brčko, I faced a tough time finding a job. The Dayton Agreement and the district status brought many international workers from the U.S. and Europe to Brčko in the postwar period. Fortunately, through some contacts, I was able to find work as a part-time security guard in OSCE [Organization for Security and Co-operation in Europe]."

Beyond this temporary and part-time post, Zilho found it difficult to gain more lucrative and secure employment within an international organization. He felt that jobs in such organizations were predominantly taken by those who lived in the town and, due to the ethnic geography of Brčko District, this meant that these organizations primarily recruited Serbs. Zilho told me:

> In that period [1995–1999], very few Bosniak families had returned to Brčko. International organizations started populating the most popular place in Bosnia: Brčko. Therefore, only Serbs had a chance to find a job in some international organizations that were dealing with return issue, employment, democratization, etc. Such a sad story! Look in OHR, how many Bosniaks and Croats are employed? Three or four and there are thirty-five local members of staff. In the UNDP [United Nations Development Programme] there are nine local staff, none of them are Bosniaks or Croats. In [the international development consultants assisting the district government] there are five employees and all of them are Serbs. [A local youth NGO] is the only multiethnic NGO, and they don't have any Croats. That is basically because, when NGOs came here, there were only Serbs in the town.

These comments contrasted with Zilho's earlier memories of "discovering" his own Bosniak identity in 1992. Zilho suggested that Serbs in Brčko, themselves often displaced from other areas of Bosnia or Croatia, should not deal with issues such as democratization or refugee return. As Zilho's anger at the recruitment of Serbs reveals, his expulsion from Brčko had led him to internalize the same ethnonational labels which he found pernicious at the outset of the conflict.

Zilho continued to struggle to find full-time employment, in spite of the initial inroads he had made at the OSCE. The privatization of the town's prewar industrial plants had failed to create the type of job opportunities within manufacturing that were open to Zilho's parents. Some of Zilho's friends sought work at Arizona Market, a large black-market site in the south of the district that had expanded out of an arms-and-goods exchange point during the war. The name Arizona Market is derived from the U.S. military name for the road on which it is built, and it was the U.S. army that originally demarcated the site of the trading area. Zilho was not attracted to the work in the market, which he said did not reflect his skills and education.

In 2001, however, an opportunity arose for better-paid employment in Brčko.

A Peace Corps volunteer came from America [to the U.S. agricultural NGO] and she was looking for a part-time translator. So my cousin called me about that and I was asking if she could arrange an interview. So she called Counterpart and they arranged an interview. So I came and had an interview for about twenty minutes and some simple questions like "Where did you learn English?" and "Am I OK with a female as boss?" The organization had four members of staff, who were all Serbs. I managed to get a job at that place. I started working for her as a part-time translator twenty hours a week, and she was here for six months. Then a new Peace Corps volunteer came and I worked for her as a part-time translator for seven months. Next, she asked our head of division if I could have a full-time job but with insurance and all the other things that everyone has already. But the lady [in the head office in Washington D.C.] approved me to work only forty hours per week and without any of the other benefits: on a per-hour basis. On April 2002, I got fired because we didn't have any volunteers. So I was asking for them to employ me as a usual employee of the NGO. They said there are no positions similar to my abilities.

Many other young people in Brčko had similar experiences of occupying NGO positions on a temporary basis and obtaining little or no training on the job. Although well-paid in comparison with other available employment—such as working in a cafe in town or a stall at Arizona Market—Zilho found that the lack of transparency between the local field office and the head office in Washington D.C. fostered suspicion and distrust among the staff team concerning the possibility of renewed contracts and the broader financial position of the NGO. At the same time, Zilho presented this NGO work as a necessary stage of his career development; through the experience he had gained, he hoped to find employment in the OHR or another intergovernmental agency.

Outside the realm of employment, Zilho often reflected on the changes in the social and political context of Brčko in the postwar period. The numbers of Bosniak residents in Brčko began to increase following the announcement of district status. Zilho and his family had returned to their prewar home in central Brčko late in 2000, rebuilding the property themselves and replanting the garden, a process he described as "very successful." In spite of this success, however, Zilho's home was the target of nationalist violence on several occasions. Zilho connected these attacks to the persuasive abilities of nationalist politicians:

I understood nationalist intimidation as a normal thing. Like the demonstrations by youth two years ago, when they smashed all the windows on my apartment, and the demonstration in schools and everything. I mean, those kids have no clue what they are doing because they are under the influence of somebody smart. And that smart person has his or her own purposes. I can't say to my friend go and jump in the well, because he is smart and he will say, "Are you crazy? *You* jump." But, if I am stupid, have no clue what is happening in politics, and I am sixteen years old and you as a politician say "Smash his windows! Then he will leave, and it will be better for us!" then I will do that—because I am stupid. If I was smart, I would say "Really, no, *you* smash his windows as it will be better for you."

Zilho thus identified nationalist violence as an irrational act, a means through which young people supported the political careers of others through the spread of fear and anxiety among returnee populations. But he did not restrict nationalist irrationality to moments of violence, nor did he see impressionable young people as sole agitators. He said that nationalist divisions permeated everyday interactions in his community:

Stupid people are making stupid things. They don't realize that, after three years, they need to live with each other. They don't realize that they need to say "Good afternoon" to their neighbor who is another ethnic group. . . . Two years ago my neighbor didn't want to say "Good afternoon" because he thought that I wouldn't be coming back to my city at all. But now he or she needs to do that if he or she wants to live in this place. There are maybe 2 percent of people who are here and they are nationalists. It is that 2 percent who are making huge problems. People who had a very strange past have moved. Why is that? Because they are afraid that someone else will see them and say "He or she did this," or "I will kill you because you were kicking my butt five years ago." Now nationalists [pause] there is less and less influence of nationalists in the city mostly because they realize that there is no future in making problems to other ethnic groups because sooner or later they need to live together.

The deployment of nationalist discourses by Bosnian political parties has been extremely effective in mobilizing voters and, subsequently, retaining

power. But the legacy of such nationalism is that politics itself, the delibera-
tion over the form and character of Bosnian society, is often viewed as a
nationalistic (and hence "irrational") enterprise. On a number of occasions
Zilho stated that he would not vote in an election, since he felt that this
would be endorsing the nationalist political system.

Instead, Zilho supported the presence of the international community
as a de facto political "opposition", since he saw the OHR and associated
institutions as providing a counterweight to excesses of nationalist political
powers:

> This whole country cannot live without the international commu-
> nity. Why is that? I don't know, they are used to it. It is not the same
> as before. A lot of people lost their friends, cousin, brother, sister in
> the war. It is not easy just to live with somebody who maybe shot
> your brother or sister. I can understand that. But I can't understand
> because I didn't lose anybody. I can't understand. But everyone
> should understand that sooner or later, but it is a process, a really
> long process.

There has been a tendency within accounts of Bosnian intervention to
set up a binary between international agencies, imagined as working to
reform and modernize the Bosnian state, and nationalist parties, who are
considered to be preventing the emergence of democratic government. But
Zilho did not simply view the presence of the international community as
a panacea for Brčko. He provided many examples of how the interests of
the international community and nationalist political parties are, in practice, often blurred and indistinct. Zilho identified the Youth Coordination
Body (YCB), an OSCE initiative to stimulate political participation, as a key
example of the international community supporting nationalist political
parties. Zilho felt that, since the OSCE contained nationalist parties and
local NGOs, it served to widen interest in nationalistic political messages.
He felt that the OSCE "wanted to look like something was being done,"
without concern for the wider implications of this initiative. A representative of Brčko Economic School, who had been part of the YCB, supported
this impression, explaining that she had left the YCB because it became
"too radical."

In 2005, Zilho's prospects improved. Building on his knowledge of English, he obtained employment on a project funded by the United States
Agency for International Development which aimed to facilitate public-sector
reform in ten municipalities around Sarajevo. Zilho felt this relocation to

the capital city, a four-hour journey from Brčko, was necessary in the context of deteriorating international interest in Brčko District. Zilho said that his new post would allow him to become a "specialized administrative reform officer" and spoke excitedly in the rhetoric of neoliberal international reform, viewing the job as a chance to help create "a state that has strong economic values and rich public and private partnership." Zilho was using his contacts, language skills, and experiences to negotiate membership of an emerging Bosnian middle class.

Zilho had also married his girlfriend Edina in 2003, and they had a baby son. Zilho had hopes for the country his son would grow up in: "We want our son to live in a prosperous Bosnia, a Bosnia that is a normal country and part of the European Union." The three generations of Zilho's family embody a vision of Yugoslav transition: from his father's upbringing under Tito's socialism, through Zilho's wartime exile and return, and on to Zilho's son's prospects of living through Bosnia's inclusion in a greater Europe.

Note

1. The empirical material in this chapter is predominantly drawn from fieldwork in Brčko between August 2002 and September 2004. A series of follow-up interviews were held with Zilho Mahić over the summer of 2006. Interviews with the following individuals are referred to in the text: the youth representative of the SDS (14 April 2003), Zilho Mahić (14 September 2002; 22 May 2003; 3 September 2006; 29 January 2007), the Director of OSCE Brčko (17 October 2002) and a representative of the Brčko Economic School student council (3 December 2002).

Further Reading

Bose, S. (2002). *Bosnia after Dayton: Nationalist Partition and International Intervention*. London: Hurst and Company.

Bringa, T. (1995). *Being Muslim the Bosnian Way: Identity and Community in a Central Bosnian Village*. Princeton, NJ: Princeton University Press.

Campbell, David. (1998). *National Deconstruction: Violence, Identity and Justice in Bosnia*. Minnesota: University of Minnesota Press.

Jeffrey, Alex. (2006). "Building State Capacity in Post-Conflict Bosnia and Herzegovina: The Case of Brčko District." *Political Geography* 25(2): 203–227.

Danny Hoffman

Rocks

A Portrait of Mohammed

Mohammed breaks rocks. It is "work" only in that it fills his days and demands much of his slender body. Smashing stone into gravel with a small hammer is one of the tasks Mohammed performs for the right to remain a squatter, a caretaker of someone else's land. What money Mohammed has comes in other unreliable and hard-won ways: hustling on the streets of Freetown; performing odd jobs for mechanics or welders; or, his most lucrative activity these days, running *djamba* [marijuana] to the Liberian border. My own visits to Freetown are sporadic and unannounced, but when they happen they mean Mohammed will temporarily have a little extra rice and cash.[1]

The fruit of Mohammed's labor will be an unfinished concrete box which will slowly evolve into the retirement home of a doctor living in the United States. Mohammed, his family, and the slow alchemy of transforming stone to gravel to concrete are the only protection the doctor has against others occupying his land. Legal land titles are a fragile guarantee against theft in Sierra Leone. More reliable are the bodies and, if necessary, the violence of young men.

Many wealthy residents of this crowded West African city have relocated to the hills to escape the noise, the pollution, and the crush of displaced victims of the country's long civil war. With them have come squatter caretakers like Mohammed. Four years ago Mohammed, Adama, and their baby, Struggle, were among the first to settle here when they put up a small *pan-bodi*, a corrugated metal shack. They are pioneers of a sort.

Fig 10.1   *Mohammed* (Photograph by Danny Hoffman)

When the houses are finished they will move on, further into the forest at the outer margins of the urban landscape or back to equally marginal spaces in the heart of the city.

Mohammed's is a rich and difficult story for me to tell. It is literally difficult: Mohammed has narrated the events of his life differently over the years. What I know (or think I know) of it comes from piecing together shreds and narrative patches that do not always cohere. My relationship with him began six years ago while I researched the pro-government Kamajor militia of which he was a part. At the time he lived in the ruins of the downtown Brookfields Hotel, one of hundreds of fighters and their dependants providing security for a government that mistrusted its own military and feared an incursion from rebels in the hills. What Mohammed has told me of the early war years is often conveyed in allusions or generalities. Like many ethnic Mendes, his stories are sequenced by theme or purpose rather than chronology. His speech also reflects the many border zones of his life. He slips without warning between the Mende dialect of the southeast and a thickly accented Liberian English; between the basic Krio of traders in Freetown or Kenema and the rough Krio slang of marginal urban youth. He can be wildly animated one minute and stop mid-sentence the next, or trail off into a mumble made rough by years of cigarettes and *djamba*. Though he knows that I circulate his image and his stories, I have never recorded a conversation with Mohammed and rarely write notes in his presence. Writing his words takes too much of the energy I need just to hear them, and he is uncomfortable with a microphone. In every sense, his voice is difficult to capture.

Mohammed's story is a challenge for more profound—and more personal—reasons. Mohammed and I are the same age. We are both fathers, and have celebrated together the births of our children. But where years, parenting, and profession have marked my own transition into adulthood, Mohammed lives and is defined by a different life calculus. He remains a "youth" in the eyes of the Sierra Leonean state and by the measures of communal existence in this West African postcolony. It is a label with political, social, and economic valences. It means that according to the logic of patronage which demarcates his social field, he has few recognized dependents of his own. It means that he has never formally married, lacking the resources to stage a wedding and to provide Adama's family with the requisite gifts and honors. And it means that he is beholden to others for his basic necessities. In return for the meager graces he receives from older, wealthier men and women, his labors are largely at their disposal. He can be called up as needed for work on the plantations or the mines, on the battlefields or in timber camps across the region—all of them dangerous locations which make the war/peace divide obsolete. When the politicians and the political parties that back them need young men to campaign (often by attacking supporters of rival parties), Mohammed and other youth will be called on to play their part. I know Mohammed too well to think of him as typical of anything. At the same time, the seemingly inescapable trap of youth in which Mohammed finds himself seems to resonate with the biographies of many young men in contemporary Sierra Leone.

Mohammed was not easy to locate after he moved up into these hills. I lost track of him, Adama, and Struggle when the last Kamajor fighters were evicted from the Brookfields Hotel in mid-2002. By the end of the next year I had heard only rumors: that he had gone to Liberia as a mercenary, that he was again selling *djamba* on the border, that he remained in the city living with the family of a friend. It was only recently that I understood that this invisibility at the far reaches of the city was both circumstantial and strategic—a point to which I will return. But on the summer evening that I first saw him there after a year out of touch, he seemed a young man determined to shape his own future.

Like other former Kamajors, Mohammed claimed that, if necessary, he was prepared to hold the land he occupied by force. "God wanted peace in this land," he said, the city and sea stretching beneath him, "so he sent the Kamajors." The reward, promised by the state and backed (in Mohammed's view) by God, is that every citizen of Sierra Leone now has a right to land. That Mohammed could speak of violently defending the territory guaranteed him as a citizen while serving as no more than a caretaker for an absentee landowner exemplified the contradictory logic of postcolonial patronage.

In the abstract, the webs of patronage to which Mohammed and other rural Mende male youth are beholden chart a relatively smooth life path. Young men achieve adulthood through a series of events that mark their progression: the various stages of initiation into men's "secret societies" like the Poro, a formal marriage, establishment of a farm and household. These are achievements facilitated by one's elders, to whom youth owe debts of respect and labor. Over time, individuals transition from clients to patrons in their own right, providing for those younger than themselves and expanding their own client networks as a mark of social status and age. The city offers a parallel tract. Children and youth labor in the home or a family business for patrons who provide them with schooling, room, and board. Rural families not uncommonly send children for fosterage to extended family or former neighbors living and prospering in the city. Rural, urban, or a combination of the two, these relationships are intended to instill in young people the knowledge to function as adults and the resources to put such knowledge into practice. Of course, one never escapes the logic of patronage, and there are always those to whom one is beholden. Nevertheless, a life well lived is said to be one that progresses from youth to adulthood, from the preponderance of one's troubles being those of a client to being those of a patron.

The abstract, however, is a fantasy in contemporary Sierra Leone. There are those who question whether there ever has been an ideal past in which elders possessed both the material riches and the goodwill to meet all of the demands placed on them by their superiors and by the young. Certainly by now the financial capacity is gone for all but a few elites. Successive economic crises have swept West Africa for decades. The long-serving president of Sierra Leone, Siaka Stevens, put the national economy in peril by using state coffers to fund his own patronage network. Structural adjustment measures further strained the resources of Sierra Leoneans across the board, and the end of Cold War era machinations by the superpowers meant a deepening of the economic crisis. A ten-year civil war, beginning in 1991, and a thriving black market in diamonds and timber have made instability the only marker of normalcy. The result for many young people is that adulthood appears as a status foreclosed by a greedy "gerontocracy" and a perpetual state of economic distress. Conversely, the agency that youth ascribe to adulthood is rarely experienced as such; senior people find themselves constrained by the demands of their dependents and by those with greater wealth or political authority.

In contrast to the orderly logic of a life structured by advancement through the patronage ranks, foreign journalists covering the war wrote that Sierra Leone was "a teenage wasteland" and "no place to be young." Scholars and many Sierra Leoneans described the situation in the country as "a crisis of youth." The language of crisis is an open signifier that implies both the threat that desperate youth pose *to* the nation and the crisis *for* youth unable to find sure footing on their own life path. Former President Joseph Momoh framed the ontological condition of young Sierra Leoneans in a pithy, but daft, proclamation: education in Sierra Leone, he said, is a privilege, not a right. Shortly thereafter the Revolutionary United Front (RUF) invaded the east of the country, led by former student radicals, marginalized youth "revolutionaries," and young Liberian mercenaries promising a vaguely articulated but brighter future for young people in Sierra Leone.

Mohammed spent the first five years of the war (1991 to 1996) as a noncombatant trading *djamba* from the forests to the villages along the Liberia border. A military coup in 1997 left him stranded in the town of Kenema. When he eventually made his way back to his village, he was taken prisoner by the progovernment Kamajor militia, who labeled him an RUF collaborator for having been so long in enemy territory. Mohammed escaped and crossed the Liberia border where he was captured again by a Kamajor contingent. This time he was sentenced to death for drug smuggling and collaboration.

From this point, Mohammed's story is illustrative of the perverse logic by which patronage functioned during the war. For some young people the disruptions of the war presented escape routes from highly exploitative relations with their elders. Young men with military experience or the bravado to make their names through violence could attract clients of their own. The combatants who surrounded them relied on the protection of these commanders and the food, medicines, and weapons they could accumulate or take by force. In return, young "rank and file" combatants gave their loyalty, their muscle, and the goods they might procure at the battlefront to their new commanders. For some who were smart and lucky, this was an opportunity to break the perceived stranglehold their elders maintained on wealth, prestige and—ultimately—adult manhood. Theirs may have been a rebellion against the patronage system, but it was hardly a revolution. At best a few young men managed to accelerate their own climb in stature and bypass years of efforts to cultivate clients of their own. They most often replicated the very relationships they sought to escape. The rhetoric of a more equitable social future did not necessarily make those young men who profited from the war more benevolent patrons than those they supplanted. Moreover, such successes were generally fleeting and dangerous. In the end, the majority experienced the war simply as an intensification of violent instabilities of patronage rather than a qualitative shift in their nature.

Mohammed's death sentence was commuted when a local commander, C.O. Bobby, intervened and agreed to "stand for" him. Though Mohammed had never met C.O. Bobby before, the man claimed that Mohammed was a distant relative for whom he would accept responsibility. It was an intervention that spared Mohammed's life, but also bound him to Bobby as his patron and as his commander. Along with the other members of Bobby's unit, Mohammed began weapons and tactical training. He was initiated into the Kamajors, a ritual induction that provided Mohammed with the knowledge and the necessary *hale* (medicine) to make his body impervious to the bullets of his enemies. Mohammed took the responsibilities and the privileges of initiation seriously; protecting the secrets of the "society" guaranteed the physical protection of occult forces at the battlefront. Giving away those secrets or failing to observe the concomitant restrictions on his behavior could very well cost him his life.

Over the next year, Mohammed fought with C.O. Bobby and his unit across the east of Sierra Leone. He spent the majority of his time on the Liberia border, ostensibly to guard against an invasion by Liberian president Charles Taylor. In practice he helped Bobby and other commanders run small-time diamond mining operations, trading rough stones with Lebanese merchants and the occasional South African buyer.

When C.O. Bobby was wounded at the battlefront, Mohammed went with him to Freetown for treatment at the capital city's Connaught Hospital. With no family in the city, it fell to Mohammed to provide for his patron's needs during his recovery. It was during this period of convalescence that Mohammed met his next patron, a young man named Junior who was barely older than Mohammed himself.

Most young combatants had no real chance of becoming commanders in their own right. Instead the war offered them two possibilities. It allowed some to violently react against their social landscape, taking vengeance against the real or symbolic individuals and structures they saw as the agents of their marginalization. In its successive waves of attacks across the country, for example, the RUF committed a number of high-profile atrocities against chiefs and chiefdom elders and spectacular destructive raids on schools, churches, and universities. The war also presented some young men with opportunities for mobility between patrons. As they were deployed around the country, units of male youth encountered one another on the battlefield as enemies or allies or sometimes both. Captured, coerced, or persuaded, combatants unwilling or unable to return home commonly served in multiple units during the course of their "careers" as fighters. The result was an often dizzyingly complex web of alliances and betrayals which never mapped easily along ethnic, sectarian, or even family lines. Over and over, the stories I was told by combatants and ex- combatants underscored that for most young people, opportunities arose from the most unlikely quarters—but even the most reliable relationships were never guaranteed.

Junior was a well-known figure within the Civil Defense Forces (CDF), the larger militia to which the Kamajors belonged. The son of a wealthy businessman in Monrovia, Junior was known for recruiting fighters from the forested border between Liberia and Sierra Leone. Though he was a patron in his own right, he was also widely regarded as a youth leader frequently at odds with the CDF leadership over their corruption and lack of regard for rank-and-file combatants. It was one such rift that landed Junior in the hospital; an assassination attempt by an elder in the CDF had failed to kill him but required emergency surgery and a six-month recovery.

Mohammed's shift in allegiance from C.O. Bobby to Junior was relatively amicable. C.O. Bobby's wounds meant that he could not lead his unit to the battlefront any longer, and his ability to provide for his "boys" was therefore severely compromised. Bobby planned to return to his village outside Kenema and the uncertain prospects of earning a living in rural, wartime Sierra Leone. Unprepared to move back to his own village, Mohammed began to assist in caring for Junior, whose future promised to be one of continued engagement in the war. Junior saw to it that Mohammed had a weapon when he went to the battlefront and enough food when he came back. Mohammed, in turn, fought when Junior needed him to fight. He surrendered to Junior what spoils he captured at the front and gave him a cut of what monies he might find through small-time hustles, odd jobs, or favorable trades. Perhaps most importantly, it was Junior who facilitated Mohammed's continued stay in the city by allowing him to barrack in the ruins of the Brookfields Hotel.

Jah Kingdom was the name for the space under the swimming pool at Brookfields. The defunct utility room was the site of a small bar where

CDF fighters could buy rum, marijuana, and cigarettes from King, a Nigerian mercenary and petty trader. Mohammed and Adama lived in one of the shower stalls of the former men's locker room.

Around the time the war "officially" ended in January 2002, Mohammed and Adama moved. The girlfriend of another Jah Kingdom resident picked a fight with Adama. Despite Adama's eight-month pregnancy, the woman kicked her in the stomach, an act against which Mohammed felt King and the other men present should have intervened. I arrived at Jah Kingdom in time to see Mohammed and Adama stuffing the last of their belongings into a duffel bag. Following them up from below the pool and toward the front gate of the hotel, I prepared to see them off for good. Instead they stopped at Block C, one of the large complexes of guest rooms. Dragging their bags to the top floor, Mohammed stopped at a room sealed with a small padlock. With a knife he pried off the latch and pushed open the door. While Adama spread their bedroll on the floor, Mohammed explained that if the previous occupants had intended to return, they would have put a stronger lock on the door. Apparently he was right. Mohammed, Adama, Struggle, and a few friends who moved in with them were still there when United Nations peacekeepers arrived to evict everyone from the hotel eight months later.

For Mohammed, leaving his home in Jah Kingdom could not have meant leaving the city of Freetown. If the war promised the possibility for young men with gumption to reconfigure their patronage ties and escape the perceived injustices meted out by a greedy gerontocracy, in the postwar period that promise lies in the city itself. The sheer number of people offers the hope of new patronage networks on a scale unthinkable in rural communities. But the city is also a qualitatively different space of possibility. When the war ended there were scores of international non-Governmental Organizations (NGOs) operating in Sierra Leone, the majority in Freetown. The streets were choked with white Toyota Landcruisers, every one embodying the promise of steady employment, training, and even sexual liaisons that could lead in unforeseeable directions. The city offered the infrastructure and knowledge base to gamble on the "DV," (Diversity Visa) the lottery-style U.S. visa give-away that signified overseas employment and possibilities for lucrative business and marriage arrangements. Like other West African cities, Freetown now hosts a slew of charismatic churches and evangelical pastors who promise phenomenal prosperity in this life through prayer and tithing. Freetown is a place of enormous risk, but it is simultaneously a space of enormous (though mysterious) possibility.

Ironically, of all of the possible futures the city makes possible, one of the most difficult and most desirable is a return to the village. Like many ex-combatants Mohammed fantasized about returning to his village as a Big Man, able to "sit down" on his family farm. This imagined future pictured Mohammed employing village youth to work his land. It enrolled him in the deliberations of the community's elder men and it gave him the opportunity for a formal marriage and the recognition of his children. Mohammed had taken steps to make this a possibility before the last RUF invasion of Freetown. Having accumulated some cash during the fighting, Mohammed sent money back to the village for local boys to clear a small plot. For a brief moment the plot made tangible Mohammed's future livelihood and the privilege and responsibilities of adulthood. The Freetown invasion and the decision to barrack the CDF at the Brookfields Hotel, however, kept Mohammed in the city. Well before he returned to the village the forest reclaimed his small farm.

Talking with Mohammed outside his *pan bodi* house, he explained that ex-combatants who came to Freetown to protect the government were abandoned there without support. The cost of living even the most rudimentary urban life meant that he now had little in the way of cash or goods. And returning to the village empty-handed is unthinkable. At best the village people would gloat and mock, saying that only a fool would go to war and to the city and come home empty-handed. At worst they would be suspicious and offended, convinced that war and urban living had indeed been profitable but that the prodigal son was too greedy to share his gains.

This was a common story, and it has meant a proliferation of young men who cultivate the city itself for their subsistence. To *dreg* in the parlance of Freetown's urban youth is to hustle, moving from point to point around the city and across the boundaries of legality. It evokes getting by through the collection of debts, the provision of favors, outsmarting or outrunning others for what one needs—a beg, borrow, or steal existence that is the fate of ex-combatants from all factions. To be a *dreg man* is to be on the move and on the lookout for new patrons and more profitable liaisons. But it is also to look for profitable opportunities beyond those relationships— opportunities to live off the fat of the urban land as an independent young person and eventually find the resources and wherewithal to become a patron in one's own right and to live as an adult or a *kpako* (big person).

As a result, for many people one of the most frustrating and worrisome aspects of the end of the war is the failure of young male combatants like Mohammed to leave Freetown and cities such as Bo, Kenema, and Makeni and return to their villages. Every neighborhood in Freetown is dotted with *potes*, the wooden stalls where young men gather to smoke djamba, drink, and talk. These social spaces for the urban poor became highly politicized at various moments in the country's history. It was in the potes that the language of revolution circulated in the waning days of the Stevens regime and from which the RUF's early leaders emerged. In the early years of the war the national army inflated its troop levels by conscripting underemployed and untrained urban youth from spaces like the potes, resulting in an escalation of atrocities committed by uniformed soldiers. Talk in the potes today is of corruption in the government and of the suffering of black men around the globe, as expressed in reggae and hip-hop song lyrics. Reservoirs of young men languishing in the city suggest that the labor pool of violence remains a real and constant threat. For other inhabitants of the city, these young men appear too readily available for use by elites-turned-warlords or disaffected politicians.

Sitting on the hillside over Freetown in late 2003, Mohammed tensed when I mentioned Junior's name. I had spoken to Junior only the day before, and knew that he planned to return briefly to Freetown from neighboring Liberia. Now an important figure in the rebel forces that had just overthrown Liberian President Charles Taylor, Junior was living in Monrovia along with many of his fighters. As the Liberia war drew to a close, each of the factions was making its final push for territory, loot, and position.

I asked Mohammed, not for the first time, why he hadn't followed Junior across the border to fight. Many of his closest friends from the Brookfields Hotel did exactly that, and a few profited handsomely from it. Mohammed's answer was what I expected: he was tired of war, his small family needed him in Freetown, he didn't trust the men going to Liberia—they were not his people. These were answers I had heard before, and I didn't disbelieve them. Yet they were more ambiguous than they appear. His implied exercise of agency in this matter masked a more complex and even dangerous set of circumstances.

Mohammed was similarly resolute when I spoke to him the previous year about campaigning for the Sierra Leone People's Party (SLPP) in the national election. After the betrayals and false promises the SLPP elite made to the nation's youth, Mohammed said, there was simply no way he would vote for the party, let along campaign on its behalf. And yet like other ex-combatants barracked at the Brookfields Hotel, when campaign season started Mohammed was among the hundreds of young people who took to the streets for the SLPP. Whatever his personal feelings about the political landscape in Sierra Leone, Mohammed was economically, socially, and politically unable to say no when asked to join the election rallies. "If he sees me, he will go," Junior told me when I mentioned that Mohammed said he was tired of fighting. "He knows I will protect him and create opportunities for him. If he sees me, he will go [to fight in Liberia]." According to Junior, once he and Mohammed reconnected in Freetown, it would only be a matter of working out the logistics and Mohammed would join the rebels across the border.

As it happened, Junior did not see Mohammed on that trip. Whatever else it may have offered him, the city provided Mohammed with a certain invisibility. His shack at the urban margins was an economic necessity, but it also enabled Mohammed to avoid seeing (or being seen by) those he might wish to avoid. Though I found Mohammed myself, it took days to do so. Junior's brief visits to Freetown to collect supplies and call up his men were insufficient to track Mohammed when the latter was determined to use the complex topography of the urban landscape to hide from an obligation he otherwise could not avoid. Patronage networks are central to every facet of existence in this part of West Africa, but there are always spaces of resistance or creative manipulation. For Mohammed and for others, that space of possibility and invisibility was a decidedly urban space. Mohammed's village on the Liberia border promised no such obscurity. Junior or his people would easily find him there. The city is often contrasted to the village as a site of opportunity versus lack, but for Mohammed and other young people the reverse can also be true: the city can stave off "opportunities" one hopes to avoid.

By late 2006 the hillside surrounding Mohammed, Adama, and Struggle's small house had become more crowded. Some of the large homes that sprouted a few years before were complete. The land had been more clearly demarcated into plots and the scale of activity—in particular the hard labor of smashing stone—had escalated. The hillside now felt less like an urban outpost and more like an industrial zone, although its marginality to the city center remained pronounced. The rutted mud pathway that connected the tarred road into town with the expanding community in the hills was no better than it had been three years before, but it extended further into the bush and now carried heavy vehicles loaded with gravel, charcoal, and timber. At the junction, the pote where Mohammed spent much of his time seemed to be constantly packed with young men.

Mohammed's small *pan bodi* was itself more crowded. Mohammed and Adama had a second son, Daniel, and Adama was pregnant with their third child. The *pan-bodi* was no longer a simple one-room lean-to but had expanded. Its zinc and wood construction was subdivided into two rooms and its walls fortified into something more solid.

Knowing that I would be traveling east the next day to rendezvous with Junior, I asked Mohammed if they had been in touch. He had not, but in contrast to our earlier conversations about his former patron, Mohammed was interested in the details of our meeting and insisted that I let Junior know where he was. The living, he had heard, was easier in Monrovia than it was in Freetown. The large United Nations peacekeeping force that was guarding the peace in Liberia meant there must be jobs, and the rumor (which I knew to be false) was that there was electricity even for the poor in the Liberian capital.

Reconnecting with Junior will be an uncertain proposition. Though his fortunes have waned considerably since the end of the fighting, Junior is still surrounded by a large number of ex-combatants and his capacity to help them is stretched thin. What's more, he is playing a dangerous role in Sierra Leone's national political dramas. He is courted by two parties, each interested in his ability to deliver the youth vote and young men for campaigning. Becoming one of Junior's "boys" again could well mean returning to violence as the next campaign season begins, or being seen as a political enemy should Junior ally with the losing side. At the same time, the doctor's house will eventually be finished and he will no longer need Mohammed to guard his plot or break his rocks. The limited autonomy offered by an absentee patron and life in Freetown have not brought the wherewithal for Mohammed to become an "adult" on his own. Yet moving closer to Junior is an uncertain course for transcending the boundaries of youth and its obligations.

Note

1. The material in this chapter is drawn from ethnographic fieldwork in Sierra Leone and Liberia that I began in the summer of 2000. Working primarily with combatants from the Kamajor, the Civil Defense Forces (CDF), and LURD (Liberians United for Reconciliation and Democracy) militias, I have focused on the ways West African male youth engage in multiple, often violent forms of labor. Mohammed is one of a group of young men with whom I lived and traveled in 2001 and 2002, and whom I have visited on shorter annual trips to the region. What I know of Mohammed's life and the lives of other combatants has come from participating in and observing the ordinary and extraordinary events of daily life. I have interviewed Mohammed extensively, but the richest insights have come from casual conversations and the relaxed talk of people simply moving through the course of a day.

Further Reading

Beah, Ismael. (2007). *A Long Way Gone: Memoirs of a Boy Soldier*. New York: Farrar, Straus and Giroux.

Gberie, Lansana. (2005). *A Dirty War in West Africa: The RUF and the Destruction of Sierra Leone*. Bloomington: Indiana University Press.

Richards, Paul. (1996). *Fighting for the Rainforest: War, Youth and Resources in Sierra Leone*. Portsmouth, NH: Heinemann and James Currey.

Craig Jeffrey

11

From Footballs to Fixer

Suresh and the New Politicians in North India

n March 2005, I was walking around Chaudhry Charan Singh University (CCSU) in Meerut City, Uttar Pradesh (U.P.), searching for a young man called Suresh. I had been told that Suresh was an especially energetic student politician, one of a small group of Dalit (ex-untouchable) "new leaders" *(naye netās)* on campus. I was interviewing these new politicians as part of a research project on student activism in north India. Students sometimes used the term "new politician" semihumorously to mock the aspirations of ambitious young men, but they often employed the term more seriously to indicate men who circulated political rhetoric on campus and assumed organizational roles within the university. Students referred to these men as "new" *(naye)* "leaders" *(netā)* because they belonged to a section of society—the Dalits—formerly excluded from higher education and youth politics in Meerut. Students also used the term new politicians to distinguish young men with political aspirations from more established politicians at the national and state level. In addition, the adjective *new* suggested the connection between these ambitious young men and notions of progress, development, and modernity that have become important within north Indian universities. Over seven months conducting research in Meerut City, I interviewed seven Dalit young men who described themselves as new leaders.

I found Suresh in his room on the first floor of a hostel in the center of CCSU. Suresh was older than I expected—about twenty-eight, four years younger than I was at the time. I was immediately struck by his appearance.

Suresh's neatly brushed hair, smart khaki trousers, and checked shirt pointed to his careful approach to self-presentation. He spoke in an animated fashion, interspersing his speech with many formal words. Suresh said that he imagined himself as a representative of his wider community and therefore as a man with a duty to behave in a "civilized" manner.

I felt nervous explaining my research to Suresh. I have been conducting research in Meerut City for twelve years, during which I time I had obtained a Ph.D. and secured a permanent job at a university. During the same period, many of the young male informants and friends in Meerut have acquired similar degree qualifications; I have met several double and one triple Ph.D. But widespread unemployment has made it impossible for all but a few students to obtain secure salaried work or establish families. With men like Suresh, I was frequently reminded of my privilege in being able "dip in and out" of an area of profound economic and social uncertainty.

Much of this uncertainty relates to the particular form of neoliberalism affecting north India. Economic reforms in India since the mid-1980s have reduced opportunities for salaried work within government and further weakened state-funded higher education. Indeed, government educational, health, and infrastructural facilities are typically in a dire condition in U.P., even in the more prosperous districts such as Meerut. This neglect of social development is linked to the class and caste structure of the state. Upper-caste Brahmins and Rajputs have dominated lucrative salaried employment, local government bureaucracies, and landownership in many parts of U.P. A second group of intermediate castes, such as the Jats and Gujars, have increasingly challenged the power of the upper castes and control landownership and local political power in many western parts of the state. The remainder of U.P.'s population is mainly comprised of Muslims, low castes slightly above "untouchables" within caste hierarchies, and Dalits. While there is a sizeable Muslim and Dalit urban elite in the state, members of this third group are typically poor and engaged in insecure manual labor.

The rich have largely controlled state power in U.P. since India became independent in 1947. But the politics of this state has been subject to considerable change during the past fifteen years. Most notably, the emergence of the pro-Dalit Bahujan Samaj Party (BSP) has altered the nature of north Indian politics. The BSP has attempted to install Dalits in the U.P. bureaucracy by improving the implementation of government reservations for Dalits in public-sector employment and increasing Dalit enrollment in education. The BSP also tried to channel development funds to Dalits, improve

their access to local state institutions, and transform the symbolic landscape of U.P., particularly through the construction of statues representing
the Dalit hero, Dr. Bhim Rao Ambedkar.

The political economy of U.P. powerfully shapes student politics in
CCSU and the practices of new politicians such as Suresh. Reflecting their
regional power, prosperous Jat or Gujar (middle-caste) young men are the
most prominent figures within student activism in Meerut and have dominated access to the CCSU student union. Of the thirty men who held one
of the top two positions in the CCSU student union between 1991 and
2004, twenty-four were Jats or Gujars. No women, Dalits, or Muslims have
obtained the post of student union president in CCSU. Dominant student
politicians rely on caste solidarities and links to regional political parties in
order to obtain student-union positions. They typically spend between
Rs.150,000 and Rs.300,000 prior to elections to raise support (Rs.150,000
was roughly equivalent to the annual salary of a low-ranking government
official in 2004).[1] Once elected, Jat and Gujar politicians build social networks with other student politicians, party politicians, the police, lawyers,
local criminals, and university and government bureaucrats. Drawing on
these social networks, CCSU dominant politicians accrue illegal incomes
of up to Rs.1,000,000 from their posts. They accumulate this money through
acting as brokers between students requiring assistance and university
bureaucrats, and by exerting pressure on the principals of colleges affiliated to CCSU to grant them seats in their institutions, which they then sell
to students seeking places at these institutions. In addition, many student
leaders extract money from building contractors constructing private colleges in Meerut. Student leaders threaten to raise questions about the quality of the construction unless the building contractors pay them "silence
money." Moreover, student union leaders are sometimes able to influence ap-
pointments to teaching and administrative positions within CCSU or affiliated colleges, and can earn money by "auctioning" posts that they control to
the highest bidder. Student leaders redistribute some of this money to their
supporters. They also invest money in hiring university professors to give
them extra-university tutorials or assist them in writing their dissertations.

Introducing Suresh

Suresh, it seemed, was different. In 2004 he was studying for a master's in
engineering at CCSU. He came from a poor background and belonged to
the Chamar caste, a Dalit caste. His parents worked as agricultural laborers
in a village 7 km from CCSU, and his father ran a small business making

footballs. As a caste formerly associated with leatherwork, the Chamars had been quite successful in moving into leather-related small-scale production in Meerut district and this area has become a center for small-scale, sports-goods manufacture. But Suresh was one of eight siblings, and his family has faced huge financial difficulties in obtaining a steady income. Suresh told me that, "We are extremely poor, constantly struggling."

Suresh's poverty marks his educational history. He attended a poorly run primary school and government high school in the village. Both schools lacked resources and diligent teachers. After passing his Twelfth Class (senior high school) examinations in 1994, the economic hardships suffered by his family forced Suresh to return to his village to assist his parents. Suresh said that between 1994 and 2000 he was *khāli*, a word that translates as "free" but also connotes the idea of being "empty." In practice, Suresh appears to have spent a great deal of this time making footballs to support his family economically. In the late 1990s, Suresh also obtained diplomas in computing and technical work from a private college in Meerut. By 2000, he had saved enough money to enroll in higher education; he obtained a single degree in physics, Hindi, and maths from a government degree college in Meerut in 2003. Commenting on his education, Suresh remembered many opportunities to obtain diplomas or move quickly through college that foundered on the rocks of his family's poverty. But Suresh was equally adamant that his parents had always supported his decisions. Suresh, "My parents told me: 'your aim is our aim.'"

In the late 1990s, Suresh tried unsuccessfully to obtain a paid position as a government clerk and then volunteered to work as the treasurer within a government *tehsīl* (subdistrict) administrative office. Suresh explained: "I knew the land revenue officer *(patwarī)* in my village. I was unemployed and asked this man for some help. He was a Brahmin, but he gave me a chance. I used his recommendation. He told the subdistrict officer *(tehsīldār)* that I should be allowed to work in the office. I worked very honestly and I was good at the job of treasurer." Suresh did not get paid for this work "But I met a lot of people, I developed a social network. I was compiling land records in the office, and I also learned a lot."

Suresh comes from a village in which over half the population belong to the Chamar caste. The numerical dominance of Chamars meant that Dalits did not experience the overt caste-based discrimination and oppression that characterizes many other villages in Meerut district. But Suresh said that higher castes have captured the lion's share of development resources in his village and remain much richer than Dalits, and this story is borne out in many recent scholarly studies of this region.

Suresh also spoke of continued caste and class discrimination in the university:

> In the past, Dalits were treated as untouchables. They could not sit with upper castes. They were not allowed to eat with upper castes. This is *slowly* changing [Suresh's emphasis]. Dalits are not below anyone here in terms of their cleanliness, living conditions, and clothing. We are also educated. But if Dalits have problems here, the administration does not help them as much. The administration is negligent. They tell us [sneering and adopting a haughty tone], "Yes, we will do your work, but come later today or come tomorrow." If you are trying to get some work done in a department, it is more difficult for Dalits.

Many other Dalits made similar complaints; there was a consensus that caste oppression had diminished but that Dalits remained subject to multiple, often subtle, forms of discrimination.

Political Goals

Suresh's aims as a new politician emerged out of an experience in high school, when he exposed the malpractice of a school clerk who was embezzling scholarship money meant for Dalit children. Issues of caste inequality and educational access are threaded through Suresh's subsequent political activity, which focuses especially on four main issues. First, Suresh has tried to widen Dalits' access to education, and at CCSU he concentrated especially on improving Dalit enrollment in postgraduate degree programs. Suresh said that department heads at the university systematically discriminate against Dalits in the allocation of Ph.D. candidate positions. In 2004, Suresh was trying to convince the university administration to establish a separate quota of Ph.D. advising positions for Dalit students. More broadly, Suresh worked hard on an everyday level to provide Dalit children in his village with information about urban educational opportunities.

Second, Suresh was determined to address equity issues that were emerging in the context of educational privatization. Between 1995 and 2005 the courses offered by CCSU have tripled in number. The vast majority of this increase has been in private (for-profit) courses run by traditional departments—such as sociology and biology—to bolster their resources. These for-profit courses are much more expensive than the traditional courses run by the university. Paralleling this development, the number of higher-educational institutions affiliated to CCSU rose from around 90 in 1995 to 380 at the beginning of 2005, and the vast majority of these institutions were offering private courses and degrees. A large number of students—especially Dalits and other relatively impoverished youth—vigorously opposed this privatization and its potential impact on poor students. This opposition sometimes brought Dalits such as Suresh into direct confrontation with the higher-caste student leaders who were profiting from privatization.

Third, Suresh was intensely concerned about the problem of unemployment among Dalits, including educated young people. According to a provision in the Indian Constitution, 25 percent of public-sector employment is reserved for Scheduled Castes (SCs) and Scheduled Tribes (STs): those castes and indigenous communities that the British identified as suffering the humiliations of untouchability. Suresh complained that this quota was not being respected in recruitment to the university administration in that places reserved for Dalits were being taken by higher castes. I was not able to verify Suresh's claims, but his argument intensified an already charged atmosphere around the issue of government jobs. Educated unemployment is one of the most profound social problems affecting contemporary north India. U.P. has played little part in the newly emerging Information Technology, outsourcing, and other new industries for which India has become renowned. Meerut students from all social backgrounds are anxious about their future employment prospects, the declining value of their degrees, and the prolonged, humiliating, and fruitless search for secure work in which they are embroiled.

Fourth, Suresh was worried about the near invisibility of the Dalit hero Dr. Bhim Rao Ambedkar on the CCSU campus. CCSU is named after the Jat politician and former prime minister of India, Chaudhry Charan Singh, whose policies as a political leader between the mid-1960s and mid-1980s benefited prosperous rurally based middle castes, such as the Jats and Gujars, and tended to marginalize the poor and Dalits. That the university is named after this politician—and that his statue faces the grand entrance to the campus—is an affront to the sensibilities of some Dalit students. Suresh was preoccupied with redressing the symbolic balance in CCSU through raising the profile of Ambedkar within the university. For example, Suresh asked the University authorities for an "Ambedkar Chair" to be established within CCSU. These symbolic demands reflect the influence of the BSP on Dalit politics in CCSU; Dalits such as Suresh married their concerns over education and employment to issues of respect and representation.

Political Strategies

Like the majority of other Dalit new politicians, Suresh had little interest in seeking election to the CCSU student union. He claimed that Jats' and Gujars' numerical dominance within the university made it almost impossible to acquire an influential position. Instead, Suresh pursued his political goals through adopting three linked strategies. First, he tried to obtain positions within the decentralized government administration. In 2001, Suresh campaigned successfully to become part of a Block Development Committee (BDC), an elected subdistrict council responsible for administering development resources to his village and surrounding settlements. Suresh said that he narrowly missed being elected to the position of vice chairperson of this committee. In the late 1990s and early 2000s he also joined the BSP. Suresh said that he had developed an understanding with two BSP politicians in Meerut and was a great admirer of the BSP leader, Mayawati.

In 2005, Suresh was looking forward to contesting the position of vice chair of the BDC for a second time.

SURESH: It is like a chain. After that, I can become chairman of the BDC and then I become a member of the legislative assembly [MLA; the state assembly in Lucknow].

CJ: But don't you need money to become an MLA?

SURESH: Yes, you usually need money. But if you are the chairman of the BDC, then it is not a problem. If you have personality, leadership skills, and status, you do not need money to run for MLA. If the public are with you and you do good work, you do not need money. I have the ability inside me. I fought for the post of BDC vice-chairman before. At that time, lots of people told me, "You will need money to contest the elections." My father got angry with the people saying this. He said, "Why does he need money? My son has the ability!" I only lost by one vote, and that was only because of dishonesty. Now I have learned a lot more, so I will certainly contest for the post of chairman in the future.

A second political strategy adopted by Suresh was to build good social networks. Like other *naye netās*, Suresh spent much time and money developing good relationships within the police, local intelligence unit, newspaper offices, and university administration. "I am well known in the university administration. I know the vice chancellor (VC), I know Dr. Manvir Singh in biology, and I know R.P. Trivedi, the head of department in physics. I also know the registrar of the university. I know so many people. I also know the district magistrate in Meerut. I can just walk into these men's offices, and they know me."

Suresh said that successful networking depended crucially on writing letters to local big-wigs. He was a prodigious correspondent and, without access to email or the money for a cell phone, he carried out his communication through the mail. Suresh said that he enjoyed letter writing because it allowed him to choose his words carefully. "Letters are my main political weapon." The sheer volume of Suresh's letter writing was startling. Often rising early in the morning, Suresh wrote six or seven letters before breakfast. But equally impressive was Suresh's accomplishment in selecting words, phrases, and aphorisms that would bolster his arguments.

A third political strategy adopted by Suresh occurred at the cultural level and involved him in circulating new discourses that questioned dominant politicians' right to represent students on campus. This politics of words and gestures was built around Dalits' claim to possess a type of cosmopolitan political skill that dominant politicians allegedly lacked. Suresh and his peers counterposed a vision of Dalit cultural versatility against a picture of leadenfooted and unimaginative higher castes. Suresh elaborated on this idea through reference to Dalits' capacity to improvise with available resources (*jugār*). Dalit new leaders conceptualized *jugār* as a process of combining—or "lashing up" —elements imagined locally as traditional with resources considered to be modern. Suresh said that *jugār* is encapsulated in the image of the rural wooden bullock cart which has been fitted with a modern engine (*jugārīi gārī*). Suresh and other new leaders went on to explain that they practiced a form of improvised politics (*jugārī rajnitī*) wherein they found deft and imaginative ways to improvise with both modern and traditional resources. For example, Suresh started a public demonstration by recounting an instance in which he used a wooden-framed rope bed and broken moped to block higher castes' access into a Dalit hostel. He then told the audience that he had become such a master of *jugār* that they should refer to him as *jugārū* (one who does *jugār*).

The idea of *jugār* provided a convenient foundation for Suresh's sense of himself as a skillful political agent in a situation in which most Dalits lacked the money required to construct images of political accomplishment through purchasing expensive consumer goods in Meerut and the muscle power necessary to confront higher castes physically. Through repeatedly emphasizing their capacity to do *jugār*, new leaders questioned assumptions among some higher castes that Dalits are inherently backward and incompetent. Ideas of being distinctively equipped to improvise contributed to Dalits' ability to "talk back" to higher castes. In particular they used ideas of themselves as experts in *jugār* to disparage Jat and Gujar politicians for their alleged dullness and parochialism.

A Dalit Revolution?

Observing similar forms of political mobilization in other parts of U.P., some commentators have been moved to write of a low-caste revolution occurring in north India. Certainly, Suresh's political strategies have posed new challenges to higher castes. Suresh used his stature as an elected government official and his access to social networks to assist Dalit students with everyday matters and counter the power of higher-caste student leaders. In a typical day, Suresh might help Dalit students to obtain examination results from an office, complain about a negligent professor, seek an application form for a scholarship, or enroll in a new course. This daily hustle involved Suresh in visiting numerous offices around campus and meeting a wide variety of university functionaries and teachers, who were mostly from prosperous middle- or upper-caste backgrounds. Suresh said that as an educated young man and local leader he is able to cultivate the requisite balance of confidence and humility required to "get work done." He spoke of his skill in remembering the likes and dislikes of numerous government officials and he boasted of his capacity to threaten uncooperative officials. In addition, Suresh acted as a successful political intermediary in his village. He diffused conflict between rural Dalits, interceded in intercaste disputes on behalf of his community, and communicated his knowledge of politics and development to rural young people. In an inversion of the characteristic relationship between age and authority in north India, older members of the Dalit community would often visit Suresh's hostel room to request his adjudication on a dispute or assistance in a matter involving the police.

Suresh had also had some success at the symbolic level. Dalits' active efforts to establish respect, in combination with the rise of the BSP, had improved their confidence and safety on campus. "We are educated people, who can now demand respect. Ambedkar helped build this country. Others know that. We are no longer afraid to raise our voices."

But Suresh's attempts to improve Dalits' access to resources and political power moderated rather than transformed processes of class and caste social reproduction within CCSU. Upper- and middle-caste Hindus, particularly the Jats, continued to dominate all formal student associations, as they did in most other higher-educational institutions in Meerut. Reflecting this dominance and their control over the means of violence in CCSU, the police usually sided with higher castes in political struggles on campus. For example, in 2004 the police and local politicians turned a blind eye when many Jats beat a group of Dalit students. Three months later they were similarly inactive when a female Dalit student was harassed by higher-caste students close to the CCSU campus. Early in 2005, the police and a local politician assisted Jats in illegally occupying a new hostel in campus. In some high-profile cases involving transparent state or university malfeasance, Dalit politicians such as Suresh tended to be on hand. But in smaller and everyday state/society interactions Suresh and his peers had to ration their time and energy according to personal considerations. Suresh had a limited stock of influence, and there were simply too few *naye netās* to serve the increasing number of poor Dalit students in their negotiations with the state, dominant politicians, and university bureaucrats.

Suresh and his compatriots also lacked a coordinated approach to changing campus politics. This point became glaringly evident in the student-union elections of fall 2004 when, after a series of factional disputes between different *netās* in the university, Dalits fielded two candidates for an influential post. With the Dalit vote split, neither candidate was successful. Broader consideration of Dalit politics in CCSU points in a similar direction: only a handful of Dalit students had shown any interest in establishing an ST/SC student union, few Dalits participated in rallies calling for increased Dalit unity on campus in the later part of 2004, and a *netā*-led campaign to improve Dalits' access to master's-level research supervision was abandoned lack of support.

Dalit initiatives also failed because *netās* sometimes prioritized their own interests over those of their caste. Suresh was widely regarded as a "community-minded" politician. But other *netās* were more inclined to use their political influence for personal gain, or else they soon abandoned socially oriented service in pursuit of more self-interested motives. For example, another Dalit *netā* who had obtained a post on the CCSU student union defined himself as a profit-seeking "broker." He admitted that he had made a substantial amount of money working as an intermediary between Dalit students and university bureaucrats. In other cases, *netās* failed to help other Chamars in spite of their best intentions. Jats and Gujars were well equipped to counter-resist lower-caste political assertion at the local level through cultivating stronger links with university bureaucrats and government officials. In university and government offices, Suresh frequently encountered higher-caste student leaders who were better qualified, more knowledgeable, and confidently sought to reassert their dominance.

In addition, higher castes counter-resisted Dalits' assertion in multiple ways. Higher castes argued that, however innovative Dalits may be in the political sphere, they retain certain distinctive markers that single them out as "backward." For example, one Jat young man told me that something "thickens the movements of Dalits," which means that they conduct political demonstrations in a clumsy manner. In other cases, higher-caste student leaders joked about the incompetence and showiness of Dalit politics, which they contrasted with their own "proper politics," and in some cases middle castes claimed that they were the true masters of *jugār*. Just as higher castes found ways to limit the influence of new politicians within associational and network-based politics, they were also well equipped to neutralize Dalit assertion in the cultural realm.

What emerged quite powerfully over my seven months of interviews and participant observation in CCSU was not just the frequency with which higher-caste dominance reasserted itself in their reactionary discourses, but also a *feeling* of continued social isolation among most Dalit students, even those like Suresh who commonly spoke of his optimism and improvisational skill. The prevailing political mood among Dalit students in CCSU, Meerut College, and the other colleges I visited in Meerut, was one of despondency, cynicism, and anger. This point surfaced toward the end of my stay in Meerut when I talked to Suresh at a tea stall outside the campus. Suresh was in a reflective mood and I took the opportunity to ask him about his future. He said that he could envisage two routes that he might take. The first would involve consolidating his position in district politics and trying to obtain power at the state level. The second would entail concentrating on his studies, seeking a "good job," and asking his parents to arrange his marriage. But Suresh said that both routes are fraught with risk. In contrast to optimistic accounts of "Dalit Revolution," Suresh argued that "Everything has changed but it is always the same."

Suresh's story offers a vivid insight into the contradictions characterizing the lives of Dalit young men in contemporary Uttar Pradesh. On the one hand, everything has indeed changed: Dalit young men have obtained increased education, heightened visibility within formal politics, and some opportunities to improve their prospects through engaging in nonagricultural work. On the other hand, things are "always the same": men like Suresh continue to experience casteism, lack access to secure employment, and find it painfully difficult to institutionalize their newfound political confidence.

In April 2007 I returned to Meerut to conduct a short period of follow-up research. I met Suresh outside the CCSU library, and we talked about how things had changed in the two years since I had last visited. I was particularly eager to ask Suresh about his involvement in student protests that occurred in 2006 over the issue of the grading of examination scripts. In that year it came to light that the CCSU administration had been sending master's theses to another university to be graded. This other university had subcontracted the grading to school students as young as eight years of age. CCSU students took to the streets in protest, and some burned their degrees. Suresh said that he had only played a small part in these protests: "It was a legal matter, the CCSU registrar was removed. Not my type of politics."

Suresh wanted to talk instead about his rising political profile *outside* the university. He had built close links with a local powerful politician and started to collect support and money for a renewed attempt to obtain a block- or district-level political post. Suresh appeared to be moving away from student activism toward concentrating on Politics with a big "P": obtaining a position within representative government. Suresh said that this political mission would require all types of shrewd improvisation *(jugār)*, but he was determined to pursue politics as a career. "I may get another job. I may become a university lecturer, but there will always be politics."

Note

1. In 2004, one U.S. dollar was roughly equivalent to 40 Indian rupees.

Further Reading

Jeffrey, Craig, Patricia Jeffery, and Roger Jeffery. (2004). "'A Useless Thing!' or 'Nectar of the Gods'? The Cultural Production of Education and Young Men's Struggles for Respect in Liberalizing North India." *Annals of the Association of American Geographers* 94(4): 961–981.

Jeffrey, Craig, Roger Jeffrey, and Patricia Jeffery. (2005). "When Schooling Fails: Young Men, Education and Low Caste Politics in North India." *Contributions to Indian Sociology* 39: 1–38.

See especially:

Jeffrey, Craig, Patricia Jeffery, and Roger Jeffery. (2008). *Degrees Without Freedom? Education, Masculinities and Unemployment in North India.* Stanford, CA: Stanford University Press.

Benjamin Gardner

Telling Nala's Story

Negotiating the Global Agendas and Local Politics of Maasai Development in Tanzania

When I finished my primary school, my father wanted me to get married and I was able to resist my family pressures, despite the fact that it was a big struggle. I stayed home for two years and refused to get married two times. I was able to get help from my cousin and two sympathetic Maasai men who were leaders at that time. When I got my way I was dedicated to go back to school with clear objectives of helping women deal with domestic violence through education and economic empowerment.

—NALA[1]

As a sixteen-year-old girl Nala helped organize Maasai women into literacy and economic support groups. In her twenties, Nala founded the Maasai Women's Forum (MWF), a grassroots organization working for Maasai women's development.[2] Today, Nala is almost thirty-six and MWF is a thriving organization with over thirty chapters and nine hundred active members. During my ethnographic research on Maasai youth, land, and development in Tanzania from 2000 to 2004,[3] Maasai leaders and community members regularly indicated that MWF was one of the most important pastoralist organizations in Tanzania.[4] As one village chairman put it, "All NGOs [nongovernmental organizations] in [this region] are not functioning, except this women's NGO. They are the only one's helping our people."

Despite her accomplishments, Nala is still considered a youth in Maasai society, where positions of authority—be they political, work related, or derived from control over a family's assets—are reserved for those individuals putatively possessing the "experience" and "wisdom" to make decisions on behalf of the community. Such experience and wisdom are grounded in social relationships that bind families across territory, kin groups, and even nationality. Being "a youth" marks one's lack of practical experience in the world, but also the supposedly limited network of social relationships upon which one can draw in times of conflict, negotiation, and compromise. Controlling household decisions over selling livestock and marriage arrangements binds elders' political economic authority to their ability to form social and political alliances necessary to speak on behalf of one's community.

As a youth, Nala is an outspoken and powerful advocate of Maasai land rights and women's rights. Nala's influence in local and national politics is an important story. Her work for girls' education and women's economic and political empowerment has reshaped the trajectories of development in Maasai communities in Tanzania. Nala's life and work are enabled by social relationships and alliances that link her local political struggles with international organizations and ideas about women, indigenous people, and development in Africa. Her own story and how it is told both enables and constrains Nala's choices and advocacy work. This youth portrait is about the ways that Nala's life is represented by others, and how those representations shape her personal, cultural, and political struggles as a young Maasai woman in Tanzania. Nala's everyday struggles in Tanzania, and with her foreign partners, also provide a lens through which to understand the cultural politics of crosscultural collaboration on "development" issues.

I first met Nala in 1992, when she was coordinating women's groups for Indigenous People of Tanzania (IPT), the first Tanzanian NGO dedicated to pastoralists and hunter-gatherers—their rights to land and natural resources and their economic and cultural development.[5] I went to Tanzania as a university student interested in the relationship between development policies and pastoralist rights and politics. I arrived in the country at a particularly important moment. The early 1990s were a time of transition in Tanzania, as liberal economic and political reforms swept through Africa, promoting free trade and foreign investment, and opening new political opportunities for NGOs to represent the needs and interests of local people. It was also a time when Maasai leaders were connecting their own struggles in Tanzania over land rights and political participation to the plight of indigenous people around the world. The leaders of these newly established organizations were educated Maasai men who previously held influential positions as national representatives, district government officials, religious leaders, or as employees for internationally funded development initiatives. Unlike many of her more educated young male coworkers, at the time Nala had only completed primary school.[6] Despite her young age and lack of experience, Nala was very effective at organizing youth and women's groups, and successfully lobbied to make women's issues a central concern for the nascent NGO.

I often asked myself: how could a young woman be such an effective advocate for women in a patriarchal society? Since first meeting Nala in 1992, I have seen how she has built and subsequently drawn on an extended network of social relationships to resolve conflicts and create social change in her community. Her story is revealing for the depth of her personal commitment and sacrifices, but also for the key role other people and organizations have played in shaping her opportunities and choices. This youth portrait explores the opportunities international alliances have opened up for individuals like Nala and organizations like MWF, as well as the challenges they create. In my analysis, I try to understand Nala's personal struggles to reconcile these opportunities and challenges.

Personal Journeys Are Political

Nala ran away from home at the age of fifteen. She loved primary school and the relative freedom it provided her from the daily chores and work expected of most young Maasai children, especially girls. Nala had earned a reputation as a strong-willed girl. She was given the nickname "half-man" by one of her uncles after she helped save her family's herd of cattle from being stolen by armed youth from a neighboring region. Joining a group of young warriors, she herded her family's cattle for two days to safety. Despite her heroic feat, tending her father's cattle was considered too important to be left to women or girls. Nala found school one of the few places where she could openly challenge male authority figures. When I asked Nala what had motivated her to work on behalf of Maasai women, she recounted the following story:

> When I was a primary school student my class teacher was a man from Moshi, Chagga, [in the] western part of Tanzania. This man was arrogant and aggressive especially to all Maasai students because they lived far from school and came to school very late. There is nothing they could have done to come early since most of them had to walk 10–15 km to the primary school.
>
> He was beating us severely and abused Maasai culture. I will always remember this direct quotation I heard over twenty years

ago. [He said] "No wonder Maasai are so backwards, you will never develop. I will beat you and if you don't like beating go back because your father has arranged marriage for you girls."

It is not very rare to see students in Tanzania collecting firewood and fetching water for teachers, especially in rural areas; this was another big struggle between me and teachers. One day I mobilized students in the whole school to refuse this activity and the students jointly demanded to know if this was a right thing for them to do in school every day. I was ruled out of school for two days. Later I came and met the village chairman who raised up the matter [with the teacher] and demanded to know why this happened.

I was determined to go further to the district council and eventually the headmaster compromised with me on behalf of all teachers. This had a big impact on me and I started discussions with my male cousin who was in secondary school on how I could get more education. My main agenda has been how to get Maasai teachers who are committed and determined to serve their brothers and sisters without abuse.

After completing primary school, Nala returned home and was to be married. Many of her brothers and male cousins were planning to attend secondary school and Nala wanted to join them. Nala was successful at postponing her marriage and tried to convince her father of the value of school. This was a difficult battle for a young woman, and she regularly consulted her male cousins. One cousin in particular, Davis, believed strongly that education was the only path for Maasai youth to help their communities and believed Nala should be allowed to go on with her schooling. Nala and Davis talked about their future, imagining themselves as the next generation of educated Maasai leaders. Nala asked Davis to intervene and convince her father to allow her to go on with her studies. As a man, Davis could sit, eat, and talk with Nala's father. But as a youth, it was almost impossible to go against his wishes or argue with him, especially when it came to something so widely accepted as a father's right to arrange his daughter's marriage. Davis tried to convince his own father, a respected *laigwanani* (traditional age group leader) to mediate on Nala's behalf. While the elder was sympathetic to Nala's desire for more education, it became clear that such culturally and politically sensitive negotiations were going to be difficult.

Davis walked 40 km to town to talk with Lepukoi and Saruni, two educated Maasai who had navigated their own complicated journeys through
kinship obligations, colonial era education in boarding schools, and the
translocal politics of representing Maasai to outsiders, while struggling to
maintain their status as legitimate community members. After months of
planning, in 1991 Davis arranged for Nala's midnight escape.[7] Dressed in
typical male attire of a red blanket, Nala made her way through her father's
gate to Saruni's waiting car, which took her to town. The next day, Saruni
and Lepukoi drove Nala to the capital city of Dar es Salaam. After only a
few weeks in Dar es Salaam, Nala flew to Toronto, Canada, for a conference
on international women's rights and journalism. Meanwhile, the two Maasai leaders who had taken their own risks to assist Nala went to speak with
her father about her future. Nala's father agreed to call off the marriage arrangements, repay the dowry, and allow Nala to work with IPT after being
assured that that she was not running off to get married. Six months after
leaving her homestead in the middle of the night, Nala returned home and
joined IPT. With her first month's salary Nala purchased blankets, beer,
and maize for her father and mother, and bought school supplies for her
younger siblings. While they did not absolve Nala of her commitments as
a daughter, these gifts and fulfilling her promise to return home went a
long way to settle the conflict between her and her family.

From Women's Groups to Maasai Women's Forum

When Lepukoi, the founder of IPT, agreed to support Nala, he saw in her
the desire and savvy to help Maasai women. As a sixteen-year-old girl,
Nala coordinated IPT's women's groups, working with women her mother
and grandmother's age. Her work allowed her to meet women and talk
with them about their problems and desires. Nala was very good at what
she did. She cared deeply for the women she worked with and shared common experiences with many of them. She could empathize with the older
women by reflecting on her mother's and aunt's lives. Unlike many international NGOs, IPT initially operated on a limited budget and Nala slept, ate,
and lived with the women she worked with. Many rural Tanzanians saw
NGO workers as urban elites who arrive in their "land rovers" for workshops
by day, and return to town to sleep in guest houses by night. Nala and her
male colleagues at IPT established reputations as being from the community,
as well as bringing new ideas and tools for social and economic change.

Lepukoi told me of the excitement when Nala returned from her travels
and came to join him in 1991. Sitting outside his home in October 2004, he

pointed to a large *ntarakwa* tree and asked me, "Do you know that tree?" He then told me his story of Nala joining IPT.

> This tree is called Nala's tree. This is where we celebrated when she came to IPT. We slaughtered [a cow], drank, and celebrated. We went all over looking for girls. Nala was the first girl we took. We got word that she was willing [to work with IPT] but her parents didn't want it. I told Saruni let's get her. We brought her here to [town] then sent her to represent IPT in Toronto. At the airport she was crying. She didn't know English. She went all the way to Toronto, transferred in Amsterdam. [My friend] was there to pick her up. That was her process of education. She spoke at the meeting and [my friend] translated. She really impressed people.

Employment with IPT gave Nala and several other young Maasai men and women opportunities to work on behalf of their families and communities, while attaining the type of professional credentials they desired. Nala and her colleagues worked tirelessly before there was even money to pay their salaries, and they saw the success of IPT as a direct reflection of themselves. Despite her enthusiasm for Maasai-led development, Nala became frustrated by what she saw as the institutionalization of Maasai gender roles and hierarchies into IPTs own work. As she tried to address women's concerns, particularly the desire to send girls to secondary school, Nala was confronted by the male-dominated hierarchy of traditional authorities and IPT's deference to what she believed were entrenched male interests.

In 1997 IPT collapsed due to allegations of mismanagement of funds, and Nala and her colleagues looked for new opportunities to carry on with their work. By this time, Maasai NGOs had become a common feature of the political landscape. Nala took the existing structure of IPT's women's groups and founded the MWF in 2000. MWF had expanded from a few women's groups providing adult-literacy classes in the mid-1990s under IPT to an organization with over nine hundred active members by 2004. Among other things, MWF started and ran six village nursery schools; nine adult-literacy centers; a revolving fund to grant small loans to women's groups; a veterinary shop and milk-separating project; a women's solidarity *boma*, where widows could live for two years and return home with their own livestock; and an extensive girls' education program. Recently MWF has been entrusted with the administration of the area's community secondary school for pastoralists and hunter-gatherer children. In just over ten years, MWF became not only one of the region's most important women's organizations, but also one of the most influential advocates on issues of poverty, education, and indigenous land rights. Most of MWF's projects can be described as local initiatives. They work closely with sub-village-based women's groups, and one of their main activities is raising funds for girls' education and convincing families of girls' rights to go to school. MWF is a relatively small organization, with five full-time staff members, and only recently received funds to buy a vehicle. Despite its low profile in regional centers like Arusha, where donors prefer to meet with their NGO partners, MWF has successfully attracted financial support from a variety of international groups.

Like many charismatic leaders, Nala helped form MWF against all odds, and its success and strength were invariably associated with her own leadership qualities. As MWF grew, its need for financial support increased. Despite MWFs democratic structure, with a local board of directors overseeing all major decisions, Nala remained the face of the organization, both in the community and to international donors. The next section of this portrait is devoted to Nala's negotiations with one of her international partners and the complicated transnational and intercultural politics of her work for Maasai women in Tanzania.

Global Agendas and Personal Biographies

Nala's work over the past twenty years has helped hundreds of Maasai girls throughout Tanzania gain unprecedented opportunities for education and salaried employment, helped women obtain livestock as personal property, and transformed the role of women as political actors. She has also played a central role in the national debate on pastoralists and other indigenous people's rights to land and natural resources. Her ability to influence such contentious issues depends largely on her personal skill at negotiating complex cultural situations in her community, as well as networking with organizations in Tanzania and Kenya. Along with her charisma, Nala's success also depends largely on the backing of international organizations and donors who provide her not only with the material resources to carry out much of her work, but with the symbolic backing that helps legitimize her activities.

In January 2005, one of MWFs donors, Aid-in-Action (AIA) sponsored Nala to travel to the United States.[8] It was a rare opportunity to intimately interact with one of her partner organizations, observe their daily operations, and see how they represent her and MWF to others. The trip brought to light many of the challenges associated with working for women's and indigenous rights locally in Tanzania while maintaining international credibility and support.

Representing Africa Abroad

Nala came to the United States for a six-week visit to promote Maasai women's rights and indigenous land rights in Tanzania, and to raise funds for the two organizations. When she arrived in the United States, Nala met staff and board members of AIA. Much of her time was scheduled for fundraising events, where she spoke at small and large gatherings and had dinners with potential donors. The events usually revolved around Nala describing her work, and the director of AIA talking about their various projects in Africa. At each event Nala would highlight different concerns of her community, but she spoke most often about girls' education. When asked by one of the AIA donors to describe her work, Nala gave the following response:

> My work is really to educate young Maasai women who are being forced to marry older men. . . . to advocate the right of Maasai women's education, because Maasai women need to do something different and not just to get married. They need to be educated to understand the world and they need to be educated to challenge assumptions within the community. . . . We have a lot of girls fleeing from forced marriages and coming to MWF because many of them need education support. . . . We are getting a lot of problems in supporting these girls because the [future] husbands are also determined to take these girls and marry them and their fathers had [already] done early arrangements to get them married. So we get a situation whereby the husband is not happy with us and the family is not happy with us, and it is just a problem. But I think it is a big potential for MWF because we need these girls to be educated, we need professionals to come back and aid their community. We need women who are able to stand and speak and represent themselves on their own behalf, and we need them to be able to understand good things about their culture and be able to retain those and also challenge the assumption[s] which are not good in the culture.

Nala is dedicated, articulate, passionate, and very successful in helping girls obtain opportunities that would be difficult to imagine without her assistance. Nala's work appeals to donors and international organizations that support women's rights, empowerment, and indigenous people, especially because she tells it so passionately and personally.

Nala's story does point the way to the potential for change in Africa. However, the neatly bound biographical narrative that emerges at such events is of Nala as a modern woman, liberated from the political and economic structures of a patriarchal society and nation-state. In a conversation I had during an AIA donor trip to Tanzania, an AIA board member said to me, "Just imagine if we had more Nalas out here, and just imagine the potential for change." While it is hard to imagine MWF's work without Nala, the organization is successful because of its grassroots operation and the efforts of hundreds of men and women to combat gender inequality and pastoralist political marginalization. While MWF deserves all of the interest it has generated from international donors and organizations, it struggles to find an identity outside its founder and spokeswoman.

What Does Women's Empowerment Look Like?

When a national women's rights organization based in Dar es Salaam came to campaign against Female Genital Mutilation (FGM) in 2001, they sought Nala and MWF to be their local partner. Nala explained that MWF was already addressing FGM in their work, but that they were not able to carry out the strategies of the national campaign. On several occasions Nala expressed her conviction that addressing FGM in the ways proposed by national organizations through enforcement of laws and widespread education campaigns would not only fail, but also jeopardize regional Maasai women's struggles. During Nala's U.S. visit, FGM was arguably the most high-profile issue for her international partners. Nala recounted her frustration about the topic during one of the fundraising events.

> I met some people here and they really wanted me to start addressing the issue of FGM. When I told them this is not our priority, they were very, very sad with me. . . . They said, "How can you advocate the rights of women if you don't stop this?" And I told them, "This is not something to stop overnight, it is something to be addressed in many ways. It is a tradition, it is a very old and long-time tradition and it takes time." And they pressured [Aid-in-Action] and

said, "How can you work with a person who doesn't believe this? Women are getting tortured." But they don't know that Maasai women have different problems, not only FGM. Sometimes donors can completely change your direction or vision because they always want to see their vision being implemented, and if an organization like MWF is not clear of what to do, it can be a big problem, because you will be implementing donor's vision instead of implementing your own objectives.

Nala believes that girls' education is the best way to confront practices such as FGM and improve women's capacity to negotiate and critique structures of patriarchal dominance. For many of her national and international partners, FGM defines a clear and violent line between male entitlement and women's rights. As Nala's own life history shows, there is no clear boundary dividing men's and women's interests, and she views international FGM campaigns as forcing a liberal gendered politics that is counterproductive to her own gendered struggles.

Anthropologist Dorothy Hodgson has written extensively about women's rights and human's rights in Africa in general, and in Maasai communities in particular. She has shown the limits of using human-rights discourses to defend women's rights in Africa, including a critique of the idea that there are universal women's issues and interests. She questions whether legal strategies and institutions are the best way to address structural inequality and violence. Despite the limitations of such frameworks, she says, "The 'women's rights as human rights' paradigm has made nation-states such as Zimbabwe and Tanzania accountable to their citizens, especially their female citizens, in new ways."[9]

Much of Nala's work is local in nature: meeting with girls, negotiating with headmasters throughout Tanzania for seats for students, bringing the District Education Director to village meetings to enforce girls' rights to go to school, securing land from the village for offices and staff housing. and dealing with the political fallout after a girl has defied her family's wishes and left for school. To defend her actions to elder men she often appeals to the law and a human-rights framework which grants girls equal opportunities to go to school and can be used to send resistant fathers to jail. She maintains strong relations with the district administrators and local police who are primarily from other regions and ethnic groups. They see Nala as a modern woman within a "backward" and " "traditional" society, and believe that helping her will transform the Maasai into "modern" Tanzanians. She relies on their support, but often resents their perception of her community, recalling her primary-school teacher's juxtaposition of modern Tanzanians and backward Maasai. It is another instance where the telling of Nala's story by strategic partners helps cement crosscultural alliances, but structures Nala's ability to define herself outside fixed notions of identity, values, and interests.

Biographies and Pictures: Circuits of Cultural Capital

Nala's trip to the United States revealed many of the inconsistencies and compromises of working across cultural and political divides for social change. Nala's work appeals broadly to international donors and their ideas about universal human rights and social and economic justice. One experience captures the contradictions between Nala's understanding of her partnership with AIA and their own understanding of their work for development in Africa.

On her first day in the United States, Nala visited the director of AIA. Michael was thrilled to have Nala meet many of AIAs donors and partners. While Nala knew Michael and several of the board members well from their frequent visits to Tanzania, she knew little about the actual workings of AIA. One of the first things that Michael shared with Nala was how much money AIA was able to raise by auctioning photos taken during a Maasai coming-of-age ceremony the previous year. Michael was thrilled that the photos drew such attention to AIA's work in Africa and brought in significant donations. The organization auctioned framed prints for between US$5,000 and $15,000 each. Michael expected Nala to feel proud that the images had raised so much money for AIA. Contrary to his own expectations, Nala told me that it was one of the worst moments of her life. At the time of the ceremony, she knew the AIA visitors were taking pictures, but she had assured the leaders of the ceremony that they were not going to sell them, and were friends of the community. She recounted some of her feelings to me.

> I was extremely sad and surprised about the use of *emanyatta* pictures. Three years ago these people came and we invited them to visit one of our emanyatta ceremonies and it is a very big thing, and a very spiritual thing, and it is a very community thing, and they took a lot of pictures. . . . And when I came here, I learned they are using these pictures to generate money for [Aid-in-Action] without even asking permission from MWF and from those people. I

learned that and was really sad about that. . . . I think this was not the right thing because we honored them to come, and see the ceremony. To take pictures of course is part of *wazungu* [European and North American] culture. . . . When others learn that they are selling people's pictures in Europe or U.S., it can completely destroy MWF and even destroy myself. It is very easy for politicians to use that, or people who are not happy with MWF work to say that this woman or this organization is not good because they are using images without permissions. This is a very serious thing to me. I managed to express my feelings and we are beginning to address this.[10]

Michael believed that raising funds for his small organization dedicated to international human rights and development was good for Africa and MWF. Nala was not so sure. While concerned about the larger social and economic issues AIA was working for, she felt that selling these images was wrong. Using images without permission posed risks to her work and reputation. The sale of the pictures also raised uncomfortable questions about the relationship between AIA and MWF and their mutual dependence. While finding and keeping donors is an essential part of running any NGO in Africa, Nala was keenly aware of the two-way relationship between donors and African NGOs. The following is a conversation I had with Nala about her relationship with donors.

BEN: Is it easy to stop working with a donor given your needs of funding projects and salaries and so forth?

NALA: It is not very easy, but if you just think about money and not your objectives you will not be achieving. It's better that you don't have money and remain with your integrity. It is not easy, but the more we work hard, the more donors need us. We can always get donors, because there are so many. I think so. I don't know.

BEN: I agree with you but how do donors need you?

NALA: We know donors need organizations that are committed to work because they need to spend their money. They always say they need to make a difference. We are depending on these donors, but they are also depending on us, they are applying funds on our behalf, on poor people's behalf. They rely on that. They need employment in their own countries. We all depend

on each other and I think it should be an equal partnership,
which it is not always.

BEN: Do donors agree with you?

NALA: Some of them don't. I think most of them don't, because not
all donors are completely transparent. They just feel like we
need their money, they have resources and they can control us
and they can make decisions for us. And you can get a very few
people who understand that, but most of them don't.

AIA's use of the images raised questions about the ethical practices of
working crossculturally for social justice. Nala realized that she had enabled AIA to gain the trust of her community and was now confronted
with what for her was the abuse of this trust. For AIA the pictures of Maasai at a cultural ceremony represented the very essence of their development goals. The framed pictures at AIA fundraising events told a particular
story of AIA and MWF and their authentic connections to local and traditional communities. While MWF benefited from its association with traditional leaders and ceremonies, Nala felt betrayed that AIA had turned these
images into commodities. This was not the first time donors had used images taken for promotional purposes of MWF or other Maasai NGOs to
generate funding and support for their own organizations.

The Agency of Biography

Nala was sitting in my living room on the last day of her trip to the United
States. She had just completed a conference call with AIA board members.
"What does sober mean?" she asked me. "Michael says everyone is now
sober to hear my concerns over their project." Members from AIA had
tried one last time to convince Nala to support their project to send a group
of U.S. filmmakers to Tanzania to document her life and struggles for Maasai women's rights in Tanzania. Nala's story was an important one and
they wanted to tell the whole world. Nala was not so sure how her story
would benefit MWF or her community and she discussed some of her concerns over the project with me.

Why do they want to teach Americans? . . . One of them said, we are
interested with Nala's life, of taking pictures, interview her mom,
her family, and relate her struggles and show how did she come to
start [Maasai Women's Forum]. They said they want to make peo-

ple aware of what is going on in Africa and the struggle you made to give women more power; and particularly we need people to go and visit Africa. . . . I told them: I was a little bit shocked in the proposal to see that you are applying for $200,000 [U.S.] dollars and this money can run MWF for almost four years.

In an era where the slogan "think globally, act locally" has inspired new forms of global engagement and connection, a film about a young African woman who has championed women's and indigenous rights seems a great way to promote greater crosscultural understandings. While Nala recognized the importance of international concern for women and indigenous people, she was unclear how telling her own life history to the global community would help her work in Tanzania. Whether she likes a particular version or not, the telling of Nala's life story, whether by me, herself, her community, or her international partners has enabled Nala to overcome some of the limits of her particular position as a young Maasai woman. But, it also presents new challenges to her ability to adapt to the changing demands of political, economic, and cultural struggles.

When I asked Nala to reflect on her relationship with donors she told me about a recent event that depicts her dilemma well. After learning about MWF's work and reputation, a large international donor offered them a grant twice the size of their annual operating budget. It would provide funds to buy two new vehicles and double the staff from five to ten. The grant was to carry out HIV/AIDS education and training. In many ways this is what MWF had hoped for: to gain the recognition as an organization capable to effect important social change throughout their community. Nala explained why they could not take the money.

> Over the last five years many donors change their focus and now want us to do work on HIV/AIDS because it is a priority in the Millennium Development Goals. But we don't have experts in that. We have so much other important work like educating girls. Sometimes if we implement their priorities and the policies of their countries we will fail to achieve our goals. If donors give you so much money they expect results that can be written in annual reports. If you don't have the capacity you will start to use the money inappropriately and when the evaluations come it will collapse, even if you do good work. When there is a misunderstanding between organizations it can destroy us.

Accepting the grant would have transformed MWF from a relatively small organization known locally as "the women's NGO" into a high-profile, nationally important development organization. Nala's experience with international partners led her to advise against the grant. She told me that "empowerment means that women are able to go to a meeting and say no, or fight for their daughters to go to school. Many donors want to see immediate results. To achieve results in our community is a long process." Nala and MWF will continue to rely on a number of partners, including international donors, to achieve their goals. As they continue to learn what others think Maasai development and empowerment should look like, Nala and MWF are better able to articulate their own mission and vision, even if they are repeatedly lost in the translation of crosscultural collaboration on development issues.

Notes

1. Nala is a pseudonym. All names of individuals and organizations in this chapter are pseudonyms.

2. MWF is a pseudonym for a Maasai women's organization officially registered as a Tanzanian NGO in 2000.

3. This portrait is based on fieldwork and interviews I conducted in Tanzania and the United States between 2000 and 2004. During that time I visited MWF projects, participated in meetings, and attended workshops. I also met with donors when they visited Tanzania, and attended donor events promoting MWF in the United States. As part of my methodology I sent the paper to Nala and have tried as best as possible to integrate her comments.

4. Pastoralism refers to a type of economic and cultural system of production, where people depend on livestock to convert semi-arid rangeland resources into milk and other products for consumption. Maasai pastoralists in Tanzania care for and manage their herds of cattle, sheep, and goats through reciprocal territorial relationships with neighboring pastoral communities.

5. IPT is a pseudonym.

6. Since that time Nala has received her Tanzanian secondary-school diploma through a correspondence course; attended, in Ireland, a year-long diploma course on development; and is currently enrolled in a bachelor's degree program in environmental studies and social sciences in Kenya.

7. Tanganyika gained its independence from Britain in 1961. In 1964 the mainland of Tanganyika formed a union with the independent island of Zanzibar creating the United Republic of Tanzania.

8. Aid-in-Action (AIA) is a pseudonym for a small nonprofit organization based in the United States which provides funding for development projects in Kenya, Tanzania, and Uganda. Ninety-five percent of their funds come from private donations. They raise funds partly through development tourism to promote their work and

cultivate relations with donors. While AIA support is important for many small organizations and projects, they do not provide funds for operational costs such as salaries and other management expenses. AIA funds supplement MWF's project budgets and help meet the costs for specific projects such as building small seasonal dams and school classrooms. AIA also directly sponsors girls' education. While providing a small part of the overall budget, AIA is an important partner enabling MWF to respond to community needs.

9. Dorothy L. Hodgson (2002), "Women's Rights as Human Rights: Women in Law and Development in Africa (WiLDAF)," *Africa Today* 49(2): 3–26.

10. Nala and AIA have since resolved the issue.

Further Reading

Cornwall, Andrea, ed. (2005). *Readings in Gender in Africa.* Oxford: James Currey.

Hodgson, Dorothy, ed. (2000). *Rethinking Pastoralism in Africa: Gender, Culture & Myth of the Patriarchal Pastoralist.* Oxford: James Currey.

Igoe, Jim, and Tim Kelsall, eds. (2005). *Between a Rock and a Hard Place: African NGOs, Donors and the State.* Durham, NC: Carolina Academic Press.

Ngcobo, Lauretta. (1999). *And They Didn't Die.* New York: Feminist Press at the City University of New York.

Oyewumi, Oyeronke. (2002). "Conceptualizing Gender: the Eurocentric Foundations of Feminist Concepts and the Challenge of African Epistemologies." *Jenda: A Journal of Culture and African Women Studies* 2(1): 1–9.

Anoop Nayak

13

Darkest Whiteness: Race, Class, and Culture in Global Times

A Portrait of Helena

Helena is a white, seventeen-year-old young woman. She has blue eyes, blonde hair, and for most of her life has lived in Lillehammer, Norway, with her Nordic mother and English father. When I met Helena, she was living away from home in the United Kingdom with just her English grandmother for company. I first got to know Helena when conducting a neighborhood ethnography investigating how the lives of new generations were being recast in the light of deindustrialization and global change. A prominent theme in this work was the question of what it meant to be young, white, and working class. In undertaking research in the North East of England, I was soon implicated in a dense network of social relations that led me to a multisite analysis of young people in various school, leisure, and community facilities. The study included interviews, observations, and interactions with young people in different spaces and was enriched by historical material and my own experience of living in an economically deprived and socially stigmatized neighborhood.

I interviewed Helena several times during my visits to the large state school she attended. Compared with the rest of England, the North East region has an ostensibly white population. Economically, it was once famous for coal mining, ship building, and mechanical engineering related to the production of armaments and industrial chemicals. Today, much of this industry has either disappeared or is severely eroded. The main economic activities are now centered on business, leisure, cultural industries, telephone call centers, and the service sector. The North East is, in many

respects, part of a "branch plant" economy where much of the profit generated does not stay in the region but tends to flow to multinational corpora-
tions whose headquarters lie elsewhere. But despite the dismantling of
much heavy industry, there is a strong sense of local identity and laboring
history among much of the population.

I interacted with Helena many times during her twelve-month stay in
the United Kingdom and watched as she navigated a committed, if occasionally naïve, race and class consciousness. Her story is significant in
demonstrating the important role that both local and global cultures play
in young people's lives. It also discloses how everyday routines, performances, and acts of embodiment can momentarily reinforce or subvert
these inequalities. While her biography cannot be said to be representative, its value lies in revealing the intricate patterning of race and class in
youth cultures. Helena shows how these processes can be reconfigured
through the living and telling of young lives.

Family Biographies

A red thread of socialist history and political protest is woven through the
rich tapestry of Helena's familial biography. Her paternal grandfather, now
deceased, had fought in World War II and been a long-serving trade union
member. He had worked in the shipping industry throughout much of his
laboring life. Helena's grandmother remains a colorful character whom I had
seen and spoken with on various occasions before I grew to know Helena.
Her grandmother had appeared several times on local news programs and in
the press protesting against the acquisition of common land by builders and
planners. I had signed many of her grandmother's petitions in an attempt to
preserve one of the few large green spaces for public use that was located near
a major shopping area in the region. At the time, I lived near this protected,
greenfield site and was similarly opposed to any attempts to sell it off to leisure and corporate business. For Helena, who was shy about publicity, her
grandmother was a high-profile, placard-waving embarrassment. And, while
the two of them shared a loving relationship, Helena flatly refused to sign up
for any of her grandmother's "silly requests" through the fear that signing
would invigorate her campaign and engender further media notoriety. In
what became a running family joke, Helena's grandmother placed her petitions in ever more prominent locations in the home in the hope that her
granddaughter would eventually sign one. Suffice to say, she did not.

Helena's father was employed at a local school in Lillehammer, and her
mother worked in the Norwegian health-care system. "Me family has always

been working class," she asserted, "always." "I'm a working-class girl. I come from a working-class family. My mum's a nurse with loads of people under her and my dad's a caretaker. It's not *that* working class," she reflected, "But I want to be working class." This desire to locate herself as a working-class subject had led Helena into socialist youth movements and provided the impetus to spend a year in North East England retracing her paternal roots and familiarizing herself with the staunch laboring culture. Norway is one of the most expensive places to live in the Western Hemisphere and though Helena's family is not wealthy, she was given a modicum of money for clothes and occasional nights out with friends.

The power of familial class biographies and the ways in which they are written into places cannot be underestimated. "I've always loved the North East 'cos me dad's like brought up there and he's said, "Helena it's the best place you can ever go." I always learned about how to like the North East." Her affiliation to the region is also politically informed. She explained how, "If it wasn't for Labour Youth, I wouldn't have come here to see my working-class background." In such ways, a working-class biography came to shape Helena's values, attitudes, and practices.

A closer examination of Helena's familial biography reveals how ethnicity also marked her family's experiences. Since the early days of the shipping trade, there have been long-standing connections between parts of North East England and Norway. It has even been argued that the lilting local dialect owes much to the undulating Nordic vocal inflection. In marrying a Norwegian woman and settling down in Lillehammer, Helena's father is an example of the diasporic movement and settlement that has taken place between these nations. However, cultural intermarriage and migratory movements across the family network extend further afield, as Helena explained: "I had a cousin who had mixed skin. Me aunt moved to South Africa, so I have a mixed family." Helena had traveled to South Africa to visit her relatives. There she discovered that her cousin Kam had endured a difficult time growing up in South Africa under the very recent shadow of apartheid. When discussing her upbringing she reflected, "I look *behind* color; that's the way my family brought me up." However, this did not mean that bonds of whiteness could not be forged in the domestic arena of her family. "My Norwegian gran is skeptical of Africans. She was saying, 'Be careful in South Africa there's loads of black people.' I was like 'Why?' But when I came back from my holidays I was like, "Whoa, what happened?"—I'd been getting racist thoughts from her. She started saying if I had a black kid how it would get bullied and everything. That's what me Dad fears anyway, he says, 'Remember what happened to Kam.'" Helena's family biography reveals how race and class may intersect with one another and how geographical mobility can engender more reflexive biographies of self and others.

Becoming Black

Growing up in Norway, Helena had developed a passion for black music through her interest in hip-hop, rap, and R&B swing. Youth markets are often saturated with ossified versions of black culture evident in the economies of signs and spaces found in the media production and consumption of contemporary music, fashion, language, and sporting iconography. In our early interviews Helena appeared drawn to at least some of the more superficial, "hip" possibilities offered by this symbolic, black, global "cool":

> I think I love the hair. It sounds so stupid, but look at this hair [grabs her long blonde strands]. I can't do nowt! It's just like straight. They [black people] can have curls, it can stand up straight, or have it really Afro. . . . It's like everything—everything's attractive.

Helena's fascination with black culture led her toward extreme forms of bodily experimentation. An example was the intensive use of tanning lotions and extended sessions on ultraviolet sun beds to achieve a deeply bronzed, near-black appearance.

> I do everything, like Michael Jackson who tries to be white, I try to be black. I dunno what's attracting me, maybe 'cos I had loads of friends. It's not only that, I dunno. I've always had my little dream since I was like a little kid like, "Dad, why can't you be black?" Even if I'd been bullied I've always wanted the black color and everything.

The desire to "be" black had become part of an embodied lifetime project tied to consumerism, where the semblance of blackness could be achieved through expensive skin products and the practice of tanning, with all its attendant health risks. The time, money, and labor spent on rigorous tanning regimes points to the way in which a reified version of "black cool," or at least a pretense at appearing exotic, is secured. Such globally mediated styles of black identity, which may have very little to do with the lives of black people themselves, demonstrate how such fictional race markers can be summoned to life, "tried on," and embodied as desirable. "I'm not saying I'm a black person in a white man's body," Helena guardedly expressed, "but I wish, and I always have, that I was more tanned."

Young people's coming-of-age is often a process of experimentation and competing identifications. Living away from her Norwegian peer group in Lillehammer, Helena gradually began to rethink her relationship to blackness, one in which blackness had been construed as the prestigious marker of cosmopolitan exotica. She explained: "I spent loads of money last year. All my money goes on sun beds, but not now. For example: sun beds, creams, stuff and everything." This reflexive critique led Helena to occasionally describe tanning as an obsessive and compulsive form of "sickness" that demonstrated her longing for a thoroughly imagined form of blackness. As time went by she grew to regard these acts as self-indulgent.

My white friends in Norway, I started it off, and now they think, "I need more tan." I started it off and now I feel so sorry 'cos they're still doing it. They're lying in the sun bed even more that me mon. They're lying there and one of my friends came with a pure black stomach and I was like, "Whoa! You're too black now, you look sickly black. No, that's not you."

It appeared that it was at the scale "closest in" that the bodily practices of tanning, hairstyles, music, and dance became a means for exhibiting a cosmopolitan "global cool." As we shall now find, the relationship between white youth and the mediated signs of blackness is partial and deeply ambivalent.

Between the Blinds: Rethinking Race and Class

In what is an ostensibly white English locality, Helena had befriended Beverly, one of the only black students in the school. "We're really close about music and we like talk about it for hours and hours and hours. Like rap to each other, we can do anything." Through her interests in music, Helena had previously developed a multiethnic friendship group in Norway. This had not been a straightforward process but involved careful navigation, demonstrating that she could travel beyond the superficial images of black global cool. Although she is now part of the dance-hall scene in Lillehammer, Norway, and in specific venues in England, Helena describes her early experience of attending these predominantly black events as isolating. "They [black people] started . . . saying, "White woman, white woman, white sheep." It gets to you sometimes. When you don't know anyone, you feel always alone."

By regularly attending musical events and thereby demonstrating a knowledge and commitment to black music, Helena overcame a suspicion that she was a "white impostor." This commitment is occasionally politicized, such as when Helena found herself challenging the white racism of her peers. She argued, "They don't say it [racist abuse] in front of me, 'cos I'll cut off their head in me words, with me arguments!" Helena explained how having black friends made her vulnerable to verbal abuse when attending mainly white venues. "I always get assumptions like from the [white] lads who say, 'This lass is trying to be cool like.' They say, 'Why are you talking to her, she's black?'" Helena recounted how she would stand up for her black friends, challenge the racism of young white males, and thus break the perceived bonds of whiteness. At such moments, she was able to vacate a stable concept of white identity that drew on a fixed allegiance to race, skin, and nation, in preference for a new, more flexible understanding of culture and ethnicity. This enables her to rework the performative circuit that continues to interpolate her as white and ascribes particular meaning to these race markers. In doing so, Helena demonstrated how she embodied particular gestures and ways of speaking, learned through her black friendship group, in order to rebut racism and a rooted notion of whiteness. As someone occasionally accused of being a "race traitor," Helena proved that she was unprepared to take up the baton of white privilege held out to her by a group of young white men who, in this instance, demanded to know why she is mixing with a multiethnic peer group.

The border crossing of a seemingly fixed racial divide was evident when Helena spoke of feeling "at home" in multicultural spaces and particularly alongside the company of black friends such as Beverly and many of her black Norwegian peers. When I asked Helena whether she felt comfortable in predominantly white circles, she replied: "No, I don't feel comfortable at all." She continued: "In black circles they haven't got this thing with snobs. They've got snobs, but they're more straightforward. Like snobs always look down on you." As the reference to "snobs" suggests, Helena is aware of the ways in which ideas of race and class come to speak through one another. "I like black circles better; in Norway I've got black friends," she divulged. As with many young people, the issue of belonging is a critical element in her life. The identifications she makes with black cultures and a particular class milieu enable Helena to perform her identity through and against competing understandings of white ethnicity.

The intertwining of race and class was further evident when the conversation turned to her stay in Britain. Here, the seemingly homogenous construction of whiteness she alludes to above was at least partially opened out.

What I like about the North East is they're really working class. It's economic. It's like ordinary people, not like snobs or anything. In

Norway we got loads of snobs in the town, everyone tries to be snobs, have the most beautiful house—really nice inside—and the best clothes for a hundred pounds for example and everything. I'm working class and I show everyone I'm lower working class.

In many respects, Helena jettisons what we might take to be a "moneyed whiteness" associated with neoliberal elites, capital accumulation, and material acquisition. This enables her to make cutting distinctions between "ordinary people" and those she depicts as self-obsessed "snobs". Helena's own life is narrated through ideas of community and shared values as opposed to an individualistic need to "get on," impress, and perform as an autonomous being. By aligning the imagined "earthy" values of North East England with the relations she claims to have encountered in black friendship circles, Helena is able to imagine new spaces for race- and class-based belonging.

A primary way in which Helena is able to stage the precarious interplay between race and class is through the recognition of mutual understandings of oppression. This became evident when Helena discussed her identifications with hip-hop music, a genre she depicted as the style of the "underclass." Helena reflected critically on the bourgeois perception of rap as simply a violent and misogynistic art form: "'Cos it's like the text in it, the words. If something was bad, it's about going to shoot off his head and everything, but if you look *under* the text at the lyrics, it's about the underclass. That's how I see it anyhow."

Rather than construe hip-hop music as either cool or dangerously excessive, Helena portrayed it as an intelligent, politically informed, and articulate mode of expression. She believed that the messages employed in hip-hop culture increased her class consciousness. She warned that, "If you get in an argument with one of these conservative people, you learn to stand up for your rights." In such ways, Helena presented hip-hop as a movement that articulates the anger and frustration of the socially and economically disenfranchised. She further explained how many of the lyrics she listened to have a particular meaning for her as a working-class young woman with a migrant history. As a foreigner coming from Norway, Helena had a peculiar status in Britain as a type of white outsider-within. By regarding hip-hop as a meaningful form of class struggle, Helena could develop a local, laboring sense of pride that resonates with the global languages of the black diaspora.

Beyond Race

Whether we can think and live beyond the modalities of race is a question that continues to haunt the postimperial present. New generations may perform the idea of race by staying resolutely within the borders of white privilege. However, engagements with stylized forms of global blackness do not necessarily render race obsolete, but can extend the optic of whiteness. This can make it difficult to move beyond the "sticky" repertoire of race signs as they continue to adhere to the everyday surface of life. Developing other ways of thinking and being is then a highly challenging path to pursue. By reading race and class through one another, Helena was able to identify with black culture and use the language of the oppressed. But she was increasingly aware of white middle-class youth who selectively appropriate what she now understands to be "her" culture. "I had me own music and now the posh ones are into it. It's horrible. They never liked it before and said, 'I hate hip-hop, it's an underclass thing.' I was like mad, really, really mad. They were stealing *my* style, *my* music and everything—it was *nothing* to do with them! That's what I thought anyway."

By identifying with an underclass and criticizing how "posh ones" gain access to black culture, Helena construes a commercially driven desire to appropriate the Other through global marketing as the enhancement of bourgeois cultural capital and a potential act of "whitening." She regarded this as a plastic, hollow form of consumption associated particularly with white appropriation. She thereby positioned herself as an "authentic" consumer of black culture and a moral guardian with a duty to prevent the cultural theft of black style. This is a politics that extends from music and clothes onto the dance floor as illustrated in the following exchange.

HELENA: Before, they [white youth] were talking behind me back about me clothes style and now everyone's wearing it and have started to hear me music. When I went on the dance floor—I, like, dance "black" or whatever you wanna call it, like butterflies and everything—and they'd say, "What the hell is she doing?" And they've now started copying my style. Everything I do, they do. I don't like that.

ANOOP: But might there be black kids who are saying, "All these white kids are stealing our style?" [. . .]

HELENA: They do say that. . . . If you say like, you like football here [the North East], lads say, "That's a man's thing to do." It's the same: you have to *prove* you like it.

Helena challenged the taken-for-granted practice of whiteness through these commitments and even deployed her body as a type of corporeal canvas for ethnic experimentation. This was evident not only in previous acts of tanning but in the choreography of her dancing and further invoked through rituals of belly-button piercing and tattooing. "I've got a Chinese tattoo on us," she revealed, "I think it's cool, Chinese signs and everything. I used to wear some Chinese clothes that were silky." Through such practices, Helena tried to define acceptable multicultural participation, which she wanted to protect from acts of white seizure. However, Helena understood her tattoo, the Chinese symbol for happiness, as embodying a deeper personal philosophy. "I thought I'd have a Chinese sign of something I really care about. That's what it means in my head. It's quite deep." Although there is often a fine gauze separating Helena's practices from those of other white peers she criticizes, what is evident is that she chooses to narrate her biography through the lens of being a politically informed and philosophically sensitive, cosmopolitan consumer. As such she remained vehemently opposed to the spectacle of consumption enacted by some white youth that is triggered only when once denigrated objects become a source of global cool.

> I like the music and everyone's like, 'Ugh, [derogatory tone]—she likes hip-hop.' There was no one else that likes it. And a couple of years ago some started to say, 'Oh, she likes hip-hop [evokes positive tone]. Wow, it's cool! She likes baggy clothes, maybe I'll wear it.' And they started wearing it.

Helena no longer views herself as an outsider looking in on black culture, but as an active participant of its many symbolic and imaginary expressions. Interestingly, she increasingly exerted a sense of ownership over these race signs and symbols. And while Helena played some role as a cultural pioneer, it is a position of privilege that emerges from the stylistic ingenuity of black youth. Reflecting on her white English peers she remarked, with no little irony, "It's funny like 'cos I'm a foreigner and suddenly everyone's taking my style!"

Despite these contradictions the possibilities for moving beyond race markers was revealed when Helena excitedly told me about a recent swing concert she attended: "There was this Asian rapper who was swinging and she had also Asian tones on the top. She was rapping, swinging a bit, she had this Asian thing too. She was brilliant! I think it's cool—it's a mixture of each culture. That's what I want, a mixture."

In this context, Helena reflected on the problematic tendency of homogenizing national cultures: "I would say like that England is a big mixture of loads of cultures combined." Indeed, her own subjectivity was informed by a series of partial identifications, including fragmented notions of blackness, working-classness, North East English, and Norwegian borrowings and imaginings. This was not a point of cultural confusion but a mark of achievement—"That's what I want, a mixture"—and it occasionally came to inform a conscious, hybrid politics of subversion. These sentiments were carried into personal friendships and imagined future relationships. "If I find a lad who I really, really love then it doesn't matter which color [he is]," Helena asserted. Although I cannot speak with any authority regarding Helena's intended intimate relations, she presented herself as a mobile cosmopolitan subject with an ability to move between and beyond the steadfast inscriptions of race logic. "I mix culture and everything. I think it's ridiculous, there's all different cultures and we should learn about each other. . . . I'm living it out, I'm a mixture! I'm not just saying it in my words and all, I'm *doing* it."

In Helena's experience, culture is not pretentious or abstract, but something that you "live out" and "do." "Doing" cultural identity in this way is a conscious celebration of intermixture that enables new meanings and points of identification to emerge. It suggests that whiteness and blackness cannot be reified as separate, impassable and homogenous race markers. They are mutually constitutive fictional race signs that are given meaning in performances that also allow for intentional and unintentional improvisation, contestation, and reappropriation. Through Helena's embodied politics of mixing we find no "original" point of production; rather, a polyglot process of global influences drawn from America, Jamaica, Africa, Britain, China, Norway, and so on. Even so, Helena's distrust of white youth who pilfer black culture is well founded and she herself is sensitive to some of the historical traces of race and class that come to inform her own biography. Moving between the light and shadow cast by the blinds of race suggests that for some young people, racial identities remain a complex, contingent, and precarious affair in global times.

Further Reading

Back, Les. (1996). *New Ethnicities and Urban Culture: Racisms and Multiculture in Young Lives*. London: UCL Press.

Nayak, Anoop. (2003). *Race, Place and Globalization: Youth Cultures in a Changing World*. Oxford: Berg.

Weis, Lois. (2004). *Class Reunion: The Remaking of the American White Working Class*. New York: Routledge.

Tracey Skelton

14

Young, Deaf, and Lesbian

A Portrait of Susannah

Susannah was born in 1978 in a northern England industrial city.[1] The city and its region at that time was experiencing economic decline which continued through to the early 1990s. Manufacturing in textiles— a mainstay of its economy—was either lost or moved to overseas centers of production. Unemployment levels were climbing and infrastructure support declining as the social costs of unemployment began to bite into the budgets of local authorities. Once the Conservatives were elected under Margaret Thatcher, cuts into public-sector provision deepened and the cost of living rose due to very high interest rates. The 1980s were a difficult time of deindustrialisation and deteriorating public services, especially for re- gions previously reliant on heavy industry and manufacturing. For people with disabilities and Deaf people, this was a particularly uncertain period. High levels of unemployment lessened their chances of employment, and there was no legislation to prevent discrimination on the basis of disability. Additionally, public services and welfare provision were harder to secure.

This specifically affected Susannah's family. Her parents are both Deaf and use British Sign Language (BSL) to communicate. Her parents had jobs, but they were poorly paid, and they had very little provision from social services as a deaf family. They were not provided with basic facili- ties such as flashing lights in place of a doorbell and smoke alarm, a mini- com machine to use with the telephone, or a qualified social worker for the Deaf. They never had access to a BSL interpreter for visits to doctors, den- tists, or hospitals.

In terms of education provision, Susannah's Local Education Authority (LEA) supported an oralist system of education. This educational practice was based on the belief that it was possible to overcome the barrier to communication that deafness caused rather than "avoid" the problem through the use of sign language. Such a stance was based on the expectation that deaf children should learn to communicate with the hearing world. The oralist system argues that with early diagnosis, high levels of amplification for hearing aids and intensive oral-language training (such as lip reading and vocalization), deaf children will develop enough spoken language to live successfully in the hearing world. In most LEAs this educational practice was delivered through local or distant (hence boarding) "schools for the deaf."

Oralism dominated the educational debates and was the dominant provision for deaf children, but it was highly controversial. The Deaf community and some children's-rights advocates argued that oralism denied children the right to their own language and that it was making deaf children fit into a hearing world rather than changing society to support the deaf. In practice, oralism helped hearing people understand deaf children, but it denied deaf children the ability to communicate with each other or other deaf people. Many deaf children leave oral systems of education with very poor linguistic ability, reading, and comprehension skills. The controversy about education continues, but in 1989 the first LEA system for deaf children adopted a bilingual policy that combines the use of sign language and spoken language to ensure that children can access the curriculum effectively and have a language for their personal and social lives.

The first time I met and interviewed Susannah was in a small teaching room of a college of further education in a city in the English Midlands.[2] Susannah was then a student of film studies and two other A levels; she was twenty-two and had returned to study after working for the post office for two and a half years, followed by a year of unemployment. Susannah had been told about our project through the college advisor for students with disabilities and had agreed to participate. My first interview with Susannah was excellent. I talked to her about her identity as a Deaf person; about her family and growing up; about her experiences of education, work, and studying at college; and her connection (or lack of it) with D/deaf and hearing communities. I discuss these further below, but first I put Susannah's interview into a definitional and methodological context.

It is important to explain the written terms Deaf, deaf, and D/deaf. D/deaf is written in this way to capture the complexity of identities that the young people involved in the project represented. A Deaf identity relates to sharing a strong sense of Deaf culture and Deaf community, and using British Sign Language. Capital-D Deaf people argue that they are not disabled but rather a linguistic minority. If hearing people used *their* language, they would not be disadvantaged. People who present a lowercase-d deaf identity usually consider themselves as disabled, use oral methods of communication such as lip reading and speaking, and spend most of their time in the hearing world. These identities are not fixed, and at different times in their lives people can slip between the two. In this chapter, where I use "Deaf," I am talking about BSL users who connect with, and feel part of, a Deaf culture. Where I use D/deaf, this indicates the inclusion of the whole range of Deaf and deaf people. I use "deaf" where the medical definition of deafness is being discussed.

Susannah and I were not alone in our interview but had a qualified BSL interpreter with us. Susannah's first and preferred language is BSL. I, as the interviewer, spoke the questions to Susannah, looking at her the whole time. Susannah watched the interpreter who "translated" my spoken words into sign language.[3] Susannah's responses were signed back to both the interpreter and myself, and the interpreter spoke what she read from the sign language. She checked frequently that she had grasped the intended meaning of what Susannah was trying to convey. The interview was recorded on audiotape, so only the hearing people's voices were captured. This process of "capturing" the interviewee's "words" is problematic in ethical terms. It renders the BSL user silent, which is precisely what a hegemonic hearing world does, and yet I was participating in a project that was focusing on vulnerability, social exclusion, and marginalization. Deaf people who use BSL as their first language cannot, or choose not to, vocalize their voices. Their hands, face, and upper bodies are their "voices" as they communicate through sign, and they "listen" through watching others sign. Susannah's deafness is such that she can hear very little, perhaps the sound of a high-speed train rushing by. Hence, communication with the hearing world is difficult because most do not use sign language. Susannah can lip read reasonably well and is an intuitive person, so she can get by in her communication with hearing people. Nevertheless, to conduct the interview in a way that produced tangible "data" and demonstrated the rigor required in research practice, interviews were tape-recorded. In the project we had planned to use a video camera, but the majority of the young D/deaf people did not want to be filmed. Additionally, the transcription of videotaped interviews would have required a great deal of time and money.

On this occasion I was working with an interpreter called Frances (a pseudonym). Frances had a feel for the goals of the project. She is a fluent

signer and an articulate speaker, and hence the quality of her interpretation is very high. Frances works extensively with Deaf people in this particular Midlands city and is well respected and trusted by them to convey
what they wish to express. Because Susannah is a strong and confident
user of BSL, and because Frances worked so well with her, this interview
was among the richest that I conducted.

I now introduce Karl to provide a counterpoint to Susannah's story. Karl
was born into a hearing family and had been through an oral system of
education. The interview with him was quite short because he could not
speak or sign very well and responded with lots of shoulder shrugs or by
saying "I don't know." Yet he seemed positive about the interview. He said
that it was an unusual experience for him to have someone who wanted to
listen to him for a long time. He told a story that proved to be quite typical
for deaf children born into hearing families, who had some degree of hearing and had been educated by oralist pedagogical methods. Karl's mother
was told that the most important thing she could do for Karl was to make
him speak and not use any form of sign language with him. He was also
forced to wear his hearing aids, which he hated and would regularly flush
down the toilet. At Karl's oralist primary school for the deaf signing was
forbidden, children were constantly told to "turn on their voices" and to
speak. The children had to wear heavy headphones, and the children were
also attached to a group aid console with an amplifier. Teachers and nursery nurses in the school could often understand what a particular child
was trying to say, but children could not hear each other. At play times
children tried to use a rudimentary sign language to communicate to each
other covertly, but teachers punished them for such activity. As a teenager
I had volunteered at this particular school and regularly saw children being made to sit on their hands to stop them from gesturing. I did not understand why deaf children were not taught signing until the oral system
was explained to me. Because at that time I did not have the language to
express my disgust at the hegemonic power of the hearing world, I stopped
volunteering and worried away at this injustice. With the ESRC grant I felt
I was able to address, in a more important way, some of these issues.

Karl is very typical of deaf pupils who go through an oral and mainstream education system: they can neither communicate effectively with
the hearing world nor can they connect with the Deaf world because they
do not have a language competence in either speech or sign. The only
children who benefit from such a system are those with high levels of social and emotional support within their home environment, and/or a good

degree of hearing, and/or are bright enough to learn and retain something from the education system. In some local authorities there is a shift in pedagogic (and political) approaches towards bilingualism. In such a system sign is taught alongside oral methods and Deaf people are now allowed to become teachers. However, many authorities are wedded to oralism and special schools or "mainstreaming" where D/deaf children are placed in hearing schools with specialist support. There is still a problem of LEAs not providing the necessary funding for bilingualism, which includes extra teachers or communication support workers and also requires training for hearing teachers to gain the necessary skills and commitment to working within a bilingual context.

In contrast to Karl, Susannah, was confident and self-assured. She had a very strong Deaf identity and was able to articulate this fluently. Toward the end of our first interview Susannah also told me that she was a lesbian. Since part of our ESRC project was to work with young lesbians and gay men, we also wanted to interview an intersecting group of young D/deaf people who were also gay. Hence, I arranged a second interview with Susannah. This next part of the chapter weaves these two interviews together to give an insight into Susannah's life, identity, and politics as a young Deaf lesbian.

Susannah was one of the few people we worked with who was born into a Deaf family. In the United Kingdom 95 percent of deaf children are born to hearing parents, a similar percentage to the number of gay people born to heterosexual parents. Both Susannah's parents are Deaf, as are her grandparents on her father's side. She is an only child, as were both her parents.

> We've got three generations of Deafness, so I don't think about being Deaf, I mean I chat to my parents, we're just Deaf that's it. . . . I felt very comfortable with communication. I missed having brothers and sisters, I got quite lonely, so my parents would take me to meet their Deaf friends, but they all had hearing children. We could manage but it wasn't perfect. . . . I really got on well with my grandfather who was Deaf, we had a really brilliant relationship and I would always ask him questions—I was a nosey, curious child.

Susannah's relationship with her grandparents was an unusual element in our research project; the majority of young deaf people do not have close relationships with their wider families due to difficulties relating to communication. Many young people had especially weak connections with their fathers, who were less likely than their mothers or siblings to put effort into communication.

As discussed earlier, there was little extra social provision for Susannah's family:

> We never had equipment for Deaf people when I was growing up, people would just wave at the window. My mum would go to the doctor herself and she would communicate by herself, then she would go with me. But as I grew up I would be the one who helped my mother; I'd be a kind of note-taker. My mum was very strong in BSL and she didn't have English skills, so that's how we managed. My English helped me with my writing and stuff like that. I was sixteen before I met someone who was actually an interpreter. The social worker used to do it before but they weren't very good, not a trained interpreter.

This lack of interpreters remains an acute problem in the United Kingdom today. There is a shortage of people willing to train for the three to four years it takes to become a fully qualified interpreter. It is an area that D/deaf charities, lobbying groups, and Deaf Clubs campaign about continually. Fully qualified interpreters such as the ones we worked with on our project are essential in supporting BSL and Sign Supported English users within a hearing world for education, health care, employment, and so forth.

The local primary school for Deaf children that Susannah attended was not a signing school. The school was part of the LEA's provision for children with a hearing impairment and it followed the oralist education pedagogy discussed above. Susannah coped with this well because her level of linguistic development established through living in a BSL family was very high. She was bright, but her parents felt that the local secondary school would not stretch her academically. At the age of eleven she passed a written entrance examination and a hearing exam for a prestigious grammar school for D/deaf children that used oral methods but had a very strong academic reputation. The school was a boarding school and a several-hour train journey away from her home. Susannah described the ways in which she and other pupils communicated in this oral school.

> Well, in our first year when we all arrived some of them [children at the school] couldn't sign, some had got sign language because they had Deaf parents and so I had a really close relationship with them, but the other children learned signing from us and so we'd

all be signing together. ... We weren't allowed to sign because it was the oral system, but secretly. ... I mean there were too many of us for them to catch us all and at bed time we could sign because they couldn't see us.

At this school, from the age of twelve to sixteen, Susannah's language of home and the language she used with her family was construed as something that was punishable. She could only use her sign language in a clandestine way in the boarding school. Susannah was intensely homesick for more than a year, but she adapted and worked hard throughout school. For a very Deaf young woman whose language is BSL, she coped well with the oral system and passed GCSE (high school) examinations that assume participants can hear.[4]

After leaving school at sixteen, and back in her home city, Susannah tried to follow an IT course in a hearing college of further education.[5] However, she found it "boring." She wanted to attend a college in the Midlands, which was a residential college for Deaf people where signing was the predominant language. However, her LEA, which had paid for the boarding school refused to pay more. They were legally entitled to refuse because Further Education (FE) colleges are not part of the compulsory education system. Susannah's parents decided to move to a nearby city with a different LEA when she was seventeen, and they got an agreement for payment for Susannah to attend the Midlands college for Deaf people. However, this did not work out very well. As this aspect of Susannah's story suggests, D/deaf young people can fall behind their hearing peers in social maturity, partly because they are trying to exist in a world that presumes hearing and tailors information and social arrangements for hearing people. D/deaf children, no matter how bright and how well connected with their families, are often cocooned from the world and tend to miss out on the social learning opportunities afforded to their hearing peers. Susannah explained some of the challenges that she faced but also conveyed the excitement she felt about being back in a signing environment:

I enjoyed the courses at college. There were other D/deaf people there but not as many as I thought. The college where we actually studied was an ordinary one for hearing people so there were more hearing in our class than D/deaf. I didn't bother with the course that much, I was seventeen, young and socializing with my mates. I thought it was brilliant to be with Deaf people and signing away all the time, but it was a bit intense. It's a small world and very gossipy and I didn't want to get into all of that. The teachers told me that I'd fail if I didn't attend and so I quit. So I went back home, I still didn't know what I wanted to do.

At the age of eighteen Susannah got a job with the post office and remained there until she was twenty, in 1998. She did not like the work; she felt isolated by her managers and took time off for "sickness." She was warned that she would be sacked and so reluctantly went back to work. She said she was arguing with her mum all the time. "I really wanted to go to college but I'd got no ambitions and didn't really know what to go for."

Susannah ended her two-year contract with the Royal Mail early. She sued them for discrimination because they would not provide her with access to a minicom (a phone system that translates speech into text), an alarm based on light rather than sound, or an interpreter for work meetings. Susannah received compensation through an out-of-court settlement. In the United Kingdom, a bitter and hard-fought campaign that used legal cases, political protest, and direct action by people with disabilities and their supporters, had forced the British government to pass the Disabilities Discrimination Act in 1995. The act outlaws discrimination on the basis of ability/disability and also provides financial support and a legal requirement for certain provision for people with disabilities to enable them to participate equally in the workforce. Although Deaf people do not recognize themselves as disabled, they are protected by this law.

Susannah returned to the college for Deaf people, but again the course did not work out for her; she just could not settle to it. She found a place to live in a neighboring city and decided to spend time sorting herself out. She decided to go to another FE college that provided good signing support, but she thought much harder about her course of study: "I thought carefully. I really love media work, I love video work, and I saw an A-level film studies course. There was also digital design and drawing, Photoshop, and so on. . . . and I do computing courses too, and that's what I've been doing since then."

Susannah appears settled in this course of study and is attending regularly. She is completing her assignments and shows a commitment that was lacking when she was seventeen. I asked her why, this time, it was working out better. It appears that she has grown more mature and is less obsessed with having a good time. She explained that she is now involved in things outside of college. Her volunteering at the local Deaf Club allowed her to use her creative skills but also give something back to other D/deaf people and the community. This was in part because the Deaf Club in her home city had been very important for her as a child. She had been able to participate in all the activities for children and so connect with other Deaf children.

> I think I've grown up, I've settled down a bit. I'm really interested in film and media. There's no one D/deaf on the course, a few in the college and a few where I live. It's part-time which suits me. I do lots of other things. I'm involved in a drama group for Deaf people and we are putting on a performance. I do the art work and design-ing. I play netball with a Deaf team; we play in a Deaf and hearing league. I play football and that's in a Deaf/hearing league. I have loads of stuff to do. I'm on the Sports Committee. I like the Deaf Club here. It's a nice mix of age, there's young and old together. There's plenty of Deaf people to sign to, and I get on with them pretty well, so it's good. . . . I feel I can go to the Deaf Club and chat to whoever I want to. . . . There's no trouble. I like to be in a place where I feel comfortable.

Susannah clearly enjoys being part of the Deaf Club and the commu-nity space it creates. She is happy to be with other Deaf people and the centrality of signing is clearly important. It reinforces her sense of identity as a Deaf person and connects her with a wider cross section of the Deaf community: "If there wasn't a Deaf Club I'd just be in pubs with my friends my own age." Susannah explained her thoughts about the Deaf community:

> Yes, there is a Deaf community because we need our own lan-guage; we need to feel that there are people with whom we can mix, that we can understand each other. There are things that peo-ple you talk to in the outside world [hearing world] they wouldn't understand, and also having to talk to people and lip reading, it's very difficult to understand each other. It's a small community and you meet up at the pub, go to a party. You have that ease of com-munication, it's a really close bond. When you communicate with the hearing world you use an interpreter or note taker, writing things down on paper. . . . It's completely different in the Deaf com-munity where you're all using the same form of communication.

At the time of our research project, there was an active campaign for the official recognition of BSL as an official language. Other countries within the European Union (EU) had put this into practice. Norway (not an

EU member) provides the main evening news in Norwegian Sign Language each evening, whereas U.K. D/deaf people have to wait until the end of the week to watch a signed version of the national news. This added to their sense of getting information later and in reduced forms compared to their hearing peers. An important part of the campaign for the official recognition of BSL was public demonstrations on the streets in London and other cities. These were important visible gatherings of Deaf people and their supporters, and they were significant in allowing Deaf people to have a voice in this political campaign about the rights of language and identity.[6]

> The London March, yes I went twice. It was fantastic and in some ways I think it will be successful, but will we get everything? In some ways I feel that's not possible. You know, in the twenty-two years since I've grown up—nothing. It's a long, slow struggle. I feel it's impossible but I guess you've got to be positive and keep going with it. More people seem to learn sign language now; it's amazing how many people can sign, a bit different from when I was a child. On the march I felt so happy; we felt like we'd taken over the road completely. You see it on television, you see it on the news, different marches happening but when it's you then you feel "right we've got people power now, we've got Deaf Pride, we've got our *own* march." There were thousands of people; it was amazing.

By way of contrast, despite the relatively high profile of these marches, Karl knew nothing about them or the campaign for the recognition of BSL as a minority language. When it was explained to him, he could not understand the meaning behind the campaign. Once again this highlights his separation from the Deaf community largely through his lack of confidence and ability in using BSL. By contrast, Susannah had very clear ideas about what she hoped would change in the future to make D/deaf people's lives better and also bring a sense of equality with hearing people. For her, progress would come about through obtaining equal access to things that she enjoyed in her life:

> With television I'm really pleased that there are more subtitles now, so much more than there was before. In the cinema they occasionally have an interpreter, but I think that would be impossible, where do you look—at the interpreter or at the screen? There should be subtitles for the cinema, in some cases there are, but not enough; I had

to go all the way down to London to be able to see the Grinch with subtitles. But it was fantastic, D/deaf and hearing people watching the same film, the same access. I could understand everything that was going on just as they could. I love to go to the cinema, films with subtitles would make such an improvement for me. I know you can go to the theater on certain nights and there is an interpreter . . . so things seem to be getting better and I hope in the future there will be 100% access . . . I was involved in a letter campaign to get the new cinema in this city to get the technology to show the subtitles—we'll have to wait and see if they do.[7]

Toward the end of the first interview I asked Susannah if she had a sense of Deaf pride—something she had mentioned a few times in the interview—and also whether she experienced discrimination in everyday social contexts:

I'm happy with who I am. I've got nothing that I think, "Oh, I wish I'd been hearing"; I don't have any regrets. I've no particular yen for music, my family are Deaf, my friends are Deaf, communications with them are totally fine for me; yeah, I'm proud to be Deaf. . . . But there can be discrimination. On trains and in taxis for example. The ticket inspectors can have a pretty rough attitude, they can be very demanding, I'll ask for a pen but they don't help me. In the taxis you can see one price on the display and they seem to be asking for something else and so I ask them to write it down, to explain, but they are never patient and some have never met a Deaf person before and you can see how their face and their body language changes, and I think "Oh come on, I'm not going to bite you for the sake of a bit of paper and pen!"

This brought the first interview to a close. Susannah had clearly articulated her sense of Deaf identity, her role in the Deaf community, her experiences of discrimination, her political activism in the BSL marches, and her hopes for communication improvements with the hearing world and equal access for Deaf people to all sorts of sectors and institutions. Susannah talked about a new television program, VeeTv, that was specifically aimed at Deaf young people. She told me that she was going to appear on it to discuss what it was like to be a lesbian. This was the first time she had mentioned her sexual identity in the interview, but it was clearly something she felt happy to share having built up a level of trust with the interpreter and myself. I wanted to explore this with her further, and so we arranged a second interview, again with Frances as the interpreter. The second interview, conducted in Susannah's home, focused much more on her lesbian identity and how this intersected and enmeshed with her Deaf identity.

Susannah could not remember an exact moment or period of time when she recognized that she was a lesbian. She spent most of her time at school with girls but saw it more as sisterly relationships. She had a few boyfriends, but the relationships did not last long. When she was at the Midlands college for Deaf people, she met Deaf people who were lesbian and gay. She found that it was easy to accept them as such and make friends with them. She often described herself as open-minded, and she felt happy to go to gay pubs with her gay Deaf friends. She was very attracted to another Deaf woman, and they had a brief affair, which ended when the other young woman decided that she was not a lesbian. Susannah felt quite hurt by this but decided to forget it and continued to socialize with a wide range of people and had encounters with both men and women. She felt at this stage, around seventeen and eighteen, that she was bisexual. She had a four-month relationship with a man when she was nineteen but did not feel right about it. She met her current partner, Kathy, when she was twenty, and at the time of this interview, they had been together for almost three years. Susannah argued that for her it has always been the person's personality rather than their gender that attracted her, but for her it was important that they were Deaf:

> I'm very strongly Deaf with Deaf people, because if I were with a hearing person I'd have a communication problem. I have to have full-time communication, twenty-four-hour communication. If I met someone who was deaf and they didn't sign, I would have to teach them to sign. I have to be able to use my language with someone I am in a relationship with.

Susannah did not really experience a singular "coming out" moment with her friends. She told a few people, or they guessed and were all okay about it, and then she supposed that "word just got around, the news spread." She said that she never felt confused or that her sexuality was a bad thing and did not experience any negative feelings about being gay. This was quite the opposite of the hearing gay people whom I interviewed. Many were full of self-loathing and had internalized the dominant negative attitudes toward homosexuality, usually termed homophobia or heterosexism. D/deaf people, as I have discussed earlier, can miss out a great deal on information and general socialization processes. This can be a disadvantage, but for those who identify as gay, it might be a positive thing. They may not be aware of the subtle and overt heterosexuality ever present in popular culture, the assumed heterosexuality evident in advertising, schoolbooks, fairy tales, and so forth. Similarly, the predominant cultural and political messages of homophobia and heterosexism can be less apparent.

While Susannah identified as being someone who was open-minded, she described her parents as antigay and homophobic, especially her mother. The other D/deaf young people we interviewed who were gay all had *hearing* parents. They argued that their parents' discovery that their child was *deaf* came as a much greater shock than that same child later telling them that they were *gay* or *lesbian*. This second realization seemed to have less of an impact. It was as though they had already come to terms with an element of difference and had worried about how their child would cope in a hearing world. Having seen their child cope with education through an oral system (the situation for the majority) and grow up in a hearing world, perhaps parents were more confident that the child would cope with other differences, such as being gay in a straight world. But Susannah's parents reacted to the news of their daughter's lesbian identity in a manner similar to that described by the hearing lesbians involved in our project. For Susannah's parents, who were both Deaf themselves, she had never appeared different from them, so her identification as a lesbian was the first time any difference became apparent. Also, because of their own deafness, they had not been exposed to the debates about tolerance or experiences of other parents of gay children. Hence, they appeared quite shocked and confused about lesbianism, and this seemed to last longer for Susannah's mother than her father. Susannah had been having flirtatious and intimate contact with Deaf girls when she was living at home after her first unsuccessful attempt at college in the Midlands. She said that the Deaf community in her home city was small and that her mum must have learned about something going on at parties.

> One Boxing Day my mum said we should go out for a walk. We were chatting and my mum said that she didn't like it when women got together. I said that there wasn't anything wrong with it, that it was all right. She asked me straight out, "How do you know?" I thought, "Oh god, I've made a slip here." My mum said "Have you done that? It's disgusting, it's horrible." I told her it was just something I was

trying out, it's not a lifetime decision. She promised not to tell my father. Then later she was at me to find out who the girl was. She suspected (and she was right) but I denied it, and I panicked. She left it for a while, then she said, "I heard that you've been with a girl at a party, that you were kissing her." This time I said, "Yes, so what?" My mother said it made her sick and that I'd told her it was a one off [isolated incident]. So to shut her up I said I had a boyfriend and really I was into men. She calmed down a bit.

When Susannah began her relationship with Kathy, she did not tell her mother. However, her mother guessed because Kathy was the only person Susannah communicated about, and the two young women were frequently together. There were incidents when Susannah's mother was rude and difficult with Kathy and even contacted Kathy's mother through the minicom to argue with her about her daughter. Susannah's mother also opened a letter that Kathy sent to Susannah at her parental address. Susannah's father, however, seemed quietly tolerant. Susannah's paternal grandparents have not discussed her sexual identity with her, but they make Kathy very welcome and always ask about her when Susannah visits on her own. Susannah's paternal family members are all Deaf, whereas her mother was born into a hearing family. It might be that Susannah's father and his parents have understood discrimination for generations and so have developed a greater tolerance of difference. It also seems from Susannah's discussion that she has a close and calmer relationship with her father and his parents than she does with her mother. Her sexual identity is another point of conflict in their mother–daughter relationship.

The kind of traumatic coming-out process that Susannah is experiencing with her mother is something that young lesbians and gay men often experience. The accepting family is a rare one. Many young people resist coming out to their families for fear of rejection, violence, or indifference. Some families work through the process over time and learn to re-accept their son or daughter, while others remain estranged for years or even permanently. For some young people who are young and still living with their parents, the coming-out process means a loss of everything all at once: they lose their family and their home. This renders them particularly vulnerable. Statutory services often overlook or ignore their gay identities, and so they do not always get appropriate support, housing, or advice. Susannah was already living independently but clearly felt hurt and confused by her mother's persistent negative reaction. Susannah feels confident about her new life and relationship, which helps her cope with her mother's attitude. Nevertheless, she knows that her mother will never completely accept her because of her sexuality and that worries and hurts her.

Susannah finds the Deaf Club an important source of support, and the Deaf Club is integral to her identity as a Deaf person. Nevertheless, she experiences tension between her involvement in the Deaf Club and her lesbian identity. Two lesbian friends advised her not to be "out" in the Deaf Club, and so she and Kathy masqueraded as friends until eventually something slipped in a discussion with friends. This did not seem to be a problem, however, and Kathy was accepted when she volunteered as a scene painter to work alongside Susannah.

As a Deaf student in a college, Susannah is assigned a communication support worker (CSW) who helps her in lectures and classes. Susannah said she had to tread carefully with the CSW because she did not know how she would react to working with a lesbian. Susannah: "I had to wait a while until we knew each other. I had to look and see what her attitude was about homosexuals. She seemed to be okay, and so then I told her, and she was okay. That was a relief."

There are several support groups for hearing lesbians and gays in contemporary Britain, usually phone lines offering advice and guidance. Susannah said that if she had needed such support, being Deaf might have been an obstacle to accessing these services. She has participated in gay pride events in London, Manchester, and in the Midlands city where she lives now.

> I'm not part of any lesbian or gay groups but I go to gay pride events. I love the fact that you can be open, you can be out, you can kiss each other, and do what you like. At pride events they always have interpreters, it's amazing. In London this one time they had a D/deaf stall where we could all meet up. The following year there wasn't a D/deaf stall and it was harder to meet up, I ended up drinking too much and getting a headache. But there was still an interpreter. I've never been to anything where they have an interpreter for *all* the events of the stage—that was so brilliant.

Interestingly, when I asked Susannah if she felt part of a gay community, she asked me, "What do you mean by being part of a community?" When I had asked the same question about a Deaf Community in the first interview, she had been able to articulate a sense of belonging and discussed the way the community was based around language—for her this was the key facet of being part of a community. So she tried to think about the concept of gay community in the same way:

> Well, I mean, there's a gay sign variety, there is a kind of camp signing which is good fun. They have a very camp sign for "shopping," "fab," things like that. You'd just use those signs with other gay people; it's for fun and to make people laugh. In terms of the other stuff you said about community, I guess I'm part-time. I don't go to just gay stuff all the time. I go to some parties but I don't go and meet the same people every week. I mix with both gay and straight communities, but the key thing is that they are all Deaf.

Susannah said she felt that she was "full-time Deaf" and "part-time gay." However, she was realistic about the ways in which different communities tolerated people from each type of community:

> I think the gay community accept[s] D/deaf people better than the Deaf community accepts gay people. I think because they have already got that gay label on them, they have that kind of discrimination as a gay person, they know what it's like to be discriminated against, so they have more empathy with D/deaf people. I've never had a problem being D/deaf in any of the gay clubs and pubs. In fact a lot of gay people, especially lesbians, are really into learning sign language.

Susannah copes extremely well in a hearing world despite being very deaf and using a communication mode that hearing people generally cannot use. She is proud of being Deaf and of having grown up in a Deaf family and feels that there is nothing strange or unusual about it. She coped well with her education because of her strong linguistic capabilities, even though at both schools she was forced to follow oralist practices and not use her own language. She has experienced discrimination as a Deaf person but has learned from each experience and has found her greatest friends, her partner, support, and fulfilment through being part of a strong and active Deaf community. Her identity as a Deaf person places her firmly within Deaf culture. It is here where she has participated in political action through the campaign to have BSL recognized as an official language. Also, she plays a role in informal politics when she volunteers within the Deaf Club in a range of activities which provide a service for members and also connects them with the hearing world through the team sports leagues.

Susannah is an example of a young, deaf person who is succeeding in a Deaf and hearing world.

Karl, on the other hand, is not yet succeeding in a hearing or in a Deaf world. He does not cope well in either one. This has a great deal to do with his oralist education, and he has never fully grasped linguistic competence. He had poor linguistic skills before he went to school and when he left. Without sign language he did not develop any linguistic confidence that could then be used within an oralist context (unlike Susannah who "understood" language through her BSL). Karl struggles to communicate with all but his closest male friends who have similar (in)abilities to his. His world is smaller, and so his opportunities for wider social and possible economic relations are fewer.

Susannah has another significant facet of her identity, her bisexual and increasingly lesbian identity, which brings her into contact with another social community. She feels she is a part-time member of this grouping even though the gay community copes with and accepts her Deafness better than the Deaf Community accepts her gayness. She currently experiences difficulties in her relationship with her mother because of the latter's homophobia. Susannah does not have a strong political sexual identity but she does participate in a range of pride activities.

Susannah is a Deaf, gay, young woman in a hearing and heterosexually dominant culture. Yet she has very strong self-esteem. She has worked out what she wants to do in her life—work in media and film—and is gaining appropriate qualifications for this. She has a partner and rents her own home. Her open-minded and positive attitude means that she rises above hearing discrimination and homophobic attitudes. Susannah blends her identities, loves her place in her community, and is optimistic about the future: hers and that of Deaf people.

> I'm an open-minded person. I respect other people. I think that's important that people respect each other so there's no discrimination. I don't discriminate against other people and so I try and understand what people are thinking and feeling. I'm laid back as a person. I don't want to be part of a clique; I like to mix with all sorts of people. That's how we learn about each other.

Notes

1. "Susannah" is a pseudonym for a young woman whom I interviewed as part of an ESRC-funded project called "Living On The Edge: Understanding The Marginalisation and Resistance of Vulnerable Youth" (award no: L134251032). This project was held jointly with Gill Valentine and Ruth Butler. The young people who were part of this project were aged sixteen to twenty-five.

2. In this chapter I avoid naming specific places and cities. This is because the D/deaf community is relatively small and tight-knit. It is important to ensure that Susannah's identity is not revealed, and the names of schools, colleges, and places of residence could prevent this chapter being "anonymous."

3. When a hearing person listens to spoken language and "changes" it into sign language it is not a *translation* but an *interpretation*. This is because the change involves a spoken language becoming a visual language using the hands, upper body, and face to express what is being conveyed. It is, therefore, much more than a direct translation of words and grammar; it is the translation of something *heard* into something *seen*.

4. There is not yet a GCSE in the BSL language as there is in English, French, Spanish, and so on. Deaf Clubs are currently campaigning for this through the legislation that outlaws disability discrimination within education.

5. In the United Kingdom postcompulsory education for those aged sixteen-plus is provided by further education (FE) colleges. Here students can re-sit any examinations they took at school, begin A level (aged sixteen–eighteen) courses for entry to university, or follow a very wide range of vocational training courses.

6. There are an estimated 250,000 people in the United Kingdom who use BSL as their first and/or preferred language (See http://www.signcommunity.org.uk/language/aboutbsl.php). The campaigning of the Deaf community and their advocates succeeded. The British government recognized BSL as an official language in its own right on 18 March 2003, but it has no legal protection. On the same day, UK£1 million was provided to start a program of initiatives to support this statement. However, recognition does not carry any process of enforcement with it. The campaign now centers on legalizing BSL so that users have the legal right to use their own language.

7. The cinema in question, part of the Cineworld Group, offers special subtitled shows on Tuesday and Sunday and only one week's notice is provided. Deaf people can use the Internet to check on the films and Deaf societies and organizations are emailed details as soon the cinema itself is advised of the program. Unfortunately, the telephone number for the cinema goes straight into a voice-activated system that D/deaf people are not able to use. There are a limited number of copies with subtitles in circulation at any one time, and so opportunities to show the films are very limited. In contrast there is full accessibility to all screens for people who use wheelchairs or have other mobility problems, and any films shown in screen 5 can be enhanced by audiodescriptive technology for people with visual impairment. These are very clear examples of D/deaf people not having equal access (either in relation to hearing people or those with disabilities) to an important resource. Although the technology exists, it is not used to its full potential.

Further Reading

Skelton, Tracey, and Gill Valentine. (2003). "'It Feels Like Being Deaf is Normal': An Exploration into the Complexities of Defining D/deafness and Young D/deaf people's Identities." *The Canadian Geographer* 47(4): 451–466.

Valentine, Gill, and Tracey Skelton. (2007). "The Right to Be Heard: Citizenship and Language." *Political Geography* 26(2): 121–140.

Valentine, Gill, Tracey Skelton, and Ruth Butler. (2003). "Coming Out and Outcomes: Negotiating Lesbian and Gay Identities with and in the Family." *Environment and Planning D: Society and Space* 21: 479–499.

Chris Philo and Kate Swanson

Afterword

Global Portraits and Local Snapshots

Mohammed's Blog

I was born in the late eighties, told that the Iraqi Iranian war ended while I was too young to even remember anything, played for a while in the street then joined primary school, I was good there, good grades like most of the pupils, we studied a lot about Saddam, the Ba'ath, the revolution, as young pupils, we didn't care so much, we didn't talk about it that much either, then came high school, where I had the most fun in my life.... [Then] what came along this simple life that I lived, was as far as I recall, three wars....

Frankly, I didn't think of anything that time, as far as I remember my head was empty of anything but fun, candy, and fun! Except that there wasn't that much candy as the economic siege [sanctions against Iraq] prevented the government from importing sugar!... I think that in 1999, there were some bombs thrown on Iraq by the US and I don't remember asking why, the only thing I remember is that we used to play soccer all the time, happy that there were no school!!!

... The year 2002 was good as I remember, because believe it or not, we had four local TV channels, three normal ones about everything, and one sports channel, they were kind of good as Uday Saddam's Alshabab TV used to bring us all US-BOX Office movies illegally.... We used to live in a bubble, for me, I never knew that there was a war in Lebanon, or something called Al-Qaeda, may be I didn't even want to know that, but there was always something missing, my father had a magnificent degree yet he never joined the Ba'ath party, he was prevented from travelling abroad by name and also from taking part in the work of any foreign company in the country, later in 2002 we started hearing stuff about an upcoming war!

Let me tell you about the day I had, two days before the war, I was at school, 8:15 A.M., I blurted something about the war . . . deep down we all knew that in a few days Saddam would be in prison . . . so we talked, and we decided to skip school for the day and have some fun of our own, we played soccer, we talked and talked, we even went to the computers lab we had that day, then left five minutes later, nothing mattered, we had fun, and two days later the war was present.

6:30 A.M., we were awakened by bombs and rockets, my mother and my sister were so scared, it's only rightful to be scared. . . . We went to Diyala, a city a little to the north of Baghdad, or that's what I think, we were afraid that it would take a long time as we didn't take but minimal necessities that could fit in our saloon car, we lived there with close relatives for about 10 days, that's when someday, we managed to tune up an old TV, it was the same moment that the statue was being pulled by the tank.

These are extracts from a blog posted on Monday, 4 June 2007, by Mohammed H. Zaid Ali, and they strike us as illustrating certain of the issues, as well as something of the spirit, running throughout the chapters in this compelling volume.[1] Now in his late teens, approaching his twenties, Mohammed is reflecting back on his school days, thereby "telling" aspects of his "young life." With a few startling phrases, he captures a sense—in part bewildered, in other ways shrewdly knowing—of how his young life in Baghdad came to be inescapably touched, in certain respects devastated, by the project of global change unleashed by the U.S.–driven "war on terror" (and by its interwoven political-economic, "imperial," and "cultural" logics). Although perhaps less political or analytical than, say, the blogs of "Riverbend," an Iraqi girl whose voice is a chilling commentary on the breakdown of Iraqi civil society since the invasion, Mohammed's words arguably pierce closer to the heart of what (we think) energizes this book.[2] We say this because Mohammed hints at three themes that we wish to tug from the preceding chapters, albeit without beginning to exhaust what could be claimed, and with an honest admission that such an act of distillation does scant justice to the richness of the thirteen young lives narrated above.

Indeed, the narratives are highly diverse, and have evidently emerged within the context of research projects harboring other immediate foci of concern: the global reach of neoliberal "reform"; the labor-market consequences of postindustrial restructuring in the global north; the traumatizing effects of war, factionalism, and routine political violence in West Africa and post-apartheid South Africa; the dynamics of caste, ethnicity, religion, and the negotiation of gender, family, and community roles in diverse situations from India to Bosnia-Herzegovina; the contradictory stances of NGOs when dealing with the traditional life-worlds of indigenous peoples; the experiences of everyday coping in U.S. streets, hostels, and apartment complexes when faced with homelessness, drug abuse, and overstretched welfare agencies; the politicized self-understandings present in such contested identities as "Scottish Muslim" and "Deaf and lesbian"; or the adopting, adapting, and subversion of multiple popular consumption practices. Even so, the young people acting as informants for these respective projects, while allowing windows on such ostensibly wider issues, have ended up becoming, as it were, *flesh-and-blood* themselves. Indeed, what emerges is their liveliness, their energy (a surprisingly common word across the chapters), in trying to make things happen, whether grand or humble. What also arises—notwithstanding the incoherence often swirling around them—is the relative coherence of their young lives as both unfolding biographies, with discernible, if sometimes tragic, patterns of cause-and-effect, and stories that the individuals concerned can clearly tell themselves about themselves. And it is these stories, shared with their academic interlocutors, that have now been so imaginatively gathered together in this volume, slipping away from the research projects that initially harnessed them, and instead reconvened in such a manner that it does become possible to see commonalities in the portraits painted.

In their introduction, Craig Jeffrey and Jane Dyson have usefully framed something of these commonalities, but, as intimated, we have three themes which we wish (briefly) to explore. First, just as Mohammed reflects on his childish play on the brink of conflict, ironically wondering if the U.S.–led invasion was perhaps somehow connected to his having had "some special fun two days before the war," so we detect a theme of crisis in the very categories of adult, youth, and child. To what extent is Mohammed being forced to grow up in the teeth of global changes pressing down so relentlessly on his young life? And how, more broadly, are youth identities today—structured from without, but also felt from within—being increasingly recast in response to larger global changes? Second, just as Mohammed's blog hints at forsaking the simplicity of childhood for the complications of late-teenage existence, rendered all the more fraught here because set within the altered realities of post-invasion Iraq, so we detect a theme of youthful identities in transition. How do he and the other young people represented in the current volume convert their "childish" hopes into strategies for tackling this transition from simplicity, with its seemingly mundane everydayness, to complexity, with the now-unavoidable need to grapple with a much expanded mesh of demands and expectations?

Third, and maybe most graphically captured by Mohammed's blog, we are concerned with the meeting of what Paula Meth (Chapter 4) refers to as "the remarkable and [the] unremarkable." Hence, it is the contrast between playing soccer and the outbreak of war, eating candy and facing economic sanctions, having childish fun and the horrific perpetrations of adult violence. This contrast is, in part, endemic to the transition forced on some young people from doing the former to experiencing the latter, but it is also one often starkly juxtaposed—Doreen Massey (2005) might say spatio-temporally juxtaposed—within the very grain of singular young lives from one moment to the next. Considering such matters provides an opportunity, moreover, for us to review claims now surfacing in the subfield of "children's geographies" about the unabashed mundaneness of everyday children's lives. These claims may potentially appear the conceit of a particular genre of theoretically inflected scholarship, and indeed a privileging of a particular form of comfortable childhood in the global north, but we draw on the preceding chapters to suggest the value of still keeping such claims, if qualified, in the picture. In so doing, we also add some notes about the transitions here narrated, in some measure from the relatively local(ized) worlds of childhood, full of things that are seemingly banal and rarely reflected on (at least by adults), to the more global(ized) worlds of young adulthood (see also Hörschelmann and Schäfer 2005).

"Crisis" in the Categories of Adult, Youth, and Child

The energies, stories, and biographies captured in this book have many echoes in the lives of young people around the world. One of these is

Olmedo, a sixteen-year-old indigenous youth who has been begging and selling on the streets since he was six years old, and whom Kate met in Ecuador several years ago. He hails from a small Andean village, where he shares a mud home with his widowed mother and three of his younger siblings. At the age of twelve, and after completing a sixth-grade education, he resolved to abandon school in order to work on the streets full time so that he could support his struggling family. In his home, Olmedo has a small black-and-white television, and every night he and his family members huddle for warmth against the cool Andean air to watch Latin American soap operas. Perched on their straw bed to watch the dramas unfold, they become bombarded by images of wealthy blondes, beautiful mansions, and fast cars, interwoven with television commercials advertising the latest fashions and gadgets for youth. Consequently, Olmedo has trouble reconciling his place in this world as compared to the imagined experiences of privileged youth elsewhere. Based on what he observes on television and experiences in the city, these wealthy youth are living and breathing youthful ideals that are "just" and "true." Meanwhile, Olmedo begs from tourists in order to support his family and maybe save up enough money to buy a secondhand bicycle.

This volume is powerful because it links the experiences of youth across global north/global south divides (see also Ansell and van Blerk 2005; *Children's Geographies* 2007; Norcup 2007; Pole, Pilcher, and Williams 2005). Stories of young people like Blacc, a homeless street kid in New York City, resonate evocatively with the experiences of Olmedo, a young indigenous beggar in Ecuador. Despite the global spread of the dominant Western constructions of childhood and youth, these constructions are often at odds with local realities. Simply put, in many parts of the world, the resources needed to reproduce these idealized forms of childhood and youth—and here we might add adulthood—are sadly lacking (see Ruddick 2003). As the narratives in the book reveal, many young people in both the global north and global south continue to experience their young lives under duress. Even though they are being indoctrinated by messages telling them that they belong in school, and that they should be fulfilling their youthful ambitions, many simply lack the means to do so. Their young lives are further complicated as they develop and grow during this period of rapid globalization, a process that clearly has profound impacts on young people's identities and their sense of where they fit in this world. There hence appear to be two broad trends affecting the lives of many of the young people in this volume. One is that in many world regions the traditional structural routes to adulthood no longer exist; or rather, in many cases the resources required for (the accepted transition to) adulthood have become impossible to obtain. This is perhaps most obvious in the stories narrated by Paula Meth and Danny Hoffman, chapters wherein both young protagonists are striving to obtain financial independence: a clear marker of adulthood. Yet, due to larger structural circumstances pertaining to war, violence, and economic crisis, Vusi and Mohammed (a different Mohammed than the young Iraqi blogger) remain reliant on their elders for economic sustenance. Mohammed's young life, in particular, has been ripped apart: at a young age, he was unwillingly coerced into the military and locked into paternalist relationships with his superiors. Until he can afford his own land—an increasingly farfetched goal—he cannot hope to become a proper adult in Sierra Leone. All the time that Mohammed is struggling to grow up by relying on traditional routes to adulthood, his chances of obtaining financial independence are slim due to ongoing economic crisis, poverty, debt, war, and violence; and as such, he is locked into a stage of perpetual youth.

The other correlated, in effect quite opposite, trend is that many young people are being pushed into adult behavior at a much younger age. Around the world, economic crises and neoliberal restructuring have deepened gaps between the rich and poor, which means that while wealthy young people are able to celebrate their birthdays at McDonald's and acquire the latest emblems of youth culture, their poorer counterparts are being pushed into the (formal or informal) workforce due to an increased demand for cash income. This process is having a significant impact on young people in many parts of the globe, north and south, but particularly in more "traditional" communities. In Andean indigenous cultures, children are commonly allowed "four years to live for free," in that up until the age of four children are not expected to contribute to household labor, but after this age families simply cannot afford to have unproductive children. In traditional agricultural settings, this worldview has long been an effective way of teaching children the crucial skills that they need to survive. Yet, when this worldview becomes transferred into a cash-based economy, it means that children as young as four years old often become incorporated into waged labor (see Swanson 2007). Young people's involvement in full-time caring responsibilities has also been intensified by neoliberal political-economic change, but particularly due to the HIV/AIDS crisis, and in Africa many young people are being forced to forego their youthful ambitions in order to care for sick and dying relatives (Robson et al. 2006).

"Crisis" in Identity and Transition

These broader structural transitions are having the most profound impacts on youth identities. Daily, young people must grapple and wade through a series of conflicting and contradictory messages: they are told they are too young to do adult things, such as have sex, work, drink, or vote; they are told to assume adult roles and responsibilities, such as care for sick relatives; they are told to become educated to maximize their earning potential; and they are told to enjoy their youth because these will be the best years of their lives. While many youth are keen to "grow up" and to set out on their own, many are also witnessing a period of prolonged adolescence due to these larger sociocultural and structural transitions. Throughout the world, as evident in the experiences of Suresh and Nala but particularly in the global north, young people are staying in school longer, living at home longer, marrying later, and overall, remaining dependent on their parents until well into their twenties (if not later). Young people are forced to filter through these mixed messages and are uncertain which to absorb, and it is inevitable that they often endure—arguably much more than did their historical forebears—agonies over their exact identity, who they should be, what they should achieve, what they should *hope* to achieve, and so on. And it is an exceptionally confusing picture as to what kind of transitions, what sorts of progressions from childhood to young person to adulthood, can or should be envisaged, and whether such transitions are then realistically attainable.

As the stories in this volume show, despite their best wishes and intents, young people often have limited control over the outcomes of their lives. In all likelihood, Iraq's young Mohammed would prefer a life of "candy and fun!" rather than a life of "bombs and rockets." Recent research in Iraq has revealed that 70 percent of Iraqi primary-school children are now suffering symptoms of post-traumatic stress disorder due to the atrocities they witness on a daily basis (Palmer 2007). What will happen as these children grow up? What will the futures of these young people be like? Despite their hopeful dreams and aspirations, the outcomes of these young people's lives may be grim. Linda McDowell (Chapter 5) also captures some of the tensions between youthful aspirations and "adult" realities. As a seventeen-year-old young man growing up in a postindustrial city, Richard is struggling to make (the increasingly agonizing) transition from childhood to adulthood. Having witnessed his father lose his job in the steel industry a decade earlier, he is determined to avoid a similar fate. However, despite his best efforts, he simply cannot find full-time, permanent work; instead, he floats from "McJob" to "McJob" as he tries to get ahead. Admittedly, Richard's real dream is to become a recording artist, but—while he has played in local pubs and has even copyrighted a song—so far this route has been far from lucrative. Despite his grand dreams, Richard is aware that he will likely have to deny his musical creativity in order to make ends meet in his "adult" world.

In reading these stories a question comes to mind: would they have been told differently had they been about the lives of chronologically younger youth? Arguably, some of the protagonists in this book may have been more optimistic about their futures, more full of youthful hopes and dreams. As an illustration, Paulina is a sixteen-year-old indigenous Ecuadorian girl whom Kate met for the first time when Paulina was twelve years old. Her story highlights some of the gendered dimensions of "growing up" in a complicated world. Four years ago, Paulina was exuberant and excited about her future. She often walked around her village with a large dictionary clutched tightly to her chest and was determined to get a highschool education. When she graduated she was going to work with computers in an office, somewhere in the city: as far as Paulina was concerned, life was going to be great. Four years later, however, Kate found her begging at a street corner in Quito. This time she was defeated in life; she had dropped out of high school, was married to an abusive husband, was missing her front teeth, and had a young child to care for. And due to limited birth control, Paulina recognized that she would continue to have children well into her future, with each one increasing demands on her and further limiting her personal possibilities. For Paulina, the reality of life's harshness had indeed sunk in. Over the last four years, a formerly optimistic narration of her young life had shifted to a pessimistic one. This capturing of transitions is precisely a key strength of this book: by following the trajectories of young people's lives, the chapters herein capably weave what might otherwise be fleeting local snapshots into more nuanced global portraits.

More than anything, many young people are left desperately trying to find their "places" in this world. As they weave their individual identities, young people must choose multiple and entangled identity paths, but the routes to these identities are complicated and fraught with personal, economic, and political conflict. On his path to becoming a leader, Kabir navigates his multiple identities as both Scottish and Muslim in an increasingly Islamophobic society; Susannah, a lesbian Deaf young woman, exists in a world that caters primarily to the hearing and the heterosexual; Helena struggles to carve out her own unique niche as a white Norwegian/English hip-hop aficionado; Sven desperately wants to fit in, get a job, and lead a normal life; while Mohammed strives to remain hidden in Freetown in order to prolong his young life. In the end, the routes that young people take reflect entangled desires: some want to be invisible, some want to be unique, some want to be leaders, some want to be followers, and others simply want to survive. As the stories in this book also demonstrate, moreover, these young people must often struggle through remarkable *and unremarkable* challenges en route to their futures.

The Remarkable and the Unremarkable

Banal Children's Geographies

One trajectory in the emerging subfield of children's geographies insists on taking us into the ostensibly most everyday, mundane, banal, unremarkable facets of lives led by children and young people. Indeed, we are asked to pause before making what might be the standard discriminations of academic social science between subject matters that are sufficiently serious and consequential to be worthy of study and those that are not. Informed by various strands of theorizing with labels such as poststructural or nonrepresentational, authors in this trajectory resist using the more familiar concepts within the social studies of childhood lexicon, regarding them as too grand, totalizing, wielded too authoritatively by self-styled academic masters, and imbued with far too much ontological coherence (i.e., made to appear far more real, far-reaching, and systematically organized than is really the case). Such authors would hence be critical of constructs such as neoliberalism, political economy, restructuring and the state; or even ones like culture, community, and family; preferring to talk more in terms of multiple, fragmentary, and contradictory processes—always specific, peculiar, and situated in time-spaces—that only fleetingly may gather in such a manner as to comprise recognizable "objects" (i.e., a neoliberal reform, a restructured old-industrial district, etc.).

Such an orientation might pose critical questions about this volume, given the organizing assumption that the young lives narrated here need to be understood within the frame of global-structural change. This assumption, it might be objected, transfers the bases for making sense of the lives under scrutiny from their own lived immediacy to these bigger structural realms, and at the same time risks abandoning too quickly the realm of mundane details (of exactly what games and music the young people play; how they relate to their siblings, parents, and friends; the "small spaces" where they spend time and energy, etc.). Furthermore, excited by tracing the tiniest filaments of emotional and affective investment that children and young people seemingly attach to the immediacy of their own social, material, and (sometimes) virtual environments, proponents of this approach to studying young lives might also worry that not enough is being said about the internal lives of the young people concerned. One result might therefore be to neglect dimensions of such lives—imaginings, reveries, and dreams perhaps—which simply cannot be straightforwardly worded (narrated) in the reflexive, often fairly knowing fashion of the chapters here. The claim might be that what is most meaningful about these lives is actually being missed, lost because basically not sought, to be replaced by an external act of meaning-making when the academic writer deploys constructs like neoliberalism, restructuring, or the state.

It would be possible to identify various sources for the critical perspective just described, but perhaps the most obvious are recent articles by John Horton and Peter Kraftl (2005, 2006a, 2006b). Horton and Kraftl persuasively—but open-handedly (theirs is no simple denunciation of *all* other possibilities)—argue for a take on children's geographies that shifts to "encompassing the un-representable, material, embodied, performative and mundane" (Horton and Kraftl 2005: 140). They wish to spotlight "*all sorts* of things-in-the-world and geographies which are habitually underestimated . . . the entire realm of small, banal, low-key, daft, happenstance things, moments, events, practices, experiences, emotions, complexities, quirks, details and who-knows-what-else? in and of everyday lives" (*ibid*: 133, emphasis in original). At the same time, they accept, up to a point, that their approach is (and should be) experimental, balking at the "trigger-happy itch to quickly analyse, distil, generalise and categorise" (*ibid*: 274); and, if this "smacks of a withdrawal from the rigours of academic research" (*ibid*: 270), then, they confess, so be it. In order to carry their claims, they have crafted one article (*ibid*) that provocatively insists on the importance of the mundane through their own joint recollections of four moments or issues from their own childhoods that really mattered to them: wearing glasses, their local parks, being clumsy, and their first days at school. It would be easy to dismiss these case studies as trivial, and we also recognize that some researchers on geographies of young lives might become quite angry about the perceived irrelevance of much that Horton and Kraftl discuss, particularly in the face of the deeply troubled young lives—ripped apart by war, violence, abuse, poverty, drugs, homelessness, and so on—such as those, in part at least, narrated in the chapters of this volume. Indeed, it would be easy, and maybe to an extent appropriate, to direct a Marxian or postcolonial critique at Horton and Kraftl for inadvertently privileging a certain version of "comfortable," suburban or provincial, predominantly white, and apparently *un*troubled childhood in the global north. Couched in this way, the current volume could then itself be positioned in support of such a countercritique of the Horton-Kraftl line.

But maybe things are not quite as simple as this, and it is worth noting Horton and Kraftl's own observation that "very similar (or very different)— yet *still* banal, mundane, material, emotive—things may matter to children and childhoods in very different and perhaps far-less-privileged circumstances" (Horton and Kraftl 2006: 272; our emphasis). Mohammed's blog, with which we started our afterword, very nicely captures this sense of what might be construed as the banal, the unremarkable: "as far as I remember my head was empty of anything but fun, candy, and fun!" Our suggestion is that such a comment, far from being regarded as trivial and irrelevant by its readers, cannot but acquire a sense of profundity precisely because of its juxtaposition with the horrors engulfing Mohammed's Iraqi homeland (Saddam's evils and economic sanctions) or soon to engulf them (the U.S.-led invasion). A riposte, however, might be to ask: why, if we accept that such "trivia" as Mohammed's watching television, playing soccer, eating candy, and having fun really do matter as the meaningful matrix of his young life, can we not extend such a verdict to the lives of other young people who are fortunate enough to be living lives that are *not* about to be ripped apart in some way? Is it indeed only through the awfulness of lives damaged that the true significance of mundane ordinariness, as something lost in the chaos of war, violence, and abuse, can be properly appreciated?

More simply, though, we would argue that there are many indications of mundane ordinariness, the unremarkable, in the chapters above. Thus, we do hear a lot about young people going about their daily business in schools, workplaces, and places of leisure, getting into (or, even more notably for the likes of Richard and Mike, *avoiding* getting into) "trouble," dealing with the anxieties of growing up, finding companionship and love, coping with diverse everyday hassles, occupying spaces to hang out for and as themselves, listening to music, dancing, laughing, fighting, crying. These are the banalities that Horton and Kraftl envisage as being shared by (and mattering for) children and young people in countless different times and places, albeit inevitably marked in particular ways, perhaps fraught with greater or lesser difficulty, depending on the exact circumstances of their young lives. And the message is that readers should not hurry past such seeming banalities on their way to what might be the "bigger" points of each chapter, maybe points folding into the broader research agendas of each academic author, but should instead linger on such "small"

details. Readers must appreciate that these bits of the stories told, these local snapshots in the global portraits, comprise the stuff of the lives lived,
often the stuff that renders these lives meaningful to the young people living them. Even the ostensibly most inconsequential moments of fun and
play, the superficially most idle and empty stretches of a young person's
time, may actually be full of significance in the forming of both their social relationships and emerging senses of self-identity. In short, the *unremarkable* here is precisely worthy of remark.

It is true that in many of the chapters above, the unremarkable banalities are juxtaposed with much more dramatic events and atrocities than
usually impact the quiet townscapes in the studies of Horton and Kraftl,
thereby throwing such banalities into stark relief in the manner of Mohammed's blog. It is also sadly true that in some cases—for Blacc, Vusi,
maybe Mike, Zilho perhaps, and the Mohammed in Chapter 10—war, violence, and abuses of all kinds have themselves become the very fabric of
everyday life, in effect morphing into the banalities of the life-worlds in
question, and thereby destabilizing the whole delineation of what is remarkable from what is unremarkable. As Derek Gregory (2004: 238) observes about some of Riverbend's less "poetic" blogs, "she describe[s] the
ordinariness and oppressiveness of everyday life under occupation." Few of
the young people featured in this volume are equivalent to the kinds of
individuals who are the model for the Horton-Kraftl articles, undergoing
relatively safe childhoods free from serious trauma, although the closest
are probably Helena and Sven with the relative luxury of enjoying music,
clothing, and styles of personal comportment as their principal everyday
concerns. For an individual like Saka, while still embedded within her
family and not having suffered physical displacement, her pivotal role as
worker, both domestically and in the fields, means that her relatively care-
less (and hopeful) world of childhood is increasingly a distant memory
(now replaced by the routine drudgery of labor and providing).

Represented Young Life-Worlds (on Their Way from the Local to the Global)

A further truth is that most of the young people featured in this volume
have ended up being quite aware of the forces shaping their lives and can
provide quite articulate, thoughtful, and reasoned accounts of their lives as
situated within the (im)balance of these forces. In part, and following what
we said earlier, some of the young people in these chapters have had little
choice but to "grow up" quickly, being compelled to deal with distinctively

"adult" issues of supporting families, caring for siblings, and formulating a thought-through approach to complex identity-politics issues (for the latter, particularly the self-analyses provided by Kabir and Susannah). In part, too, some of these young people, notably those who are now not so young, such as Zilho, Suresh, and Nala, give sustained reflections on their longer-term strategies for negotiating their own status, complete with opportunities sought for material-symbolic advancement on behalf of themselves and their family, caste, or ethnic groupings. One implication is that these individuals *are* capable of representing their young lives in terms easily recognizable to adults, and indeed in a verbal currency favored by academic researchers, which almost inevitably sets them at a distance from Horton-Kraftl's "*non*representational" living of banalities. It is not so much that they have ceased to be enmeshed in such banalities—surely we all are so enmeshed, whoever we are, young or old, since how could it be otherwise?—but it is that they can see beyond these banalities and their immediate, often quite local(ized) contexts. As a result, the understandings that many of these young people develop regarding their life-worlds are unavoidably saturated by knowledge of the broader forces impacting on their lives, as just mentioned, and perhaps too by comparisons with places and circumstances elsewhere (possibly places with which their own worlds are networked materially or virtually). That being said, though, it does not follow that much of the meaning that they derive from their worlds, that nourish them through the day or at least energize them, cease to arise precisely in the commonly unspoken nooks and crannies of existence (in and among things, peoples, achievements, upsets, etc.).

Phrasing it this way, though, begs a final question about what, then, after all, is so *different* about young people and those characterized as adults? And to ask this question is of course to return to the start of our first substantive section of comments: when addressing the crisis in categorizations of children, young people, and adults (and, in fact, in any division of people according to periods referencing their chrono-biological time alive). Nobody can really avoid living in the immediate here-and-nowness of their own life-worlds, however much some of us may pretend or represent ourselves otherwise, claiming that we are living a life of the mind, or of spirituality, or of politics, shaped by ideas, injunctions, and philosophies seemingly beamed into our lives from wherever. But maybe a key difference is that the younger we are and the more we approximate the category conventionally taken as "child", the more physically, mentally, and emotionally dependent we are on the banal resources available to us locally in the near-at-hand (even if this near-at-hand may now include images projected on television or computer screens). At the same time, the younger we are, the less we have learned, the less we can recognize such immediacy, the less we can reflect on it, distance ourselves from it, appreciate how much it is itself structured by influences and flows from without. Similarly, the less we can articulate the meanings that we derive from our local(ized) contexts, the more it seems we are at one with the mundaneness of these contexts—even if filled with suffering and terror—and not separated off from them by the acts of cognition, reflection, and representation.

Maybe if the current volume had entailed the telling of rather younger lives, an unknowing immersion in the here-and-now would have been more apparent, with chapters possessing more the feel of local snapshots than of global portraits. Indeed, as already asked above in a different context, it is interesting to ponder how the chapters would have looked if drawing on the first-hand accounts, perhaps including diaries, drawings, and mental maps, of children aged, say, five to twelve. As it happens, the current volume is based on the testimony of older young people, in some cases people whose positioning as youths is an artifice of their standing within regional traditions of what constitutes independent adulthood. The upshot is that their accounts commonly embody—hardly unsurprisingly—a sense of transition: of individuals in the process of transition from childhood, complete with its thoroughly situated banalities, to younger adulthood, all too often now weighed down with cares, a loss of innocent hopes, the devising of strategies, and, more broadly, the formulating of political-cultural identities over and against the prevailing moment (in large measure constituted precisely through the articulation of local experience and global forces). Given that many if not all of the chapters contain an element of individual biography, a window is opened not just on the childhoods of the young people concerned but also on how they *now* remember, revisit, and interpret their own childhoods. This means that the thread of transitions is all the more prominent. The distinctiveness of the volume arguably lies here, then, in the scars to which it bears witness of lost and local(ized) childhoods, ones like Mohammed's full of "fun, candy, and fun!" as well as vaguely held hopes for the future, all swept away in the face of changes that are partially just those of growing up but that have also been—in all of these chapters—indelibly structured by the crosscutting of globe-spanning political-economic forces and sociocultural pressures.

Acknowledgments

Thanks to Craig and Jane for inviting us to add this Afterword to their excellent volume.

Notes

1. See http://iloveuirag.blogspot.com (accessed June 20, 2007).
2. See http://riverbendblog.blogspot.com; Gregory 2004, esp. pp. 213, 238, 240, 245, 247.

References

Ansell, Nicola, and Lorraine van Blerk. (2005). Theme Section on "Children and Youth in Developing Areas." *Children's Geographies* 3(2): 145–218.

Children's Geographies. (2007). Special Issue on "Global Childhoods: Why Children? Why Now?" *Children's Geographies* 5(1–2): 1–187.

Gregory, Derek. (2004). *The Colonial Present: Afghanistan, Palestine, Iraq.* Oxford: Blackwell.

Hörschelmann, Kathrin, and Nadine Schäfer. (2005). "Performing the Local through the Global: Globalisation and Individualisation in the Spatial Practices of Young East Germans." *Children's Geographies* 3(2): 219–242.

Horton, John, and Peter Kraftl. (2005). "For More-than-usefulness: Six Overlapping Points about Children's Geographies." *Children's Geographies* 3(2): 131–143.

———. (2006a). "What Else? Some More Ways of Thinking and Doing 'Children's Geographies.'" *Children's Geographies* 4(1): 69–96.

———. (2006b). "Not Just Growing Up, but Going On: Materials, Spacings, Bodies, Situations." *Children's Geographies* 4(3): 259–276.

Massey, Doreen. (2005). *For Space.* London: Sage.

Norcup, Jo. (2007). "Book Review of Pole, Pilcher and Williams." *Children's Geographies* 5(4): 489.

Palmer, James. (2007). "Trauma Severe for Iraqi Children." *USA Today,* April 16, 2007, 1A.

Pole, Christopher., Jane Pilcher, and John Williams (eds.). (2005). *Young People in Transition: Becoming Citizens?* New York: Palgrave MacMillan.

Robson, Elsbeth, Nicola Ansell, Ulli S. Huber, William T. S. Gould, and Lorraine van Blerk. (2006). "Young Caregivers in the Context of the HIV/AIDS Pandemic in Sub-Saharan Africa." *Population, Space and Place* 12(2): 93–111.

Ruddick, Susan. (2003). "The Politics of Aging: Globalization and the Restructuring of Youth and Childhood." *Antipode* 35(2): 334–362.

Swanson, Kate. (2007). "'Bad Mothers' and 'Delinquent Children': Unravelling Anti-begging Rhetoric in the Ecuadorian Andes." *Gender, Place and Culture* 14(6): 703–720.

About the Contributors

Stuart Aitken is a professor of Geography and director of the Center for Interdisciplinary Studies of Youth and Space (ISYS) at San Diego State University, an adjunct professor at the Department of Geography and the National Child Research Centre (NOSEB) in Trondheim, Norway, and an honorary professor of Geography at the University of Wales, Aberystwth. His research interests include urban, social and film geography with an emphasis on families and communities, children and youth. He has written and edited numerous books on these areas. He is an editor of the journal, *Children's Geographies*.

Sean Crotty recently graduated from San Diego State University with an M.A. in Geography and is currently a Ph.D. candidate there.

Jane Dyson is an affiliate assistant professor at the Jackson School of International Studies, University of Washington. She received her Ph.D. from Cambridge University in 2006. Her research examines children's work, youth identities, and the political ecology of development, with a particular focus on India and the Himalayan region. Most recently, she published the article "Harvesting Identities: Youth, Work and Gender in the Indian Himalayas" in *Annals of the Association of American Geographers* 98(1) 2008.

Benjamin Gardner is an assistant professor in the Department of Interdisciplinary Arts and Sciences at the University of Washington Bothell. He received his Ph.D. in Geography at the University of California Berkeley in 2007. His research interests include the cultural politics of development, environmental politics, the post-colonial nation-state, and East Africa. He has published in edited book volumes and peer reviewed journals about gender and development, land rights and transnational investment, and the links between community, landscapes, and activism.

Kristina Gibson is an assistant professor in residence of Urban and Community Studies at the University of Connecticut. She received her Ph.D. in Geography at the University of Colorado, Boulder. She specializes in urban and youth geographies, public space, homeless youth, and street outreach/social work. Recently, she completed a three-year ethnographic investigation of street outreach organizations in New York City. She is also currently an acting board member of Stage 2, which is an outreach nonprofit working with minority and LGBTQ (lesbian, gay, bisexual, transgender, and queer/questioning) street youth.

Danny Hoffman is an assistant professor in the Department of Anthropology at the University of Washington. He received his Ph.D. at Duke University in 2004. His research interests include visual anthropology, violence and militarism, experimental ethnography, and West Africa. He has been published in various academic journals. Most recently, he published an article ("The City as Barracks: Freetown, Monrovia, and the Organization of Violence in Postcolonial African Cities") in *Cultural Anthropology* 22(3) 2007.

Peter Hopkins is a lecturer in Social Geography in the School of Geography, Politics and Sociology, Newcastle University, UK. His main research interests include urban geographies of race, ethnicity and religion, geographies and sociologies of religion, and critical perspectives on young people's geographies. The majority of his work is informed by qualitative research. He is the author of *Islam, Youth, Masculinity* (Edwin Mellen Press); co-editor (with Cara Aitchison and Mei-Po Kwan) of *Geographies of Muslim identities: gender, diaspora, belonging* (Ashgate); co-editor (with Richard Gale) of *Muslims in Britain: race, place and identities* (Edinburgh University Press); and has published articles in a range of peer-reviewed journal (e.g., *Transactions of the Institute of British Geographers, Environment and Planning A, Ethnicities* and *Area*).

Kathrin Horschelmann is associate director of the Centre for the Study of Cities and Regions, as well as a lecturer in the Department of Geography for Durham University. Her research interests include gender and feminist geographies, geographies of the media, and youth culture and globalization. She has published articles in many books and journals, including *Transactions of the Institute of British Geographers, Antipode, Environment and Planning A* and *Political Geography*. She is also the co-editor of *Spaces of Masculinities* (Routledge, 2005).

Alex Jeffrey is a lecturer in Human Geography at Newcastle University in the School of Geography, Politics and Sociology. He received his Ph.D. from the Department of Geography at Durham University in 2005. His research interests include the fragmentation of Yugoslavia, civil society, international intervention, and nongovernmental organizations. He has recently published articles in *Review of International Political Economy, Political Geography* and *Development and Change*. He is co-author, with Professor Joe Painter, of *Political Geography: an Introduction to Space and Power* (Sage, 2009).

Craig Jeffrey is an associate professor at the Department of Geography and Jackson School of International Studies, University of Washington. His research examines the cultural geography and political anthropology of youth, education, and caste, with particular attention to

India. He has published numerous articles and a book, *Degrees Without Freedom: Education, Masculinities and Unemployment in North India* (Stanford University Press, 2008) with Patricia Jeffery and Roger Jeffery. Craig is also using his interests in global youth to reflect on critical pedagogy, especially how drama might be used to transform students' learning experiences in India and the United States.

Linda McDowell is a professor of Human Geography at Oxford University. She is also the joint coordinator of the Transformations: Economy, Society, and Place research cluster. Her research interests include the connections between economic restructuring, labor market change, and class and gender divisions in Great Britain. She is the author of numerous books, including *Redundant Masculinities?* (Blackwell, 2003) and *Hard Labour* (UCL Press, 2005). She is also a trustee of the Foundation for Urban and Regional Studies.

Paula Meth is a lecturer in Town and Regional Planning at the University of Sheffield. She completed her Ph.D. in Geography at the University of Cambridge and has since worked across the subjects of Geography, Development Studies, and Planning. Her main research interests are the social and spatial experiences of marginalized people within the Global South, with a current focus on gender and violence in South Africa. Paula also has an interest in the politics and practice of qualitative methodology (particularly the use of diaries). She has published in books and academic journals and is one of the co-authors of the forthcoming book, *Geographies of the Global South* (Routledge). Paula has been the treasurer of the Developing Areas Research Group, part of the Institute of British Geographers since September 2004.

Katharyne Mitchell is professor of Geography and the Simpson Professor in the Public Humanities at the University of Washington. She is the founding director of the Reclaiming Childhood project, an interdisciplinary and community-oriented collaboration examining the changing nature of American childhood. See www.reclaimingchildhood. org. In addition to her research on childhood and education, she has also examined the role of the public intellectual in western society and has a forthcoming edited book on this theme: *Practicing Public Scholarship*. Other monographs and edited volumes include: *Crossing the Neoliberal Line: Pacific Rim Migration and the Metropolis*; *Life's Work: Geographies of Social Reproduction*; and *A Companion to Political Geography*.

Christopher Moreno is an adjunct professor of Anthropology and Geography at Miramar College and a Ph.D. candidate at San Diego State University. He is also on the editorial board of *Aether: The Journal of Media Geography*.

Anoop Nayak is a reader in Social and Cultural Geography at Newcastle University. His research interests are in the fields of race, migration and asylum; youth cultural studies; masculinities, education and labor; and whiteness, nationalism and new theories of social class. He is author of the monograph *Race, Place and Globalization: Youth Cultures in a Changing World* (Berg, 2003) and has recently published a book with Mary Jane Kehily entitled *Gender, Youth and Culture: Young Masculinities and Femininities* (Palgrave, 2008).

Chris Philo is a professor of Geography at the University of Glasgow. He received his Ph.D. from the University of Cambridge in 1992. His research focuses on the historical, cultural, and rural geographies of mental-ill health, and children geographies. He has published numerous articles in a variety of books and scholarly journals. His most recent publication was the article "Scaling the Asylum: Three Different Geographies of Craig Dunain Lunatic Asylum" in *Psychiatric Spaces: Architecture, Madness and the Built Environment* (Routledge, 2007).

Tracey Skelton is currently associate professor of human geography at the National University of Singapore and professor of Critical Geographies at Loughborough University. Her research work interweaves young people's geographies, feminist geography, cultural geography, development studies, and cultural studies. Her current research is exploring the ways in which young people in Auckland, New Zealand and Singapore connect or disconnect with their home cities and notions of citizenship and how they narrate and anticipate their global futures and engagements with globalization. She has published extensively in numerous scholarly journals and books including *Cool Places* and *Global Childhoods*. She is the Viewpoints Editor for *Children's Geographies*.

Kate Swanson is an assistant professor in the Department of Geography at San Diego State University. She received her Ph.D. in Geography from the University of Toronto in 2005. Her research interests include urban restructuring and exclusion, labor migration, youth identities and childhood, and racialization of indigenous people. She has published articles in various scholarly journals, including "Revanchist Urbanism Heads South: The Regulation of Indigenous Beggars and Street Vendors in Ecuador" in *Antipode: A Radical Journal of Geography* (2007).

Index